SUPER HOROSCOPE
CAPRICORN

2011

DECEMBER 21 - JANUARY 19

BERKLEY BOOKS, NEW YORK

THE BERKLEY PUBLISHING GROUP
Published by the Penguin Group
Penguin Group (USA) Inc.
375 Hudson Street, New York, New York 10014, USA
Penguin Group (Canada), 90 Eglinton Avenue East, Suite 700, Toronto, Ontario M4P 2Y3, Canada
(a division of Pearson Penguin Canada Inc.)
Penguin Books Ltd., 80 Strand, London WC2R 0RL, England
Penguin Group Ireland, 25 St. Stephen's Green, Dublin 2, Ireland (a division of Penguin Books Ltd.)
Penguin Group (Australia), 250 Camberwell Road, Camberwell, Victoria 3124, Australia
(a division of Pearson Australia Group Pty. Ltd.)
Penguin Books India Pvt. Ltd., 11 Community Centre, Panchsheel Park, New Delhi—110 017, India
Penguin Group (NZ), 67 Apollo Drive, Rosedale, North Shore 0632, New Zealand
(a division of Pearson New Zealand Ltd.)
Penguin Books (South Africa) (Pty.) Ltd., 24 Sturdee Avenue, Rosebank, Johannesburg 2196,
South Africa

Penguin Books Ltd., Registered Offices: 80 Strand, London WC2R 0RL, England

The publishers regret that they cannot answer individual letters requesting personal horoscope information.

2011 SUPER HOROSCOPE CAPRICORN

PRINTING HISTORY
Berkley trade paperback edition / July 2010

Berkley trade paperback ISBN: 978-0-425-23294-1

Library of Congress Cataloging-in-Publication Data

ISSN: 1535-8941

PRINTED IN THE UNITED STATES OF AMERICA

10 9 8 7 6 5 4 3 2 1

Contents

THE CUSP-BORN CAPRICORN

Are you *really* a Capricorn? If your birthday falls around Christmas, at the very beginning of Capricorn, will you still retain the traits of Sagittarius, the sign of the Zodiac before Capricorn? And what if you were born during the third week of January—arc you more Aquarius than Capricorn? Many people born at the edge, or cusp, of a sign have great difficulty determining exactly what sign they are. If you are one of these people, here's how you can figure it out, once and for all.

Consult the cusp table on the facing page, then locate the year of your birth. The table will tell you the precise days on which the Sun entered and left your sign for the year of your birth. In that way you can determine if you are a true Capricorn—or whether you are a Sagittarius or Aquarius—according to the variations in cusp dates from year to year (see also page 17).

Whether you were born at the beginning or end of Capricorn, yours is a lifetime reflecting a process of subtle transformation. Your life on Earth will symbolize a significant change in consciousness, for you are either about to enter a whole new way of living, or are leaving one behind.

If you were born at the beginning of Capricorn, you may want to read the horoscope book for Sagittarius as well as Capricorn, for Sagittarius is a deep—often hidden—part of your spirit. You were born with the special gift of being able to bring your dreams into reality and put your talents and ambitions to practical use. You need to conquer worry and depression and learn to take life seriously, but without losing your sense of humor and hope. You need to find a balance between believing nothing and believing too much. You need to find the middle ground between cynicism and idealism.

If you were born at the end of Capricorn, you may want to read the horoscope book on Aquarius, for you are a dynamic mixture of both the Capricorn and Aquarius natures. You are in a transitional state of consciousness, about to enter a whole new way of living, but still duty-bound to perform responsibilities before you are set free. You are bound by two lifestyles, one conservative, the other freedom-oriented. You combine the talents of regularity and discipline with rebellious spontaneity and flashing genius. You can be troubled by reversals and setbacks, despite your serious planning, and find great conflict between strong, personal ambitions and deep desires for freedom.

You have a great pull toward the future, but you are powerfully drawn back to society and cultural conditioning. Try to concentrate on your newly found enthusiasms and build a solid foundation on which to achieve the success you long for.

THE CUSPS OF CAPRICORN

DATES SUN ENTERS CAPRICORN (LEAVES SAGITTARIUS)

December 22 every year from 1900 to 2015, except for the following:

December 21

1912	1944	1964	1977	1989	2000	2010
16	48	65	80	92	2001	2012
20	52	68	81	93	2002	2013
23	53	69	84	94	2004	2014
28	56	72	85	96	2005	
32	57	73	86	97	2006	
36	60	76	88	98	2008	
40	61				2009	

DATES SUN LEAVES CAPRICORN (ENTERS AQUARIUS)

January 20 every year from 1900 to 2015, except for the following:

January 19			January 21		
1977	1989	2001	1903	1920	1932
81	93	2005	04	24	36
85	97	2009	08	28	44
		2013	12		

THE ASCENDANT: CAPRICORN RISING

Could you be a "double" Capricorn? That is, could you have Capricorn as your Rising sign as well as your Sun sign? The tables on pages 8–9 will tell you Capricorns what your Rising sign happens to be. Just find the hour of your birth, then find the day of your birth, and you will see which sign of the Zodiac is your Ascendant, as the Rising sign is called. The Ascendant is called that because it is the sign rising on the eastern horizon at the time of your birth. For a more detailed discussion of the Rising sign and the twelve houses of the Zodiac, see pages 17–20.

The Ascendant, or Rising sign, is placed on the 1st house in a horoscope, of which there are twelve houses. The 1st house represents your response to the environment—your unique response. Call it identity, personality, ego, self-image, facade, come-on, body-mind-spirit—whatever term best conveys to you the meaning of the you that acts and reacts in the world. It is a you that is always changing, discovering a new you. Your identity started with birth and early environment, over which you had little conscious control, and continues to experience, to adjust, to express itself. The 1st house also represents how others see you. Has anyone ever guessed your sign to be your Rising sign? People may respond to that personality, that facade, that body type governed by your Rising sign.

Your Ascendant, or Rising sign, modifies your basic Sun sign personality, and it affects the way you act out the daily predictions for your Sun sign. If your rising sign is indeed Capricorn, what follows is a description of its effects on your horoscope. If your Rising sign is not Capricorn, but some other sign of the Zodiac, you may wish to read the horoscope book for that sign.

For those of you with Capricorn Rising, that is, in the 1st house, the planet that is rising in the 1st house is Saturn, ruler of Capricorn. Saturn here gives you an extraordinary philosophical capacity and at the same a penchant for lone pursuits. You can see reality from many perspectives, and you feel impelled to test the viability of each framework you discover. But you would rather do it your own way, not other people's, and be accountable only to yourself,

CAPRICORN RISING / 7

not to anyone else. Saturn in this position also gives you a melancholy turn of mind.

You have an immense respect for the best order of things, for the way people should relate to each other in order to support each other. And you want to weave this order and support not only into the fabric of your own life but also into the larger tapestry of society as a whole. Thus you are very social, but your underlying drive is to integrate concepts of how people should behave with your self-concept. You start with a principle and you try to expand it. You are not concerned with peer pressure or popularity. Indeed, your aloofness, combined with your solitary habits, taciturn moods, and great powers of concentration, make some people think that you do not care at all or that you have an undeveloped conscience. Quite the opposite is true.

Because of these traits you have a remarkable ability to create far-reaching plans and to see them through. You can put kaleidoscopic images into focus, you can galvanize scattered energies into a powerful momentum. You are an excellent manipulator of ideas and a good manager of people. You are happiest when such tasks face you and when you have unlimited responsibility to carry them out. A family or a company is grist for your mill. Power to you means the ability to achieve your aims. Power is not fame, fortune, fondness, or any other measure of how people judge you. You are your own judge.

On the other hand, Capricorn Rising individuals are quite sensitive to the ways in which people treat your principles. In your mind your identity and your principles are merged, so when your ideas are insulted, you are insulted. You dislike rule breakers, and for that you may earn a reputation for sternness. You detest traitors, philanderers, cheats of all kinds, and for that you may be called rigid or old-fashioned. You consider a breach of support or trust dishonorable because it is harmful, and you can be pitiless in your scorn of the perpetrator.

Your persona may be so identified with your principles that you check impulses, shun spontaneity. You could refuse to let mirth show in your face even though you are probably the first peson to see humor in a situation. You could insulate your feelings because they don't seem to fit your preconceptions; contradiction is a theme you seldom tolerate. And only until you have generalized the meaning of an event, an interaction, an emotion, will you then relax into it.

The key words for those of you with Capricorn Rising are form and focus. Your own uphill struggle is a model of success for those who would despair and give in. Don't conserve your talents in seclusion.

RISING SIGNS FOR CAPRICORN

Hour of Birth*	Date of Birth		
	December 21–26	December 27–31	January 1–5
Midnight	Virgo;	Libra	Libra
1 AM	Libra 12/22	Libra	Libra
2 AM	Libra	Libra; Scorpio 12/29	Scorpio
3 AM	Scorpio	Scorpio	Scorpio
4 AM	Scorpio	Scorpio	Scorpio; Sagittarius 1/5
5 AM	Sagittarius	Sagittarius	Sagittarius
6 AM	Sagittarius	Sagittarius	Sagittarius
7 AM	Sagittarius	Capricorn	Capricorn
8 AM	Capricorn	Capricorn	Capricorn
9 AM	Capricorn; Aquarius 12/26	Aquarius	Aquarius
10 AM	Aquarius	Aquarius	Aquarius; Pisces 1/2
11 AM	Pisces	Pisces	Pisces
Noon	Pisces; Aries 12/22	Aries	Aries
1 PM	Aries; Taurus 12/26	Taurus	Taurus
2 PM	Taurus	Taurus	Gemini
3 PM	Gemini	Gemini	Gemini
4 PM	Gemini	Gemini	Cancer
5 PM	Cancer	Cancer	Cancer
6 PM	Cancer	Cancer	Cancer
7 PM	Cancer; Leo 12/22	Leo	Leo
8 PM	Leo	Leo	Leo
9 PM	Leo	Leo; Virgo 12/30	Virgo
10 PM	Virgo	Virgo	Virgo
11 PM	Virgo	Virgo	Virgo

*Hour of birth given here is for Standard Time in any time zone. If your hour of birth was recorded in Daylight Saving Time, subtract one hour from it and consult that hour in the table above. For example, if you were born at 6 AM D.S.T., see 5 AM above.

RISING SIGNS FOR CAPRICORN

Hour of Birth*	Date of Birth		
	January 6–10	January 11–15	January 16–21
Midnight	Libra	Libra	Libra
1 AM	Libra	Libra; Scorpio 1/13	Libra
2 AM	Scorpio	Scorpio	Scorpio
3 AM	Scorpio	Scorpio	Scorpio; Sagittarius 1/21
4 AM	Sagittarius	Sagittarius	Sagittarius
5 AM	Sagittarius	Sagittarius	Sagittarius
6 AM	Sagittarius; Capricorn 1/7	Capricorn	Capricorn
7 AM	Capricorn	Capricorn	Capricorn
8 AM	Capricorn; Aquarius 1/7	Aquarius	Aquarius
9 AM	Aquarius	Aquarius	Aquarius; Pisces 1/17
10 AM	Pisces	Pisces	Pisces; Aries 1/21
11 AM	Aries	Aries	Aries
Noon	Aries; Taurus 1/10	Taurus	Taurus
1 PM	Taurus	Taurus; Gemini 1/15	Gemini
2 PM	Gemini	Gemini	Gemini
3 PM	Gemini	Gemini; Cancer 1/15	Cancer
4 PM	Cancer	Cancer	Cancer
5 PM	Cancer	Cancer	Cancer; Leo 1/21
6 PM	Leo	Leo	Leo
7 PM	Leo	Leo	Leo
8 PM	Leo	Leo; Virgo 1/14	Virgo
9 PM	Virgo	Virgo	Virgo
10 PM	Virgo	Virgo	Virgo; Libra 1/21
11 PM	Libra	Libra	Libra

*See note on facing page.

THE PLACE OF ASTROLOGY IN TODAY'S WORLD

Does astrology have a place in the fast-moving, ultra-scientific world we live in today? Can it be justified in a sophisticated society whose outriders are already preparing to step off the moon into the deep space of the planets themselves? Or is it just a hangover of ancient superstition, a psychological dummy for neurotics and dreamers of every historical age?

These are the kind of questions that any inquiring person can be expected to ask when they approach a subject like astrology which goes beyond, but never excludes, the materialistic side of life.

The simple, single answer is that astrology works. It works for many millions of people in the western world alone. In the United States there are 10 million followers and in Europe, an estimated 25 million. America has more than 4000 practicing astrologers, Europe nearly three times as many. Even down-under Australia has its hundreds of thousands of adherents. In the eastern countries, astrology has enormous followings, again, because it has been proved to work. In India, for example, brides and grooms for centuries have been chosen on the basis of their astrological compatibility.

Astrology today is more vital than ever before, more practicable because all over the world the media devotes much space and time to it, more valid because science itself is confirming the precepts of astrological knowledge with every new exciting step. The ordinary person who daily applies astrology intelligently does not have to wonder whether it is true nor believe in it blindly. He can see it working for himself. And, if he can use it—and this book is designed to help the reader to do just that—he can make living a far richer experience, and become a more developed personality and a better person.

Astrology and Relationships

Astrology is the science of relationships. It is not just a study of planetary influences on man and his environment. It is the study of man himself.

We are at the center of our personal universe, of all our relationships. And our happiness or sadness depends on how we act, how we relate to the people and things that surround us. The emotions that we generate have a distinct effect—for better or worse—on the world around us. Our friends and our enemies will confirm this. Just look in the mirror the next time you are angry. In other words, each of us is a kind of sun or planet or star radiating our feelings on the environment around us. Our influence on our personal universe, whether loving, helpful, or destructive, varies with our changing moods, expressed through our individual character.

Our personal "radiations" are potent in the way they affect our moods and our ability to control them. But we usually are able to throw off our emotion in some sort of action—we have a good cry, walk it off, or tell someone our troubles—before it can build up too far and make us physically ill. Astrology helps us to understand the universal forces working on us, and through this understanding, we can become more properly adjusted to our surroundings so that we find ourselves coping where others may flounder.

The Challenge of Love

The challenge of love lies in recognizing the difference between infatuation, emotion, sex, and, sometimes, the intentional deceit of the other person. Mankind, with its record of broken marriages, despair, and disillusionment, is obviously not very good at making these distinctions.

Can astrology help?

Yes. In the same way that advance knowledge can usually help in any human situation. And there is probably no situation as human, as poignant, as pathetic and universal, as the failure of man's love.

Love, of course, is not just between man and woman. It involves love of children, parents, home, and friends. But the big problems usually involve the choice of partner.

Astrology has established degrees of compatibility that exist between people born under the various signs of the Zodiac. Because people are individuals, there are numerous variations and modifications. So the astrologer, when approached on mate and marriage matters, makes allowances for them. But the fact remains that some groups of people are suited for each other and some are not, and astrology has expressed this in terms of characteristics we all can study and use as a personal guide.

No matter how much enjoyment and pleasure we find in the different aspects of each other's character, if it is not an overall compatibility, the chances of our finding fulfillment or enduring happiness in each other are pretty hopeless. And astrology can help us to find someone compatible.

Astrology and Science

Closely related to our emotions is the "other side" of our personal universe, our physical welfare. Our body, of course, is largely influenced by things around us over which we have very little control. The phone rings, we hear it. The train runs late. We snag our stocking or cut our face shaving. Our body is under a constant bombardment of events that influence our daily lives to varying degrees.

The question that arises from all this is, what makes each of us act so that we have to involve other people and keep the ball of activity and evolution rolling? This is the question that both science and astrology are involved with. The scientists have attacked it from different angles: anthropology, the study of human evolution as body, mind and response to environment; anatomy, the study of bodily structure; psychology, the science of the human mind; and so on. These studies have produced very impressive classifications and valuable information, but because the approach to the problem is fragmented, so is the result. They remain "branches" of science. Science generally studies effects. It keeps turning up wonderful answers but no lasting solutions. Astrology, on the other hand, approaches the question from the broader viewpoint. Astrology began its inquiry with the totality of human experience and saw it as an effect. It then looked to find the cause, or at least the prime movers, and during thousands of years of observation of man and his *universal* environment came up with the extraordinary principle of planetary influence—or astrology, which, from the Greek, means the science of the stars.

Modern science, as we shall see, has confirmed much of astrology's foundations—most of it unintentionally, some of it reluctantly, but still, indisputably.

It is not difficult to imagine that there must be a connection between outer space and Earth. Even today, scientists are not too sure how our Earth was created, but it is generally agreed that it is only a tiny part of the universe. And as a part of the universe, people on Earth see and feel the influence of heavenly bodies in almost every aspect of our existence. There is no doubt that the Sun has the greatest influence on life on this planet. Without it there would be no life, for without it there would be no warmth, no division into day and night, no cycles of time or season at all. This is clear and easy to see. The influence of the Moon, on the other hand, is more subtle, though no less definite.

There are many ways in which the influence of the Moon manifests itself here on Earth, both on human and animal life. It is a well-known fact, for instance, that the large movements of water on our planet—that is the ebb and flow of the tides—are caused by the Moon's gravitational pull. Since this is so, it follows that these water movements do not occur only in the oceans, but that all bodies of water are affected, even down to the tiniest puddle.

The human body, too, which consists of about 70 percent water, falls within the scope of this lunar influence. For example the menstrual cycle of most women corresponds to the 28-day lunar month; the period of pregnancy in humans is 273 days, or equal to nine lunar months. Similarly, many illnesses reach a crisis at the change of the Moon, and statistics in many countries have shown that the crime rate is highest at the time of the Full Moon. Even human sexual desire has been associated with the phases of the Moon. But it is in the movement of the tides that we get the clearest demonstration of planetary influence, which leads to the irresistible correspondence between the so-called metaphysical and the physical.

Tide tables are prepared years in advance by calculating the future positions of the Moon. Science has known for a long time that the Moon is the main cause of tidal action. But only in the last few years has it begun to realize the possible extent of this influence on mankind. To begin with, the ocean tides do not rise and fall as we might imagine from our personal observations of them. The Moon as it orbits around Earth sets up a circular wave of attraction which pulls the oceans of the world after it, broadly in an east to west direction. This influence is like a phantom wave crest, a loop of power stretching from pole to pole which passes over and around the Earth like an invisible shadow. It travels with equal effect across the land masses and, as scientists were recently amazed to observe, caused oysters placed in the dark in the middle of the United States where there is no sea to open their shells to receive the nonexistent tide. If the land-locked oysters react to this invisible signal, what effect does it have on us who not so long ago in evolutionary time came out of the sea and still have its salt in our blood and sweat?

Less well known is the fact that the Moon is also the primary force behind the circulation of blood in human beings and animals, and the movement of sap in trees and plants. Agriculturists have established that the Moon has a distinct influence on crops, which explains why for centuries people have planted according to Moon cycles. The habits of many animals, too, are directed by the movement of the Moon. Migratory birds, for instance, depart only at or near the time of the Full Moon. And certain sea creatures, eels in particular, move only in accordance with certain phases of the Moon.

Know Thyself—Why?

In today's fast-changing world, everyone still longs to know what the future holds. It is the one thing that everyone has in common: rich and poor, famous and infamous, all are deeply concerned about tomorrow.

But the key to the future, as every historian knows, lies in the past. This is as true of individual people as it is of nations. You cannot understand your future without first understanding your past, which is simply another way of saying that you must first of all know yourself.

The motto "know thyself" seems obvious enough nowadays, but it was originally put forward as the foundation of wisdom by the ancient Greek philosophers. It was then adopted by the "mystery religions" of the ancient Middle East, Greece, Rome, and is still used in all genuine schools of mind training or mystical discipline, both in those of the East, based on yoga, and those of the West. So it is universally accepted now, and has been through the ages.

But how do you go about discovering what sort of person you are? The first step is usually classification into some sort of system of types. Astrology did this long before the birth of Christ. Psychology has also done it. So has modern medicine, in its way.

One system classifies people according to the source of the impulses they respond to most readily: the muscles, leading to direct bodily action; the digestive organs, resulting in emotion; or the brain and nerves, giving rise to thinking. Another such system says that character is determined by the endocrine glands, and gives us such labels as "pituitary," "thyroid," and "hyperthyroid" types. These different systems are neither contradictory nor mutually exclusive. In fact, they are very often different ways of saying the same thing.

Very popular, useful classifications were devised by Carl Jung, the eminent disciple of Freud. Jung observed among the different faculties of the mind, four which have a predominant influence on character. These four faculties exist in all of us without exception, but not in perfect balance. So when we say, for instance, that someone is a "thinking type," it means that in any situation he or she tries to be rational. Emotion, which may be the opposite of thinking, will be his or her weakest function. This thinking type can be sensible and reasonable, or calculating and unsympathetic. The emotional type, on the other hand, can often be recognized by exaggerated language—everything is either marvelous or terrible—and in extreme cases they even invent dramas and quarrels out of nothing just to make life more interesting.

The other two faculties are intuition and physical sensation. The sensation type does not only care for food and drink, nice clothes and furniture; he or she is also interested in all forms of physical experience. Many scientists are sensation types as are athletes and nature-lovers. Like sensation, intuition is a form of perception and we all possess it. But it works through that part of the mind which is not under conscious control—consequently it sees meanings and connections which are not obvious to thought or emotion. Inventors and original thinkers are always intuitive, but so, too, are superstitious people who see meanings where none exist.

Thus, sensation tells us what is going on in the world, feeling (that is, emotion) tells us how important it is to ourselves, thinking enables us to interpret it and work out what we should do about it, and intuition tells us what it means to ourselves and others. All four faculties are essential, and all are present in every one of us. But some people are guided chiefly by one, others by another. In addition, Jung also observed a division of the human personality into the extrovert and the introvert, which cuts across these four types.

A disadvantage of all these systems of classification is that one cannot tell very easily where to place oneself. Some people are reluctant to admit that they act to please their emotions. So they deceive themselves for years by trying to belong to whichever type they think is the "best." Of course, there is no best; each has its faults and each has its good points.

The advantage of the signs of the Zodiac is that they simplify classification. Not only that, but your date of birth is personal—it is unarguably yours. What better way to know yourself than by going back as far as possible to the very moment of your birth? And this is precisely what your horoscope is all about, as we shall see in the next section.

WHAT IS A HOROSCOPE?

If you had been able to take a picture of the skies at the moment of your birth, that photograph would be your horoscope. Lacking such a snapshot, it is still possible to recreate the picture—and this is at the basis of the astrologer's art. In other words, your horoscope is a representation of the skies with the planets in the exact positions they occupied at the time you were born.

The year of birth tells an astrologer the positions of the distant, slow-moving planets Jupiter, Saturn, Uranus, Neptune, and Pluto. The month of birth indicates the Sun sign, or birth sign as it is commonly called, as well as indicating the positions of the rapidly moving planets Venus, Mercury, and Mars. The day and time of birth will locate the position of our Moon. And the moment—the exact hour and minute—of birth determines the houses through what is called the Ascendant, or Rising sign.

With this information the astrologer consults various tables to calculate the specific positions of the Sun, Moon, and other planets relative to your birthplace at the moment you were born. Then he or she locates them by means of the Zodiac.

The Zodiac

The Zodiac is a band of stars (constellations) in the skies, centered on the Sun's apparent path around the Earth, and is divided into twelve equal segments, or signs. What we are actually dividing up is the Earth's path around the Sun. But from our point of view here on Earth, it seems as if the Sun is making a great circle around our planet in the sky, so we say it is the Sun's apparent path. This twelvefold division, the Zodiac, is a reference system for the astrologer. At any given moment the planets—and in astrology both the Sun and Moon are considered to be planets—can all be located at a specific point along this path.

Now where in all this are you, the subject of the horoscope? Your character is largely determined by the sign the Sun is in. So that is where the astrologer looks first in your horoscope, at your Sun sign.

The Sun Sign and the Cusp

There are twelve signs in the Zodiac, and the Sun spends approximately one month in each sign. But because of the motion of the Earth around the Sun—the Sun's apparent motion—the dates when the Sun enters and leaves each sign may change from year to year. Some people born near the cusp, or edge, of a sign have difficulty determining which is their Sun sign. But in this book a Table of Cusps is provided for the years 1900 to 2015 (page 5) so you can find out what your true Sun sign is.

Here are the twelve signs of the Zodiac, their ancient zodiacal symbol, and the dates when the Sun enters and leaves each sign for the year 2011. Remember, these dates may change from year to year.

ARIES	Ram	March 20–April 20
TAURUS	Bull	April 20–May 21
GEMINI	Twins	May 21–June 21
CANCER	Crab	June 21–July 22
LEO	Lion	July 23–August 23
VIRGO	Virgin	August 23–September 23
LIBRA	Scales	September 23–October 23
SCORPIO	Scorpion	October 23–November 22
SAGITTARIUS	Archer	November 22–December 22
CAPRICORN	Sea Goat	December 22–January 20
AQUARIUS	Water Bearer	January 20–February 18
PISCES	Fish	February 18–March 20

It is possible to draw significant conclusions and make meaningful predictions based simply on the Sun sign of a person. There are many people who have been amazed at the accuracy of the description of their own character based only on the Sun sign. But an astrologer needs more information than just your Sun sign to interpret the photograph that is your horoscope.

The Rising Sign and the Zodiacal Houses

An astrologer needs the exact time and place of your birth in order to construct and interpret your horoscope. The illustration on the next page shows the flat chart, or natural wheel, an astrologer uses. Note the inner circle of the wheel labeled 1 through 12. These 12 divisions are known as the houses of the Zodiac.

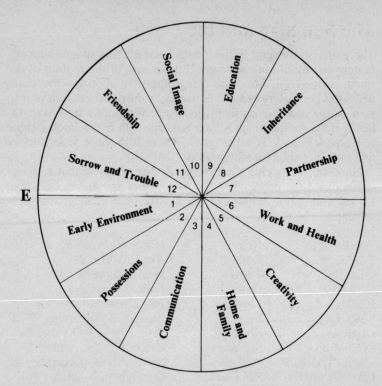

The 1st house always starts from the position marked E, which corresponds to the eastern horizon. The rest of the houses 2 through 12 follow around in a "counterclockwise" direction. The point where each house starts is known as a cusp, or edge.

The cusp, or edge, of the 1st house (point E) is where an astrologer would place your Rising sign, the Ascendant. And, as already noted, the exact time of your birth determines your Rising sign. Let's see how this works.

As the Earth rotates on its axis once every 24 hours, each one of the twelve signs of the Zodiac appears to be "rising" on the horizon, with a new one appearing about every 2 hours. Actually it is the turning of the Earth that exposes each sign to view, but in our astrological work we are discussing apparent motion. This Rising sign marks the Ascendant, and it colors the whole orientation of a horoscope. It indicates the sign governing the 1st house of the chart, and will thus determine which signs will govern all the other houses.

To visualize this idea, imagine two color wheels with twelve divisions superimposed upon each other. For just as the Zodiac is divided into twelve constellations that we identify as the signs, another twelvefold division is used to denote the houses. Now imagine one wheel (the signs) moving slowly while the other wheel (the houses) remains still. This analogy may help you see how the signs keep shifting the "color" of the houses as the Rising sign continues to change every two hours. To simplify things, a Table of Rising Signs has been provided (pages 8–9) for your specific Sun sign.

Once your Rising sign has been placed on the cusp of the 1st house, the signs that govern the rest of the 11 houses can be placed on the chart. In any individual's horoscope the signs do not necessarily correspond with the houses. For example, it could be that a sign covers part of two adjacent houses. It is the interpretation of such variations in an individual's horoscope that marks the professional astrologer.

But to gain a workable understanding of astrology, it is not necessary to go into great detail. In fact, we just need a description of the houses and their meanings, as is shown in the illustration above and in the table below.

THE 12 HOUSES OF THE ZODIAC

1st	Individuality, body appearance, general outlook on life	Personality house
2nd	Finance, possessions, ethical principles, gain or loss	Money house
3rd	Relatives, communication, short journeys, writing, education	Relatives house
4th	Family and home, parental ties, land and property, security	Home house
5th	Pleasure, children, creativity, entertainment, risk	Pleasure house
6th	Health, harvest, hygiene, work and service, employees	Health house
7th	Marriage and divorce, the law, partnerships and alliances	Marriage house
8th	Inheritance, secret deals, sex, death, regeneration	Inheritance house
9th	Travel, sports, study, philosophy, religion	Travel house
10th	Career, social standing, success and honor	Business house
11th	Friendship, social life, hopes and wishes	Friends house
12th	Troubles, illness, secret enemies, hidden agendas	Trouble house

The Planets in the Houses

An astrologer, knowing the exact time and place of your birth, will use tables of planetary motion in order to locate the planets in your horoscope chart. He or she will determine which planet or planets are in which sign and in which house. It is not uncommon, in an individual's horoscope, for there to be two or more planets in the same sign and in the same house.

The characteristics of the planets modify the influence of the Sun according to their natures and strengths.

Sun: Source of life. Basic temperament according to the Sun sign. The conscious will. Human potential.
Moon: Emotions. Moods. Customs. Habits. Changeable. Adaptive. Nurturing.
Mercury: Communication. Intellect. Reasoning power. Curiosity. Short travels.
Venus: Love. Delight. Charm. Harmony. Balance. Art. Beautiful possessions.
Mars: Energy. Initiative. War. Anger. Adventure. Courage. Daring. Impulse.
Jupiter: Luck. Optimism. Generous. Expansive. Opportunities. Protection.
Saturn: Pessimism. Privation. Obstacles. Delay. Hard work. Research. Lasting rewards after long struggle.
Uranus: Fashion. Electricity. Revolution. Independence. Freedom. Sudden changes. Modern science.
Neptune: Sensationalism. Theater. Dreams. Inspiration. Illusion. Deception.
Pluto: Creation and destruction. Total transformation. Lust for power. Strong obsessions.

Superimpose the characteristics of the planets on the functions of the house in which they appear. Express the result through the character of the Sun sign, and you will get the basic idea.

Of course, many other considerations have been taken into account in producing the carefully worked out predictions in this book: the aspects of the planets to each other; their strength according to position and sign; whether they are in a house of exaltation or decline; whether they are natural enemies or not; whether a planet occupies its own sign; the position of a planet in relation to its own house or sign; whether the sign is male or female; whether the sign is a fire, earth, water, or air sign. These are only a few of the colors on the astrologer's pallet which he or she must mix with the inspiration of the artist and the accuracy of the mathematician.

How To Use These Predictions

A person reading the predictions in this book should understand that they are produced from the daily position of the planets for a group of people and are not, of course, individually specialized. To get the full benefit of them our readers should relate the predictions to their own character and circumstances, coordinate them, and draw their own conclusions from them.

If you are a serious observer of your own life, you should find a definite pattern emerging that will be a helpful and reliable guide.

The point is that we always retain our free will. The stars indicate certain directional tendencies but we are not compelled to follow. We can do or not do, and wisdom must make the choice.

We all have our good and bad days. Sometimes they extend into cycles of weeks. It is therefore advisable to study daily predictions in a span ranging from the day before to several days ahead.

Daily predictions should be taken very generally. The word "difficult" does not necessarily indicate a whole day of obstruction or inconvenience. It is a warning to you to be cautious. Your caution will often see you around the difficulty before you are involved. This is the correct use of astrology.

In another section (pages 78–84), detailed information is given about the influence of the Moon as it passes through each of the twelve signs of the Zodiac. There are instructions on how to use the Moon Tables (pages 85–92), which provide Moon Sign Dates throughout the year as well as the Moon's role in health and daily affairs. This information should be used in conjunction with the daily forecasts to give a fuller picture of the astrological trends.

HISTORY OF ASTROLOGY

The origins of astrology have been lost far back in history, but we do know that reference is made to it as far back as the first written records of the human race. It is not hard to see why. Even in primitive times, people must have looked for an explanation for the various happenings in their lives. They must have wanted to know why people were different from one another. And in their search they turned to the regular movements of the Sun, Moon, and stars to see if they could provide an answer.

It is interesting to note that as soon as man learned to use his tools in any type of design, or his mind in any kind of calculation, he turned his attention to the heavens. Ancient cave dwellings reveal dim crescents and circles representative of the Sun and Moon, rulers of day and night. Mesopotamia and the civilization of Chaldea, in itself the foundation of those of Babylonia and Assyria, show a complete picture of astronomical observation and well-developed astrological interpretation.

Humanity has a natural instinct for order. The study of anthropology reveals that primitive people—even as far back as prehistoric times—were striving to achieve a certain order in their lives. They tried to organize the apparent chaos of the universe. They had the desire to attach meaning to things. This demand for order has persisted throughout the history of man. So that observing the regularity of the heavenly bodies made it logical that primitive peoples should turn heavenward in their search for an understanding of the world in which they found themselves so random and alone.

And they did find a significance in the movements of the stars. Shepherds tending their flocks, for instance, observed that when the cluster of stars now known as the constellation Aries was in sight, it was the time of fertility and they associated it with the Ram. And they noticed that the growth of plants and plant life corresponded with different phases of the Moon, so that certain times were favorable for the planting of crops, and other times were not. In this way, there grew up a tradition of seasons and causes connected with the passage of the Sun through the twelve signs of the Zodiac.

Astrology was valued so highly that the king was kept informed of the daily and monthly changes in the heavenly bodies, and the results of astrological studies regarding events of the future. Head astrologers were clearly men of great rank and position, and the office was said to be a hereditary one.

Omens were taken, not only from eclipses and conjunctions of the Moon or Sun with one of the planets, but also from storms and earthquakes. In the eastern civilizations, particularly, the reverence inspired by astrology appears to have remained unbroken since the very earliest days. In ancient China, astrology, astronomy, and religion went hand in hand. The astrologer, who was also an astronomer, was part of the official government service and had his own corner in the Imperial Palace. The duties of the Imperial astrologer, whose office was one of the most important in the land, were clearly defined, as this extract from early records shows:

This exalted gentleman must concern himself with the stars in the heavens, keeping a record of the changes and movements of the Planets, the Sun and the Moon, in order to examine the movements of the terrestrial world with the object of prognosticating good and bad fortune. He divides the territories of the nine regions of the empire in accordance with their dependence on particular celestial bodies. All the fiefs and principalities are connected with the stars and from this their prosperity or misfortune should be ascertained. He makes prognostications according to the twelve years of the Jupiter cycle of good and evil of the terrestrial world. From the colors of the five kinds of clouds, he determines the coming of floods or droughts, abundance or famine. From the twelve winds, he draws conclusions about the state of harmony of heaven and earth, and takes note of good and bad signs that result from their accord or disaccord. In general, he concerns himself with five kinds of phenomena so as to warn the Emperor to come to the aid of the government and to allow for variations in the ceremonies according to their circumstances.

The Chinese were also keen observers of the fixed stars, giving them such unusual names as Ghost Vehicle, Sun of Imperial Concubine, Imperial Prince, Pivot of Heaven, Twinkling Brilliance, Weaving Girl. But, great astrologers though they may have been, the Chinese lacked one aspect of mathematics that the Greeks applied to astrology—deductive geometry. Deductive geometry was the basis of much classical astrology in and after the time of the Greeks, and this explains the different methods of prognostication used in the East and West.

Down through the ages the astrologer's art has depended, not so much on the uncovering of new facts, though this is important, as on the interpretation of the facts already known. This is the essence of the astrologer's skill.

But why should the signs of the Zodiac have any effect at all on the formation of human character? It is easy to see why people thought they did, and even now we constantly use astrological expressions in our everyday speech. The thoughts of "lucky star," "ill-fated," "star-crossed," "mooning around," are interwoven into the very structure of our language.

Wherever the concept of the Zodiac is understood and used, it could well appear to have an influence on the human character. Does this mean, then, that the human race, in whose civilization the idea of the twelve signs of the Zodiac has long been embedded, is divided into only twelve types? Can we honestly believe that it is really as simple as that? If so, there must be pretty wide ranges of variation within each type. And if, to explain the variation, we call in heredity and environment, experiences in early childhood, the thyroid and other glands, and also the four functions of the mind together with extroversion and introversion, then one begins to wonder if the original classification was worth making at all. No sensible person believes that his favorite system explains everything. But even so, he will not find the system much use at all if it does not even save him the trouble of bothering with the others.

In the same way, if we were to put every person under only one sign of the Zodiac, the system becomes too rigid and unlike life. Besides, it was never intended to be used like that. It may be convenient to have only twelve types, but we know that in practice there is every possible gradation between aggressiveness and timidity, or between conscientiousness and laziness. How, then, do we account for this?

A person born under any given Sun sign can be mainly influenced by one or two of the other signs that appear in their individual horoscope. For instance, famous persons born under the sign of Gemini include Henry VIII, whom nothing and no one could have induced to abdicate, and Edward VIII, who did just that. Obviously, then, the sign Gemini does not fully explain the complete character of either of them.

Again, under the opposite sign, Sagittarius, were both Stalin, who was totally consumed with the notion of power, and Charles V, who freely gave up an empire because he preferred to go into a monastery. And we find under Scorpio many uncompromising characters such as Luther, de Gaulle, Indira Gandhi, and Montgomery, but also Petain, a successful commander whose name later became synonymous with collaboration.

A single sign is therefore obviously inadequate to explain the differences between people; it can only explain resemblances, such as the combativeness of the Scorpio group, or the far-reaching devotion of Charles V and Stalin to their respective ideals—the Christian heaven and the Communist utopia.

But very few people have only one sign in their horoscope chart. In addition to the month of birth, the day and, even more, the hour to the nearest minute if possible, ought to be considered. Without this, it is impossible to have an actual horoscope, for the word horoscope literally means "a consideration of the hour."

The month of birth tells you only which sign of the Zodiac was occupied by the Sun. The day and hour tell you what sign was occupied by the Moon. And the minute tells you which sign was rising on the eastern horizon. This is called the Ascendant, and, as some astrologers believe, it is supposed to be the most important thing in the whole horoscope.

The Sun is said to signify one's heart, that is to say, one's deepest desires and inmost nature. This is quite different from the Moon, which signifies one's superficial way of behaving. When the ancient Romans referred to the Emperor Augustus as a Capricorn, they meant that he had the Moon in Capricorn. Or, to take another example, a modern astrologer would call Disraeli a Scorpion because he had Scorpio Rising, but most people would call him Sagittarius because he had the Sun there. The Romans would have called him Leo because his Moon was in Leo.

So if one does not seem to fit one's birth month, it is always worthwhile reading the other signs, for one may have been born at a time when any of them were rising or occupied by the Moon. It also seems to be the case that the influence of the Sun develops as life goes on, so that the month of birth is easier to guess in people over the age of forty. The young are supposed to be influenced mainly by their Ascendant, the Rising sign, which characterizes the body and physical personality as a whole.

It is nonsense to assume that all people born at a certain time will exhibit the same characteristics, or that they will even behave in the same manner. It is quite obvious that, from the very moment of its birth, a child is subject to the effects of its environment, and that this in turn will influence its character and heritage to a decisive extent. Also to be taken into account are education and economic conditions, which play a very important part in the formation of one's character as well.

People have, in general, certain character traits and qualities which, according to their environment, develop in either a positive or a negative manner. Therefore, selfishness (inherent selfishness, that is) might emerge as unselfishness; kindness and consideration as cruelty and lack of consideration toward others. In the same way, a naturally constructive person may, through frustration, become destructive, and so on. The latent characteristics with which people are born can, therefore, through environment and good or bad training, become something that would appear to be its opposite, and so give the lie to the astrologer's description of their character. But this is not the case. The true character is still there, but it is buried deep beneath these external superficialities.

Careful study of the character traits of various signs of the Zodiac are of immeasurable help, and can render beneficial service to the intelligent person. Undoubtedly, the reader will already have discovered that, while he is able to get on very well with some people, he just "cannot stand" others. The causes sometimes seem inexplicable. At times there is intense dislike, at other times immediate sympathy. And there is, too, the phenomenon of love at first sight, which is also apparently inexplicable. People appear to be either sympathetic or unsympathetic toward each other for no apparent reason.

Now if we look at this in the light of the Zodiac, we find that people born under different signs are either compatible or incompatible with each other. In other words, there are good and bad interrelating factors among the various signs. This does not, of course, mean that humanity can be divided into groups of hostile camps. It would be quite wrong to be hostile or indifferent toward people who happen to be born under an incompatible sign. There is no reason why everybody should not, or cannot, learn to control and adjust their feelings and actions, especially after they are aware of the positive qualities of other people by studying their character analyses, among other things.

Every person born under a certain sign has both positive and negative qualities, which are developed more or less according to our free will. Nobody is entirely good or entirely bad, and it is up to each of us to learn to control ourselves on the one hand and at the same time to endeavor to learn about ourselves and others.

It cannot be emphasized often enough that it is free will that determines whether we will make really good use of our talents and abilities. Using our free will, we can either overcome our failings or allow them to rule us. Our free will enables us to exert sufficient willpower to control our failings so that they do not harm ourselves or others.

Astrology can reveal our inclinations and tendencies. Astrology can tell us about ourselves so that we are able to use our free will to overcome our shortcomings. In this way astrology helps us do our best to become needed and valuable members of society as well as helpmates to our family and our friends. Astrology also can save us a great deal of unhappiness and remorse.

Yet it may seem absurd that an ancient philosophy could be a prop to modern men and women. But below the materialistic surface of modern life, there are hidden streams of feeling and thought. Symbology is reappearing as a study worthy of the scholar; the psychosomatic factor in illness has passed from the writings of the crank to those of the specialist; spiritual healing in all its forms is no longer a pious hope but an accepted phenomenon. And it is into this context that we consider astrology, in the sense that it is an analysis of human types.

Astrology and medicine had a long journey together, and only parted company a couple of centuries ago. There still remain in medical language such astrological terms as "saturnine," "choleric," and "mercurial," used in the diagnosis of physical tendencies. The herbalist, for long the handyman of the medical profession, has been dominated by astrology since the days of the Greeks. Certain herbs traditionally respond to certain planetary influences, and diseases must therefore be treated to ensure harmony between the medicine and the disease.

But the stars are expected to foretell and not only to diagnose.

Astrological forecasting has been remarkably accurate, but often it is wide of the mark. The brave person who cares to predict world events takes dangerous chances. Individual forecasting is less clear cut; it can be a help or a disillusionment. Then we come to the nagging question: if it is possible to foreknow, is it right to foretell? This is a point of ethics on which it is hard to pronounce judgment. The doctor faces the same dilemma if he finds that symptoms of a mortal disease are present in his patient and that he can only prognosticate a steady decline. How much to tell an individual in a crisis is a problem that has perplexed many distinguished scholars. Honest and conscientious astrologers in this modern world, where so many people are seeking guidance, face the same problem.

Five hundred years ago it was customary to call in a learned man who was an astrologer who was probably also a doctor and a philosopher. By his knowledge of astrology, his study of planetary influences, he felt himself qualified to guide those in distress. The world has moved forward at a fantastic rate since then, and yet people are still uncertain of themselves. At first sight it seems fantastic in the light of modern thinking that they turn to the most ancient of all studies, and get someone to calculate a horoscope for them. But is it really so fantastic if you take a second look? For astrology is concerned with tomorrow, with survival. And in a world such as ours, tomorrow and survival are the keywords for the twenty-first century.

SPECIAL OVERVIEW 2011–2020

The second decade of the twenty-first century opens on major planetary shifts that set the stage for challenge, opportunity, and change. The personal planets—notably Jupiter and Saturn—and the generational planets—Uranus, Neptune, and Pluto—have all moved forward into new signs of the zodiac. These fresh planetary influences act to shape unfolding events and illuminate pathways to the future.

Jupiter, the big planet that attracts luck, spends about one year in each zodiacal sign. It takes approximately twelve years for Jupiter to travel through all twelve signs of the zodiac in order to complete a cycle. In 2011 a new Jupiter cycle is initiated with Jupiter transiting Aries, the first sign of the zodiac. As each year progresses over the course of the decade, Jupiter moves forward into the next sign, following the natural progression of the zodiac. Jupiter visits Taurus in 2012, Gemini in 2013, Cancer in 2014, Leo in 2015, Virgo in 2016, Libra in 2017, Scorpio in 2018, Sagittarius in 2019, Capricorn in 2020. Then in late December 2020 Jupiter enters Aquarius just two weeks before the decade closes. Jupiter's vibrations are helpful and fruitful, a source of good luck and a protection against bad luck. Opportunity swells under Jupiter's powerful rays. Learning takes leaps of faith.

Saturn, the beautiful planet of reason and responsibility, spends about two and a half years in each zodiacal sign. A complete Saturn cycle through all twelve signs of the zodiac takes about twenty-nine to thirty years. Saturn is known as the lawgiver: setting boundaries and codes of conduct, urging self-discipline and structure within a creative framework. The rule of law, the role of government, the responsibility of the individual are all sourced from Saturn. Saturn gives as it takes. Once a lesson is learned, Saturn's reward is just and full.

Saturn transits Libra throughout 2011 until early autumn of 2012. Here Saturn seeks to harmonize, to balance, to bring order out of chaos. Saturn in Libra ennobles the artist, the judge, the high-minded, the honest. Saturn next visits Scorpio from autumn 2012 until late December 2014. With Saturn in Scorpio, tactic and strategy combine to get workable solutions and desired results. Saturn's problem-solving tools here can harness dynamic energy for the common good. Saturn in Sagittarius, an idealistic and humanistic transit that stretches from December 2014 into the last day of autumn 2017, promotes activism over mere dogma and debate. Saturn in Sagittarius can be a driving force for good. Saturn tours Capricorn, the sign that Saturn rules, from the first day of winter 2017 into early spring 2020. Saturn in Capricorn is a consolidating transit, bringing things forth and into fruition. Here a plan can be made right, made whole, then launched for success. Saturn starts to visit Aquarius, a sign that Saturn corules and a very good sign for Saturn to visit, in the very last year of the decade. Saturn in Aquarius fosters team spirit, the unity of effort amid diversity. The transit of Saturn in Aquarius until early 2023 represents a period of enlightened activism and unprecedented growth.

Uranus, Neptune, and Pluto spend more than several years in each sign. They produce the differences in attitude, belief, behavior, and taste that distinguish one generation from another—and so are called the generational planets.

Uranus, planet of innovation and surprise, is known as the awakener. Uranus spends seven to eight years in each sign. Uranus started a new cycle when it entered Aries, the first sign of the zodiac, in May 2010. Uranus tours Aries until May 2018. Uranus in Aries accents originality, freedom, independence, unpredictability. There can be a start-stop quality to undertakings given this transit. Despite contradiction and confrontation, significant invention and productivity mark this transit. Uranus next visits Taurus through the end of the decade into 2026. Strategic thinking and timely action characterize the transit of Uranus in Taurus. Here intuition is backed up by common sense, leading to fresh discoveries upon which new industries can be built.

Neptune spends about fourteen years in each sign. Neptune, the visionary planet, enters Pisces, the sign Neptune rules and the final sign of the zodiac, in early April 2011. Neptune journeys through Pisces until 2026 to complete the Neptune cycle of visiting all twelve zodiacal signs. Neptune's tour of Pisces ushers in a long period of great potentiality: universal understanding, universal good, universal love, universal generosity, universal forgiveness—the universal spirit affects all. Neptune in Pisces can oversee the fruition of such noble aims as human rights for all and liberation from all forms of tyranny. Neptune in Pisces is a pervasive influence that changes concepts, consciences, attitudes, actions. The impact of Neptune in Pisces is to illuminate and to inspire.

Pluto, dwarf planet of beginnings and endings, entered the earthy sign of Capricorn in 2008 and journeys there for sixteen years into late 2024. Pluto in Capricorn over the course of this extensive visit has the capacity to change the landscape as well as the humanscape. The transforming energy of Pluto combines with the persevering power of Capricorn to give depth and character to potential change. Pluto in Capricorn brings focus and cohesion to disparate, diverse creativities. As new forms arise and take root, Pluto in Capricorn organizes the rebuilding process. Freedom versus limitation, freedom versus authority is in the framework during this transit. Reasonableness struggles with recklessness to solve divisive issues. Pluto in Capricorn teaches important lessons about adversity, and the lessons will be learned.

THE SIGNS OF THE ZODIAC

Dominant Characteristics

Aries: March 21–April 20

The Positive Side of Aries

The Aries has many positive points to his character. People born under this first sign of the Zodiac are often quite strong and enthusiastic. On the whole, they are forward-looking people who are not easily discouraged by temporary setbacks. They know what they want out of life and they go out after it. Their personalities are strong. Others are usually quite impressed by the Ram's way of doing things. Quite often they are sources of inspiration for others traveling the same route. Aries men and women have a special zest for life that can be contagious; for others, they are a fine example of how life should be lived.

The Aries person usually has a quick and active mind. He is imaginative and inventive. He enjoys keeping busy and active. He generally gets along well with all kinds of people. He is interested in mankind, as a whole. He likes to be challenged. Some would say he thrives on opposition, for it is when he is set against that he often does his best. Getting over or around obstacles is a challenge he generally enjoys. All in all, Aries is quite positive and young-thinking. He likes to keep abreast of new things that are happening in the world. Aries are often fond of speed. They like things to be done quickly, and this sometimes aggravates their slower colleagues and associates.

The Aries man or woman always seems to remain young. Their whole approach to life is youthful and optimistic. They never say

die, no matter what the odds. They may have an occasional setback, but it is not long before they are back on their feet again.

The Negative Side of Aries

Everybody has his less positive qualities—and Aries is no exception. Sometimes the Aries man or woman is not very tactful in communicating with others; in his hurry to get things done he is apt to be a little callous or inconsiderate. Sensitive people are likely to find him somewhat sharp-tongued in some situations. Often in his eagerness to get the show on the road, he misses the mark altogether and cannot achieve his aims.

At times Aries can be too impulsive. He can occasionally be stubborn and refuse to listen to reason. If things do not move quickly enough to suit the Aries man or woman, he or she is apt to become rather nervous or irritable. The uncultivated Aries is not unfamiliar with moments of doubt and fear. He is capable of being destructive if he does not get his way. He can overcome some of his emotional problems by steadily trying to express himself as he really is, but this requires effort.

Taurus: April 21–May 20

The Positive Side of Taurus

The Taurus person is known for his ability to concentrate and for his tenacity. These are perhaps his strongest qualities. The Taurus man or woman generally has very little trouble in getting along with others; it's his nature to be helpful toward people in need. He can always be depended on by his friends, especially those in trouble.

Taurus generally achieves what he wants through his ability to persevere. He never leaves anything unfinished but works on something until it has been completed. People can usually take him at his word; he is honest and forthright in most of his dealings. The Taurus person has a good chance to make a success of his life because of his many positive qualities. The Taurus who aims high seldom falls short of his mark. He learns well by experience. He is thorough and does not believe in shortcuts of any kind. The Bull's thoroughness pays off in the end, for through his deliberateness he learns how to rely on himself and what he has learned. The Taurus person tries to get along with others, as a rule.

He is not overly critical and likes people to be themselves. He is a tolerant person and enjoys peace and harmony—especially in his home life.

Taurus is usually cautious in all that he does. He is not a person who believes in taking unnecessary risks. Before adopting any one line of action, he will weigh all of the pros and cons. The Taurus person is steadfast. Once his mind is made up it seldom changes. The person born under this sign usually is a good family person—reliable and loving.

The Negative Side of Taurus

Sometimes the Taurus man or woman is a bit too stubborn. He won't listen to other points of view if his mind is set on something. To others, this can be quite annoying. Taurus also does not like to be told what to do. He becomes rather angry if others think him not too bright. He does not like to be told he is wrong, even when he is. He dislikes being contradicted.

Some people who are born under this sign are very suspicious of others—even of those persons close to them. They find it difficult to trust people fully. They are often afraid of being deceived or taken advantage of. The Bull often finds it difficult to forget or forgive. His love of material things sometimes makes him rather avaricious and petty.

Gemini: May 21–June 20

The Positive Side of Gemini

The person born under this sign of the Heavenly Twins is usually quite bright and quick-witted. Some of them are capable of doing many different things. The Gemini person very often has many different interests. He keeps an open mind and is always anxious to learn new things.

Gemini is often an analytical person. He is a person who enjoys making use of his intellect. He is governed more by his mind than by his emotions. He is a person who is not confined to one view; he can often understand both sides to a problem or question. He knows how to reason, how to make rapid decisions if need be.

He is an adaptable person and can make himself at home almost anywhere. There are all kinds of situations he can adapt to. He is a person who seldom doubts himself; he is sure of his talents and his ability to think and reason. Gemini is generally most satisfied when he is in a situation where he can make use of his intellect. Never short of imagination, he often has strong talents for invention. He is rather a modern person when it comes to life; Gemini almost always moves along with the times—perhaps that is why he remains so youthful throughout most of his life.

Literature and art appeal to the person born under this sign. Creativity in almost any form will interest and intrigue the Gemini man or woman.

The Gemini is often quite charming. A good talker, he often is the center of attraction at any gathering. People find it easy to like a person born under this sign because he can appear easygoing and usually has a good sense of humor.

The Negative Side of Gemini

Sometimes the Gemini person tries to do too many things at one time—and as a result, winds up finishing nothing. Some Twins are easily distracted and find it rather difficult to concentrate on one thing for too long a time. Sometimes they give in to trifling fancies and find it rather boring to become too serious about any one thing. Some of them are never dependable, no matter what they promise.

Although the Gemini man or woman often appears to be well-versed on many subjects, this is sometimes just a veneer. His knowledge may be only superficial, but because he speaks so well he gives people the impression of erudition. Some Geminis are sharp-tongued and inconsiderate; they think only of themselves and their own pleasure.

Cancer: June 21–July 20

The Positive Side of Cancer

The Moon Child's most positive point is his understanding nature. On the whole, he is a loving and sympathetic person. He would never go out of his way to hurt anyone. The Cancer man or woman is often very kind and tender; they give what they can to others. They hate to see others suffering and will do what they can to help someone in less fortunate circumstances than themselves. They are often very concerned about the world. Their interest in people generally goes beyond that of just their own families and close friends; they have a deep sense of community and respect humanitarian values. The Moon Child means what he says, as a rule; he is honest about his feelings.

The Cancer man or woman is a person who knows the art of patience. When something seems difficult, he is willing to wait until the situation becomes manageable again. He is a person who knows how to bide his time. Cancer knows how to concentrate on one thing at a time. When he has made his mind up he generally sticks with what he does, seeing it through to the end.

Cancer is a person who loves his home. He enjoys being surrounded by familiar things and the people he loves. Of all the signs, Cancer is the most maternal. Even the men born under this sign often have a motherly or protective quality about them. They like to take care of people in their family—to see that they are well loved and well provided for. They are usually loyal and faithful. Family ties mean a lot to the Cancer man or woman. Parents and in-laws are respected and loved. Young Cancer responds very well to adults who show faith in him. The Moon Child has a strong sense of tradition. He is very sensitive to the moods of others.

The Negative Side of Cancer

Sometimes Cancer finds it rather hard to face life. It becomes too much for him. He can be a little timid and retiring, when things don't go too well. When unfortunate things happen, he is apt to just shrug and say, "Whatever will be will be." He can be fatalistic to a fault. The uncultivated Cancer is a bit lazy. He doesn't have very much ambition. Anything that seems a bit difficult he'll gladly leave to others. He may be lacking in initiative. Too sensitive, when he feels he's been injured, he'll crawl back into his shell and nurse his imaginary wounds. The immature Moon Child often is given to crying when the smallest thing goes wrong.

Some Cancers find it difficult to enjoy themselves in environments outside their homes. They make heavy demands on others, and need to be constantly reassured that they are loved. Lacking such reassurance, they may resort to sulking in silence.

Leo: July 21–August 21

The Positive Side of Leo

Often Leos make good leaders. They seem to be good organizers and administrators. Usually they are quite popular with others. Whatever group it is that they belong to, the Leo man or woman is almost sure to be or become the leader. Loyalty, one of the Lion's noblest traits, enables him or her to maintain this leadership position.

Leo is generous most of the time. It is his best characteristic. He or she likes to give gifts and presents. In making others happy, the Leo person becomes happy himself. He likes to splurge when spending money on others. In some instances it may seem that the Lion's generosity knows no boundaries. A hospitable person, the Leo man or woman is very fond of welcoming people to his house and entertaining them. He is never short of company.

Leo has plenty of energy and drive. He enjoys working toward some specific goal. When he applies himself correctly, he gets what he wants most often. The Leo person is almost never unsure of himself. He has plenty of confidence and aplomb. He is a person who is direct in almost everything he does. He has a quick mind and can make a decision in a very short time.

He usually sets a good example for others because of his ambitious manner and positive ways. He knows how to stick to something once he's started. Although Leo may be good at making a joke, he is not superficial or glib. He is a loving person, kind and thoughtful.

There is generally nothing small or petty about the Leo man or woman. He does what he can for those who are deserving. He is a person others can rely upon at all times. He means what he says. An honest person, generally speaking, he is a friend who is valued and sought out.

The Negative Side of Leo

Leo, however, does have his faults. At times, he can be just a bit too arrogant. He thinks that no one deserves a leadership position except him. Only he is capable of doing things well. His opinion of himself is often much too high. Because of his conceit, he is sometimes rather unpopular with a good many people. Some Leos are too materialistic; they can only think in terms of money and profit.

Some Leos enjoy lording it over others—at home or at their place of business. What is more, they feel they have the right to. Egocentric to an impossible degree, this sort of Leo cares little about how others think or feel. He can be rude and cutting.

Virgo: August 22–September 22

The Positive Side of Virgo

The person born under the sign of Virgo is generally a busy person. He knows how to arrange and organize things. He is a good planner. Above all, he is practical and is not afraid of hard work.

Often called the sign of the Harvester, Virgo knows how to attain what he desires. He sticks with something until it is finished. He never shirks his duties, and can always be depended upon. The Virgo person can be thoroughly trusted at all times.

The man or woman born under this sign tries to do everything to perfection. He doesn't believe in doing anything halfway. He always aims for the top. He is the sort of a person who is always learning and constantly striving to better himself—not because he wants more money or glory, but because it gives him a feeling of accomplishment.

The Virgo man or woman is a very observant person. He is sensitive to how others feel, and can see things below the surface of a situation. He usually puts this talent to constructive use.

It is not difficult for the Virgo to be open and earnest. He believes in putting his cards on the table. He is never secretive or underhanded. He's as good as his word. The Virgo person is generally plainspoken and down to earth. He has no trouble in expressing himself.

The Virgo person likes to keep up to date on new developments in his particular field. Well-informed, generally, he sometimes has a keen interest in the arts or literature. What he knows, he knows well. His ability to use his critical faculties is well-developed and sometimes startles others because of its accuracy.

Virgos adhere to a moderate way of life; they avoid excesses. Virgo is a responsible person and enjoys being of service.

The Negative Side of Virgo

Sometimes a Virgo person is too critical. He thinks that only he can do something the way it should be done. Whatever anyone else does is inferior. He can be rather annoying in the way he quibbles over insignificant details. In telling others how things should be done, he can be rather tactless and mean.

Some Virgos seem rather emotionless and cool. They feel emotional involvement is beneath them. They are sometimes too tidy, too neat. With money they can be rather miserly. Some Virgos try to force their opinions and ideas on others.

Libra: September 23–October 22

The Positive Side of Libra

Libras love harmony. It is one of their most outstanding character traits. They are interested in achieving balance; they admire beauty and grace in things as well as in people. Generally speaking, they are kind and considerate people. Libras are usually very sympathetic. They go out of their way not to hurt another person's feelings. They are outgoing and do what they can to help those in need.

People born under the sign of Libra almost always make good friends. They are loyal and amiable. They enjoy the company of others. Many of them are rather moderate in their views; they believe in keeping an open mind, however, and weighing both sides of an issue fairly before making a decision.

Alert and intelligent, Libra, often known as the Lawgiver, is always fair-minded and tries to put himself in the position of the other person. They are against injustice; quite often they take up for the underdog. In most of their social dealings, they try to be tactful and kind. They dislike discord and bickering, and most Libras strive for peace and harmony in all their relationships.

The Libra man or woman has a keen sense of beauty. They appreciate handsome furnishings and clothes. Many of them are artistically inclined. Their taste is usually impeccable. They know how to use color. Their homes are almost always attractively arranged and inviting. They enjoy entertaining people and see to it that their guests always feel at home and welcome.

Libra gets along with almost everyone. He is well-liked and socially much in demand.

The Negative Side of Libra

Some people born under this sign tend to be rather insincere. So eager are they to achieve harmony in all relationships that they will even go so far as to lie. Many of them are escapists. They find facing the truth an ordeal and prefer living in a world of make-believe.

In a serious argument, some Libras give in rather easily even when they know they are right. Arguing, even about something they believe in, is too unsettling for some of them.

Libras sometimes care too much for material things. They enjoy possessions and luxuries. Some are vain and tend to be jealous.

Scorpio: October 23–November 22

The Positive Side of Scorpio

The Scorpio man or woman generally knows what he or she wants out of life. He is a determined person. He sees something through to the end. Scorpio is quite sincere, and seldom says anything he doesn't mean. When he sets a goal for himself he tries to go about achieving it in a very direct way.

The Scorpion is brave and courageous. They are not afraid of hard work. Obstacles do not frighten them. They forge ahead until they achieve what they set out for. The Scorpio man or woman has a strong will.

Although Scorpio may seem rather fixed and determined, inside he is often quite tender and loving. He can care very much for others. He believes in sincerity in all relationships. His feelings about someone tend to last; they are profound and not superficial.

The Scorpio person is someone who adheres to his principles no matter what happens. He will not be deterred from a path he believes to be right.

Because of his many positive strengths, the Scorpion can often achieve happiness for himself and for those that he loves.

He is a constructive person by nature. He often has a deep understanding of people and of life, in general. He is perceptive and unafraid. Obstacles often seem to spur him on. He is a positive person who enjoys winning. He has many strengths and resources; challenge of any sort often brings out the best in him.

The Negative Side of Scorpio

The Scorpio person is sometimes hypersensitive. Often he imagines injury when there is none. He feels that others do not bother to recognize him for his true worth. Sometimes he is given to excessive boasting in order to compensate for what he feels is neglect.

Scorpio can be proud, arrogant, and competitive. They can be sly when they put their minds to it and they enjoy outwitting persons or institutions noted for their cleverness.

Their tactics for getting what they want are sometimes devious and ruthless. They don't care too much about what others may think. If they feel others have done them an injustice, they will do their best to seek revenge. The Scorpion often has a sudden, violent temper; and this person's interest in sex is sometimes quite unbalanced or excessive.

Sagittarius: November 23–December 20

The Positive Side of Sagittarius

People born under this sign are honest and forthright. Their approach to life is earnest and open. Sagittarius is often quite adult in his way of seeing things. They are broad-minded and tolerant people. When dealing with others the person born under the sign of the Archer is almost always open and forthright. He doesn't believe in deceit or pretension. His standards are high. People who associate with Sagittarius generally admire and respect his tolerant viewpoint.

The Archer trusts others easily and expects them to trust him. He is never suspicious or envious and almost always thinks well of others. People always enjoy his company because he is so friendly and easygoing. The Sagittarius man or woman is often good-humored. He can always be depended upon by his friends, family, and coworkers.

The person born under this sign of the Zodiac likes a good joke every now and then. Sagittarius is eager for fun and laughs, which makes him very popular with others.

A lively person, he enjoys sports and outdoor life. The Archer is fond of animals. Intelligent and interesting, he can begin an ani-

mated conversation with ease. He likes exchanging ideas and discussing various views.

He is not selfish or proud. If someone proposes an idea or plan that is better than his, he will immediately adopt it. Imaginative yet practical, he knows how to put ideas into practice.

The Archer enjoys sport and games, and it doesn't matter if he wins or loses. He is a forgiving person, and never sulks over something that has not worked out in his favor.

He is seldom critical, and is almost always generous.

The Negative Side of Sagittarius

Some Sagittarius are restless. They take foolish risks and seldom learn from the mistakes they make. They don't have heads for money and are often mismanaging their finances. Some of them devote much of their time to gambling.

Some are too outspoken and tactless, always putting their feet in their mouths. They hurt others carelessly by being honest at the wrong time. Sometimes they make promises which they don't keep. They don't stick close enough to their plans and go from one failure to another. They are undisciplined and waste a lot of energy.

Capricorn: December 21–January 19

The Positive Side of Capricorn

The person born under the sign of Capricorn, known variously as the Mountain Goat or Sea Goat, is usually very stable and patient. He sticks to whatever tasks he has and sees them through. He can always be relied upon and he is not averse to work.

An honest person, Capricorn is generally serious about whatever he does. He does not take his duties lightly. He is a practical person and believes in keeping his feet on the ground.

Quite often the person born under this sign is ambitious and knows how to get what he wants out of life. The Goat forges ahead and never gives up his goal. When he is determined about something, he almost always wins. He is a good worker—a hard worker. Although things may not come easy to him, he will not complain, but continue working until his chores are finished.

He is usually good at business matters and knows the value of money. He is not a spendthrift and knows how to put something away for a rainy day; he dislikes waste and unnecessary loss.

Capricorn knows how to make use of his self-control. He can apply himself to almost anything once he puts his mind to it. His ability to concentrate sometimes astounds others. He is diligent and does well when involved in detail work.

The Capricorn man or woman is charitable, generally speaking, and will do what is possible to help others less fortunate. As a friend, he is loyal and trustworthy. He never shirks his duties or responsibilities. He is self-reliant and never expects too much of the other fellow. He does what he can on his own. If someone does him a good turn, then he will do his best to return the favor.

The Negative Side of Capricorn

Like everyone, Capricorn, too, has faults. At times, the Goat can be overcritical of others. He expects others to live up to his own high standards. He thinks highly of himself and tends to look down on others.

His interest in material things may be exaggerated. The Capricorn man or woman thinks too much about getting on in the world and having something to show for it. He may even be a little greedy.

He sometimes thinks he knows what's best for everyone. He is too bossy. He is always trying to organize and correct others. He may be a little narrow in his thinking.

Aquarius: January 20–February 18

The Positive Side of Aquarius

The Aquarius man or woman is usually very honest and forthright. These are his two greatest qualities. His standards for himself are generally very high. He can always be relied upon by others. His word is his bond.

Aquarius is perhaps the most tolerant of all the Zodiac personalities. He respects other people's beliefs and feels that everyone is entitled to his own approach to life.

He would never do anything to injure another's feelings. He is never unkind or cruel. Always considerate of others, the Water

Bearer is always willing to help a person in need. He feels a very strong tie between himself and all the other members of mankind.

The person born under this sign, called the Water Bearer, is almost always an individualist. He does not believe in teaming up with the masses, but prefers going his own way. His ideas about life and mankind are often quite advanced. There is a saying to the effect that the average Aquarius is fifty years ahead of his time.

Aquarius is community-minded. The problems of the world concern him greatly. He is interested in helping others no matter what part of the globe they live in. He is truly a humanitarian sort. He likes to be of service to others.

Giving, considerate, and without prejudice, Aquarius have no trouble getting along with others.

The Negative Side of Aquarius

Aquarius may be too much of a dreamer. He makes plans but seldom carries them out. He is rather unrealistic. His imagination has a tendency to run away with him. Because many of his plans are impractical, he is always in some sort of a dither.

Others may not approve of him at all times because of his unconventional behavior. He may be a bit eccentric. Sometimes he is so busy with his own thoughts that he loses touch with the realities of existence.

Some Aquarius feel they are more clever and intelligent than others. They seldom admit to their own faults, even when they are quite apparent. Some become rather fanatic in their views. Their criticism of others is sometimes destructive and negative.

Pisces: February 19–March 20

The Positive Side of Pisces

Known as the sign of the Fishes, Pisces has a sympathetic nature. Kindly, he is often dedicated in the way he goes about helping others. The sick and the troubled often turn to him for advice and assistance. Possessing keen intuition, Pisces can easily understand people's deepest problems.

He is very broad-minded and does not criticize others for their faults. He knows how to accept people for what they are. On the whole, he is a trustworthy and earnest person. He is loyal to his friends and will do what he can to help them in time of need. Generous and good-natured, he is a lover of peace; he is often willing to help others solve their differences. People who have taken a wrong turn in life often interest him and he will do what he can to persuade them to rehabilitate themselves.

He has a strong intuitive sense and most of the time he knows how to make it work for him. Pisces is unusually perceptive and often knows what is bothering someone before that person, himself, is aware of it. The Pisces man or woman is an idealistic person, basically, and is interested in making the world a better place in which to live. Pisces believes that everyone should help each other. He is willing to do more than his share in order to achieve cooperation with others.

The person born under this sign often is talented in music or art. He is a receptive person; he is able to take the ups and downs of life with philosophic calm.

The Negative Side of Pisces

Some Pisces are often depressed; their outlook on life is rather glum. They may feel that they have been given a bad deal in life and that others are always taking unfair advantage of them. Pisces sometimes feel that the world is a cold and cruel place. The Fishes can be easily discouraged. The Pisces man or woman may even withdraw from the harshness of reality into a secret shell of his own where he dreams and idles away a good deal of his time.

Pisces can be lazy. He lets things happen without giving the least bit of resistance. He drifts along, whether on the high road or on the low. He can be lacking in willpower.

Some Pisces people seek escape through drugs or alcohol. When temptation comes along they find it hard to resist. In matters of sex, they can be rather permissive.

Sun Sign Personalities

ARIES: Hans Christian Andersen, Pearl Bailey, Marlon Brando, Wernher Von Braun, Charlie Chaplin, Joan Crawford, Da Vinci, Bette Davis, Doris Day, W.C. Fields, Alec Guinness, Adolf Hitler, William Holden, Thomas Jefferson, Nikita Khrushchev, Elton John, Arturo Toscanini, J.P. Morgan, Paul Robeson, Gloria Steinem, Sarah Vaughn, Vincent van Gogh, Tennessee Williams

TAURUS: Fred Astaire, Charlotte Brontë, Carol Burnett, Irving Berlin, Bing Crosby, Salvador Dali, Tchaikovsky, Queen Elizabeth II, Duke Ellington, Ella Fitzgerald, Henry Fonda, Sigmund Freud, Orson Welles, Joe Louis, Lenin, Karl Marx, Golda Meir, Eva Peron, Bertrand Russell, Shakespeare, Kate Smith, Benjamin Spock, Barbra Streisand, Shirley Temple, Harry Truman

GEMINI: Ruth Benedict, Josephine Baker, Rachel Carson, Carlos Chavez, Walt Whitman, Bob Dylan, Ralph Waldo Emerson, Judy Garland, Paul Gauguin, Allen Ginsberg, Benny Goodman, Bob Hope, Burl Ives, John F. Kennedy, Peggy Lee, Marilyn Monroe, Joe Namath, Cole Porter, Laurence Olivier, Harriet Beecher Stowe, Queen Victoria, John Wayne, Frank Lloyd Wright

CANCER: "Dear Abby," Lizzie Borden, David Brinkley, Yul Brynner, Pearl Buck, Marc Chagall, Princess Diana, Babe Didrikson, Mary Baker Eddy, Henry VIII, John Glenn, Ernest Hemingway, Lena Horne, Oscar Hammerstein, Helen Keller, Ann Landers, George Orwell, Nancy Reagan, Rembrandt, Richard Rodgers, Ginger Rogers, Rubens, Jean-Paul Sartre, O.J. Simpson

LEO: Neil Armstrong, James Baldwin, Lucille Ball, Emily Brontë, Wilt Chamberlain, Julia Child, William J. Clinton, Cecil B. De Mille, Ogden Nash, Amelia Earhart, Edna Ferber, Arthur Goldberg, Alfred Hitchcock, Mick Jagger, George Meany, Annie Oakley, George Bernard Shaw, Napoleon, Jacqueline Onassis, Henry Ford, Francis Scott Key, Andy Warhol, Mae West, Orville Wright

VIRGO: Ingrid Bergman, Warren Burger, Maurice Chevalier, Agatha Christie, Sean Connery, Lafayette, Peter Falk, Greta Garbo, Althea Gibson, Arthur Godfrey, Goethe, Buddy Hackett, Michael Jackson, Lyndon Johnson, D.H. Lawrence, Sophia Loren, Grandma Moses, Arnold Palmer, Queen Elizabeth I, Walter Reuther, Peter Sellers, Lily Tomlin, George Wallace

LIBRA: Brigitte Bardot, Art Buchwald, Truman Capote, Dwight D. Eisenhower, William Faulkner, F. Scott Fitzgerald, Gandhi, George Gershwin, Micky Mantle, Helen Hayes, Vladimir Horowitz, Doris Lessing, Martina Navratalova, Eugene O'Neill, Luciano Pavarotti, Emily Post, Eleanor Roosevelt, Bruce Springsteen, Margaret Thatcher, Gore Vidal, Barbara Walters, Oscar Wilde

SCORPIO: Vivien Leigh, Richard Burton, Art Carney, Johnny Carson, Billy Graham, Grace Kelly, Walter Cronkite, Marie Curie, Charles de Gaulle, Linda Evans, Indira Gandhi, Theodore Roosevelt, Rock Hudson, Katherine Hepburn, Robert F. Kennedy, Billie Jean King, Martin Luther, Georgia O'Keeffe, Pablo Picasso, Jonas Salk, Alan Shepard, Robert Louis Stevenson

SAGITTARIUS: Jane Austen, Louisa May Alcott, Woody Allen, Beethoven, Willy Brandt, Mary Martin, William F. Buckley, Maria Callas, Winston Churchill, Noel Coward, Emily Dickinson, Walt Disney, Benjamin Disraeli, James Doolittle, Kirk Douglas, Chet Huntley, Jane Fonda, Chris Evert Lloyd, Margaret Mead, Charles Schulz, John Milton, Frank Sinatra, Steven Spielberg

CAPRICORN: Muhammad Ali, Isaac Asimov, Pablo Casals, Dizzy Dean, Marlene Dietrich, James Farmer, Ava Gardner, Barry Goldwater, Cary Grant, J. Edgar Hoover, Howard Hughes, Joan of Arc, Gypsy Rose Lee, Martin Luther King, Jr., Rudyard Kipling, Mao Tse-tung, Richard Nixon, Gamal Nasser, Louis Pasteur, Albert Schweitzer, Stalin, Benjamin Franklin, Elvis Presley

AQUARIUS: Marian Anderson, Susan B. Anthony, Jack Benny, John Barrymore, Mikhail Baryshnikov, Charles Darwin, Charles Dickens, Thomas Edison, Clark Gable, Jascha Heifetz, Abraham Lincoln, Yehudi Menuhin, Mozart, Jack Nicklaus, Ronald Reagan, Jackie Robinson, Norman Rockwell, Franklin D. Roosevelt, Gertrude Stein, Charles Lindbergh, Margaret Truman

PISCES: Edward Albee, Harry Belafonte, Alexander Graham Bell, Chopin, Adelle Davis, Albert Einstein, Golda Meir, Jackie Gleason, Winslow Homer, Edward M. Kennedy, Victor Hugo, Mike Mansfield, Michelangelo, Edna St. Vincent Millay, Liza Minelli, John Steinbeck, Linus Pauling, Ravel, Renoir, Diana Ross, William Shirer, Elizabeth Taylor, George Washington

The Signs and Their Key Words

		POSITIVE	NEGATIVE
ARIES	self	courage, initiative, pioneer instinct	brash rudeness, selfish impetuosity
TAURUS	money	endurance, loyalty, wealth	obstinacy, gluttony
GEMINI	mind	versatility	capriciousness, unreliability
CANCER	family	sympathy, homing instinct	clannishness, childishness
LEO	children	love, authority, integrity	egotism, force
VIRGO	work	purity, industry, analysis	faultfinding, cynicism
LIBRA	marriage	harmony, justice	vacillation, superficiality
SCORPIO	sex	survival, regeneration	vengeance, discord
SAGITTARIUS	travel	optimism, higher learning	lawlessness
CAPRICORN	career	depth	narrowness, gloom
AQUARIUS	friends	human fellowship, genius	perverse unpredictability
PISCES	confine-ment	spiritual love, universality	diffusion, escapism

The Elements and Qualities of The Signs

Every sign has both an *element* and a *quality* associated with it. The element indicates the basic makeup of the sign, and the quality describes the kind of activity associated with each.

Element	Sign	Quality	Sign
FIRE...........	ARIES LEO SAGITTARIUS	CARDINAL	ARIES LIBRA CANCER CAPRICORN
EARTH	TAURUS VIRGO CAPRICORN	FIXED	TAURUS LEO SCORPIO AQUARIUS
AIR..............	GEMINI LIBRA AQUARIUS		
WATER	CANCER SCORPIO PISCES	MUTABLE	GEMINI VIRGO SAGITTARIUS PISCES

Signs can be grouped together according to their element and quality. Signs of the same element share many basic traits in common. They tend to form stable configurations and ultimately harmonious relationships. Signs of the same quality are often less harmonious, but they share many dynamic potentials for growth as well as profound fulfillment.

Further discussion of each of these sign groupings is provided on the following pages.

The Fire Signs

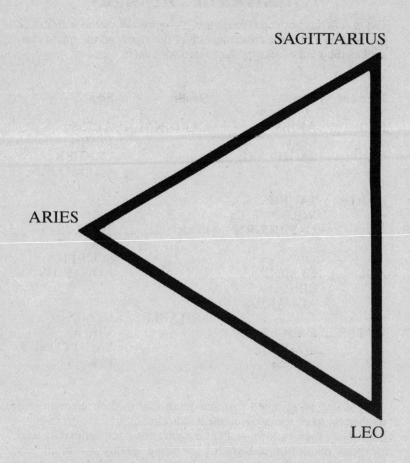

This is the fire group. On the whole these are emotional, volatile types, quick to anger, quick to forgive. They are adventurous, powerful people and act as a source of inspiration for everyone. They spark into action with immediate exuberant impulses. They are intelligent, self-involved, creative, and idealistic. They all share a certain vibrancy and glow that outwardly reflects an inner flame and passion for living.

The Earth Signs

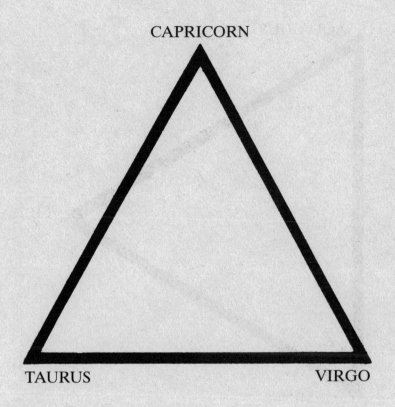

CAPRICORN

TAURUS   VIRGO

This is the earth group. They are in constant touch with the material world and tend to be conservative. Although they are all capable of spartan self-discipline, they are earthy, sensual people who are stimulated by the tangible, elegant, and luxurious. The thread of their lives is always practical, but they do fantasize and are often attracted to dark, mysterious, emotional people. They are like great cliffs overhanging the sea, forever married to the ocean but always resisting erosion from the dark, emotional forces that thunder at their feet.

The Air Signs

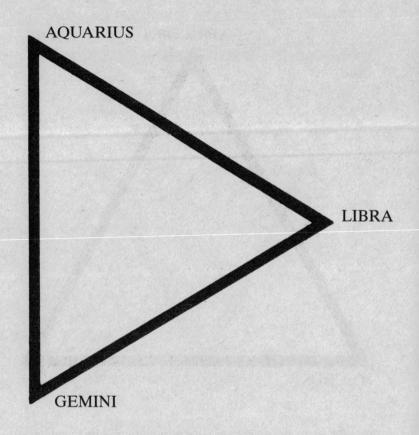

This is the air group. They are light, mental creatures desirous of contact, communication, and relationship. They are involved with people and the forming of ties on many levels. Original thinkers, they are the bearers of human news. Their language is their sense of word, color, style, and beauty. They provide an atmosphere suitable and pleasant for living. They add change and versatility to the scene, and it is through them that we can explore new territory of human intelligence and experience.

The Water Signs

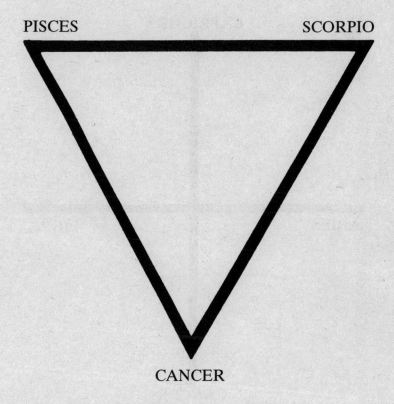

PISCES   SCORPIO

CANCER

This is the water group. Through the water people, we are all joined together on emotional, nonverbal levels. They are silent, mysterious types whose magic hypnotizes even the most determined realist. They have uncanny perceptions about people and are as rich as the oceans when it comes to feeling, emotion, or imagination. They are sensitive, mystical creatures with memories that go back beyond time. Through water, life is sustained. These people have the potential for the depths of darkness or the heights of mysticism and art.

The Cardinal Signs

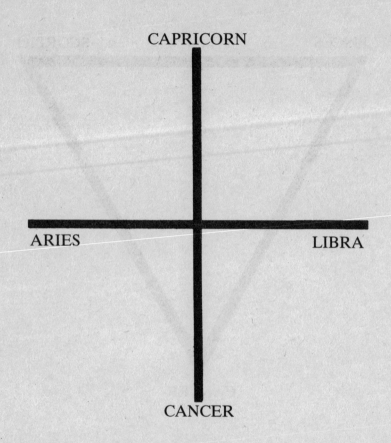

Put together, this is a clear-cut picture of dynamism, activity, tremendous stress, and remarkable achievement. These people know the meaning of great change since their lives are often characterized by significant crises and major successes. This combination is like a simultaneous storm of summer, fall, winter, and spring. The danger is chaotic diffusion of energy; the potential is irrepressible growth and victory.

The Fixed Signs

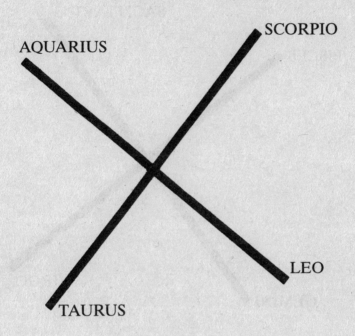

Fixed signs are always establishing themselves in a given place or area of experience. Like explorers who arrive and plant a flag, these people claim a position from which they do not enjoy being deposed. They are staunch, stalwart, upright, trusty, honorable people, although their obstinacy is well-known. Their contribution is fixity, and they are the angels who support our visible world.

The Mutable Signs

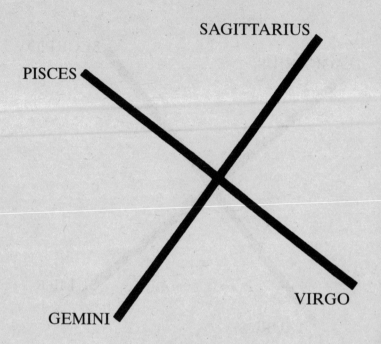

Mutable people are versatile, sensitive, intelligent, ner vous, and deeply curious about life. They are the translators of all energy. They often carry out or complete tasks initiated by others. Combinations of these signs have highly developed minds; they are imaginative and jumpy and think and talk a lot. At worst their lives are a Tower of Babel. At best they are adaptable and ready creatures who can assimilate one kind of experience and enjoy it while anticipating coming changes.

THE PLANETS
OF THE SOLAR SYSTEM

This section describes the planets of the solar system. In astrology, both the Sun and the Moon are considered to be planets. Because of the Moon's influence in our day-to-day lives, the Moon is described in a separate section following this one.

The Planets and the Signs They Rule

The signs of the Zodiac are linked to the planets in the following way. Each sign is governed or ruled by one or more planets. No matter where the planets are located in the sky at any given moment, they still rule their respective signs, and when they travel through the signs they rule, they have special dignity and their effects are stronger.

Following is a list of the planets and the signs they rule. After looking at the list, read the definitions of the planets and see if you can determine how the planet ruling *your* Sun sign has affected your life.

SIGNS	RULING PLANETS
Aries	Mars, Pluto
Taurus	Venus
Gemini	Mercury
Cancer	Moon
Leo	Sun
Virgo	Mercury
Libra	Venus
Scorpio	Mars, Pluto
Sagittarius	Jupiter
Capricorn	Saturn
Aquarius	Saturn, Uranus
Pisces	Jupiter, Neptune

Characteristics of the Planets

The following pages give the meaning and characteristics of the planets of the solar system. They all travel around the Sun at different speeds and different distances. Taken with the Sun, they all distribute individual intelligence and ability throughout the entire chart.

The planets modify the influence of the Sun in a chart according to their own particular natures, strengths, and positions. Their positions must be calculated for each year and day, and their function and expression in a horoscope will change as they move from one area of the Zodiac to another.

We start with a description of the sun.

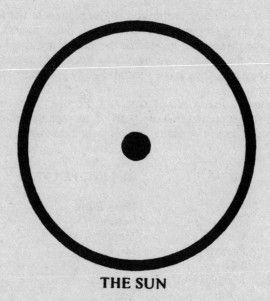

THE SUN

SUN

This is the center of existence. Around this flaming sphere all the planets revolve in endless orbits. Our star is constantly sending out its beams of light and energy without which no life on Earth would be possible. In astrology it symbolizes everything we are trying to become, the center around which all of our activity in life will always revolve. It is the symbol of our basic nature and describes the natural and constant thread that runs through everything that we do from birth to death on this planet.

To early astrologers, the Sun seemed to be another planet because it crossed the heavens every day, just like the rest of the bodies in the sky.

It is the only star near enough to be seen well—it is, in fact, a dwarf star. Approximately 860,000 miles in diameter, it is about ten times as wide as the giant planet Jupiter. The next nearest star is nearly 300,000 times as far away, and if the Sun were located as far away as most of the bright stars, it would be too faint to be seen without a telescope.

Everything in the horoscope ultimately revolves around this singular body. Although other forces may be prominent in the charts of some individuals, still the Sun is the total nucleus of being and symbolizes the complete potential of every human being alive. It is vitality and the life force. Your whole essence comes from the position of the Sun.

You are always trying to express the Sun according to its position by house and sign. Possibility for all development is found in the Sun, and it marks the fundamental character of your personal radiations all around you.

It is the symbol of strength, vigor, wisdom, dignity, ardor, and generosity, and the ability for a person to function as a mature individual. It is also a creative force in society. It is consciousness of the gift of life.

The underdeveloped solar nature is arrogant, pushy, undependable, and proud, and is constantly using force.

MERCURY

Mercury is the planet closest to the Sun. It races around our star, gathering information and translating it to the rest of the system. Mercury represents your capacity to understand the desires of your own will and to translate those desires into action.

In other words it is the planet of mind and the power of communication. Through Mercury we develop an ability to think, write, speak, and observe—to become aware of the world around us. It colors our attitudes and vision of the world, as well as our capacity to communicate our inner responses to the outside world. Some people who have serious disabilities in their power of verbal communication have often wrongly been described as people lacking intelligence.

Although this planet (and its position in the horoscope) indicates your power to communicate your thoughts and perceptions to the world, intelligence is something deeper. Intelligence is distributed throughout all the planets. It is the relationship of the planets to each other that truly describes what we call intelligence. Mercury rules speaking, language, mathematics, draft and design, students, messengers, young people, offices, teachers, and any pursuits where the mind of man has wings.

VENUS

Venus is beauty. It symbolizes the harmony and radiance of a rare and elusive quality: beauty itself. It is refinement and delicacy, softness and charm. In astrology it indicates grace, balance, and the aesthetic sense. Where Venus is we see beauty, a gentle drawing in of energy and the need for satisfaction and completion. It is a special touch that finishes off rough edges. It is sensitivity, and affection, and it is always the place for that other elusive phenomenon: love. Venus describes our sense of what is beautiful and loving. Poorly developed, it is vulgar, tasteless, and self-indulgent. But its ideal is the flame of spiritual love—Aphrodite, goddess of love, and the sweetness and power of personal beauty.

MARS

Mars is raw, crude energy. The planet next to Earth but outward from the Sun is a fiery red sphere that charges through the horoscope with force and fury. It represents the way you reach out for new adventure and new experience. It is energy and drive, initiative, courage, and daring. It is the power to start something and see it through. It can be thoughtless, cruel and wild, angry and hostile, causing cuts, burns, scalds, and wounds. It can stab its way through a chart, or it can be the symbol of healthy spirited adventure, well-channeled constructive power to begin and keep up the drive. If you have trouble starting things, if you lack the get-up-and-go to start the ball rolling, if you lack aggressiveness and self-confidence, chances are there's another planet influencing your Mars. Mars rules soldiers, butchers, surgeons, salesmen—any field that requires daring, bold skill, operational technique, or self-promotion.

JUPITER

This is the largest planet of the solar system. Scientists have recently learned that Jupiter reflects more light than it receives from the Sun. In a sense it is like a star itself. In astrology it rules good luck and good cheer, health, wealth, optimism, happiness, success, and joy. It is the symbol of opportunity and always opens the way for new possibilities in your life. It rules exuberance, enthusiasm, wisdom, knowledge, generosity, and all forms of expansion in general. It rules actors, statesmen, clerics, professional people, religion, publishing, and the distribution of many people over large areas.

Sometimes Jupiter makes you think you deserve everything, and you become sloppy, wasteful, careless and rude, prodigal and lawless, in the illusion that nothing can ever go wrong. Then there is the danger of overconfidence, exaggeration, undependability, and overindulgence.

Jupiter is the minimization of limitation and the emphasis on spirituality and potential. It is the thirst for knowledge and higher learning.

SATURN

Saturn circles our system in dark splendor with its mysterious rings, forcing us to be awakened to what ever we have neglected in the past. It will present real puzzles and problems to be solved, causing delays, obstacles, and hindrances. By doing so, Saturn stirs our own sensitivity to those areas where we are laziest.

Here we must patiently develop *method*, and only through pains-taking effort can our ends be achieved. It brings order to a horoscope and imposes reason just where we are feeling least reasonable. By creating limitations and boundary, Saturn shows the consequences of being human and demands that we accept the changing cycles inevitable in human life. Saturn rules time, old age, and sobriety. It can bring depression, gloom, jealousy, and greed, or serious ac cep tance of responsibilities out of which success will develop. With Saturn there is nothing to do but face facts. It rules laborers, stones, granite, rocks, and crystals of all kinds.

THE OUTER PLANETS:
URANUS, NEPTUNE, PLUTO

Uranus, Neptune, Pluto are the outer planets. They liberate human beings from cultural conditioning, and in that sense are the lawbreakers. In early times it was thought that Saturn was the last planet of the system—the outer limit beyond which we could never go. The discovery of the next three planets ushered in new phases of human history, revolution, and technology.

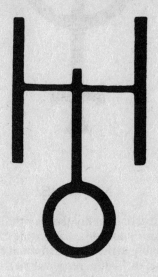

URANUS

Uranus rules unexpected change, upheaval, revolution. It is the symbol of total independence and asserts the freedom of an individual from all restriction and restraint. It is a breakthrough planet and indicates talent, originality, and genius in a horoscope. It usually causes last-minute reversals and changes of plan, unwanted separations, accidents, catastrophes, and eccentric behavior. It can add irrational rebelliousness and perverse bohemianism to a personality or a streak of unaffected brilliance in science and art. It rules technology, aviation, and all forms of electrical and electronic advancement. It governs great leaps forward and topsy-turvy situations, and *always* turns things around at the last minute. Its effects are difficult to predict, since it rules sudden last-minute decisions and events that come like lightning out of the blue.

NEPTUNE

Neptune dissolves existing reality the way the sea erodes the cliffs beside it. Its effects are subtle like the ringing of a buoy's bell in the fog. It suggests a reality higher than definition can usually describe. It awakens a sense of higher responsibility often causing guilt, worry, anxieties, or delusions. Neptune is associated with all forms of escape and can make things seem a certain way so convincingly that you are absolutely sure of something that eventually turns out to be quite different.

It is the planet of illusion and therefore governs the invisible realms that lie beyond our ordinary minds, beyond our simple factual ability to prove what is "real." Treachery, deceit, disillusionment, and disappointment are linked to Neptune. It describes a vague reality that promises eternity and the divine, yet in a manner so complex that we cannot really fathom it at all. At its worst Neptune is a cheap intoxicant; at its best it is the poetry, music, and inspiration of the higher planes of spiritual love. It has dominion over movies, photographs, and much of the arts.

PLUTO

Pluto lies at the outpost of our system and therefore rules finality in a horoscope—the final closing of chapters in your life, the passing of major milestones and points of development from which there is no return. It is a final wipeout, a closeout, an evacuation. It is a distant, subtle but powerful catalyst in all transformations that occur. It creates, destroys, then re creates. Sometimes Pluto starts its influence with a minor event or insignificant incident that might even go unnoticed. Slowly but surely, little by little, everything changes, until at last there has been a total transformation in the area of your life where Pluto has been operating. It rules mass thinking and the trends that society first rejects, then adopts, and finally outgrows.

Pluto rules the dead and the underworld—all the powerful forces of creation and destruction that go on all the time beneath, around, and above us. It can bring a lust for power with strong obsessions.

It is the planet that rules the metamorphosis of the caterpillar into a butterfly, for it symbolizes the capacity to change totally and forever a person's lifestyle, way of thought, and behavior.

THE MOON IN EACH SIGN

The Moon is the nearest planet to the Earth. It exerts more observable influence on us from day to day than any other planet. The effect is very personal, very intimate, and if we are not aware of how it works it can make us quite unstable in our ideas. And the annoying thing is that at these times we often see our own instability but can do nothing about it. A knowledge of what can be expected may help considerably. We can then be prepared to stand strong against the Moon's negative influences and use its positive ones to help us to get ahead. Who has not heard of going with the tide?

The Moon reflects, has no light of its own. It reflects the Sun—the life giver—in the form of vital movement. The Moon controls the tides, the blood rhythm, the movement of sap in trees and plants. Its nature is inconstancy and change so it signifies our moods, our superficial behavior—walking, talking, and especially thinking. Being a true reflector of other forces, the Moon is cold, watery like the surface of a still lake, brilliant and scintillating at times, but easily ruffled and disturbed by the winds of change.

The Moon takes about 27⅓ days to make a complete transit of the Zodiac. It spends just over 2¼ days in each sign. During that time it reflects the qualities, energies, and characteristics of the sign and, to a degree, the planet which rules the sign. When the Moon in its transit occupies a sign incompatible with our own birth sign, we can expect to feel a vague uneasiness, perhaps a touch of irritableness. We should not be discouraged nor let the feeling get us down, or, worse still, allow ourselves to take the discomfort out on others. Try to remember that the Moon has to change signs within 55 hours and, provided you are not physically ill, your mood will probably change with it. It is amazing how frequently depression lifts with the shift in the Moon's position. And, of course, when the Moon is transiting a sign compatible or sympathetic to yours, you will probably feel some sort of stimulation or just be plain happy to be alive.

In the horoscope, the Moon is such a powerful indicator that competent astrologers often use the sign it occupied at birth as the birth sign of the person. This is done particularly when the Sun is on the cusp, or edge, of two signs. Most experienced astrologers, however, coordinate both Sun and Moon signs by reading and confirming from one to the other and secure a far more accurate and personalized analysis.

For these reasons, the Moon tables which follow this section (see pages 86–92) are of great importance to the individual. They show the days and the exact times the Moon will enter each sign of the Zodiac for the year. Remember, you have to adjust the indicated times to local time. The corrections, already calculated for most of the main cities, are at the beginning of the tables. What follows now is a guide to the influences that will be reflected to the Earth by the Moon while it transits each of the twelve signs. The influence is at its peak about 26 hours after the Moon enters a sign. As you read the daily forecast, check the Moon sign for any given day and glance back at this guide.

MOON IN ARIES
This is a time for action, for reaching out beyond the usual self-imposed limitations and faint-hearted cautions. If you have plans in your head or on your desk, put them into practice. New ventures, applications, new jobs, new starts of any kind—all have a good chance of success. This is the period when original and dynamic impulses are being reflected onto Earth. Such energies are extremely vital and favor the pursuit of pleasure and adventure in practically every form. Sick people should feel an improvement. Those who are well will probably find themselves exuding confidence and optimism. People fond of physical exercise should find their bodies growing with tone and well-being. Boldness, strength, determination should characterize most of your activities with a readiness to face up to old challenges. Yesterday's problems may seem petty and exaggerated—so deal with them. Strike out alone. Self-reliance will attract others to you. This is a good time for making friends. Business and marriage partners are more likely to be impressed with the man and woman of action. Opposition will be overcome or thrown aside with much less effort than usual. CAUTION: Be dominant but not domineering.

MOON IN TAURUS
The spontaneous, action-packed person of yesterday gives way to the cautious, diligent, hardworking "thinker." In this period ideas will probably be concentrated on ways of improving finances. A great deal of time may be spent figuring out and going over schemes and plans. It is the right time to be careful with detail.

People will find themselves working longer than usual at their desks. Or devoting more time to serious thought about the future. A strong desire to put order into business and financial arrangements may cause extra work. Loved ones may complain of being neglected and may fail to appreciate that your efforts are for their ultimate benefit. Your desire for system may extend to criticism of arrangements in the home and lead to minor upsets. Health may be affected through overwork. Try to secure a reasonable amount of rest and relaxation, although the tendency will be to "keep going" despite good advice. Work done conscientiously in this period should result in a solid contribution to your future security. CAUTION: Try not to be as serious with people as the work you are engaged in.

MOON IN GEMINI

The humdrum of routine and too much work should suddenly end. You are likely to find yourself in an expansive, quicksilver world of change and self-expression. Urges to write, to paint, to experience the freedom of some sort of artistic outpouring, may be very strong. Take full advantage of them. You may find yourself finishing something you began and put aside long ago. Or embarking on something new which could easily be prompted by a chance meeting, a new acquaintance, or even an advertisement. There may be a yearning for a change of scenery, the feeling to visit another country (not too far away), or at least to get away for a few days. This may result in short, quick journeys. Or, if you are planning a single visit, there may be some unexpected changes or detours on the way. Familiar activities will seem to give little satisfaction unless they contain a fresh element of excitement or expectation. The inclination will be toward untried pursuits, particularly those that allow you to express your inner nature. The accent is on new faces, new places. CAUTION: Do not be too quick to commit yourself emotionally.

MOON IN CANCER

Feelings of uncertainty and vague insecurity are likely to cause problems while the Moon is in Cancer. Thoughts may turn frequently to the warmth of the home and the comfort of loved ones. Nostalgic impulses could cause you to bring out old photographs and letters and reflect on the days when your life seemed to be much more rewarding and less demanding. The love and understanding of parents and family may be important, and, if it is not forthcoming, you may have to fight against bouts of self-pity. The cordiality of friends and the thought of good times with them that are sure to be repeated will help to restore you to a happier frame of mind. The desire to be alone may follow minor setbacks or rebuffs at this time, but solitude is unlikely to help. Better to get on the telephone or visit someone. This period often causes peculiar dreams and upsurges of imaginative thinking which can be helpful to authors of occult and mystical works. Preoccupation with the personal world of simple human needs can overshadow any material strivings. CAUTION: Do not spend too much time thinking— seek the company of loved ones or close friends.

MOON IN LEO
New horizons of exciting and rather extravagant activity open up. This is the time for exhilarating entertainment, glamorous and lavish parties, and expensive shopping sprees. Any merrymaking that relies upon your generosity as a host has every chance of being a spectacular success. You should find yourself right in the center of the fun, either as the life of the party or simply as a person whom happy people like to be with. Romance thrives in this heady atmosphere and friendships are likely to explode unexpectedly into serious attachments. Children and younger people should be attracted to you and you may find yourself organizing a picnic or a visit to a fun-fair, the movies, or the beach. The sunny company and vitality of youthful companions should help you to find some unsuspected energy. In career, you could find an opening for promotion or advancement. This should be the time to make a direct approach. The period favors those engaged in original research. CAUTION: Bask in popularity, not in flattery.

MOON IN VIRGO
Off comes the party cap and out steps the busy, practical worker. He wants to get his personal affairs straight, to rearrange them, if necessary, for more efficiency, so he will have more time for more work. He clears up his correspondence, pays outstanding bills, makes numerous phone calls. He is likely to make inquiries, or sign up for some new insurance and put money into gilt-edged investment. Thoughts probably revolve around the need for future security—to tie up loose ends and clear the decks. There may be a tendency to be "finicky," to interfere in the routine of others, particularly friends and family members. The motive may be a genuine desire to help with suggestions for updating or streamlining their affairs, but these will probably not be welcomed. Sympathy may be felt for less fortunate sections of the community and a flurry of some sort of voluntary service is likely. This may be accompanied by strong feelings of responsibility on several fronts and health may suffer from extra efforts made. CAUTION: Everyone may not want your help or advice.

MOON IN LIBRA

These are days of harmony and agreement and you should find
yourself at peace with most others. Relationships tend to be
smooth and sweet-flowing. Friends may become closer and bonds
deepen in mutual understanding. Hopes will be shared. Progress
by cooperation could be the secret of success in every sphere. In
business, established partnerships may flourish and new ones get
off to a good start. Acquaintances could discover similar interests that lead to congenial discussions and rewarding exchanges
of some sort. Love, as a unifying force, reaches its optimum. Marriage partners should find accord. Those who wed at this time face
the prospect of a happy union. Cooperation and tolerance are felt
to be stronger than dissension and impatience. The argumentative
are not quite so loud in their bellowings, nor as inflexible in their
attitudes. In the home, there should be a greater recognition of
the other point of view and a readiness to put the wishes of the
group before selfish insistence. This is a favorable time to join an
art group. CAUTION: Do not be too independent—let others help
you if they want to.

MOON IN SCORPIO

Driving impulses to make money and to economize are likely to
cause upsets all around. No area of expenditure is likely to be
spared the ax, including the household budget. This is a time when
the desire to cut down on extravagance can become near fanatical.
Care must be exercised to try to keep the aim in reasonable perspective. Others may not feel the same urgent need to save and may
retaliate. There is a danger that possessions of sentimental value
will be sold to realize cash for investment. Buying and selling of
stock for quick profit is also likely. The attention turns to organizing, reorganizing, tidying up at home and at work. Neglected jobs
could suddenly be done with great bursts of energy. The desire for
solitude may intervene. Self-searching thoughts could disturb. The
sense of invisible and mysterious energies in play could cause some
excitability. The reassurance of loves ones may help. CAUTION:
Be kind to the people you love.

MOON IN SAGITTARIUS

These are days when you are likely to be stirred and elevated by
discussions and reflections of a religious and philosophical nature.
Ideas of faraway places may cause unusual response and excitement. A decision may be made to visit someone overseas, perhaps
a person whose influence was important to your earlier character
development. There could be a strong resolution to get away from

present intellectual patterns, to learn new subjects, and to meet more interesting people. The superficial may be rejected in all its forms. An impatience with old ideas and unimaginative contacts could lead to a change of companions and interests. There may be an upsurge of religious feeling and metaphysical inquiry. Even a new insight into the significance of astrology and other occult studies is likely under the curious stimulus of the Moon in Sagittarius. Physically, you may express this need for fundamental change by spending more time outdoors: sports, gardening, long walks appeal. CAUTION: Try to channel any restlessness into worthwhile study.

MOON IN CAPRICORN

Life in these hours may seem to pivot around the importance of gaining prestige and honor in the career, as well as maintaining a spotless reputation. Ambitious urges may be excessive and could be accompanied by quite acquisitive drives for money. Effort should be directed along strictly ethical lines where there is no possibility of reproach or scandal. All endeavors are likely to be characterized by great earnestness, and an air of authority and purpose which should impress those who are looking for leadership or reliability. The desire to conform to accepted standards may extend to sharp criticism of family members. Frivolity and unconventional actions are unlikely to amuse while the Moon is in Capricorn. Moderation and seriousness are the orders of the day. Achievement and recognition in this period could come through community work or organizing for the benefit of some amateur group. CAUTION: Dignity and esteem are not always self-awarded.

MOON IN AQUARIUS

Moon in Aquarius is in the second last sign of the Zodiac where ideas can become disturbingly fine and subtle. The result is often a mental "no-man's land" where imagination cannot be trusted with the same certitude as other times. The dangers for the individual are the extremes of optimism and pessimism. Unless the imagination is held in check, situations are likely to be misread, and rosy conclusions drawn where they do not exist. Consequences for the unwary can be costly in career and business. Best to think twice and not speak or act until you think again. Pessimism can be a cruel self-inflicted penalty for delusion at this time. Between the two extremes are strange areas of self-deception which, for example, can make the selfish person think he is actually being generous. Eerie dreams which resemble the reality and even seem to continue into the waking state are also possible. CAUTION: Look for the fact and not just for the image in your mind.

MOON IN PISCES

Everything seems to come to the surface now. Memory may be crystal clear, throwing up long-forgotten information which could be valuable in the career or business. Flashes of clairvoyance and intuition are possible along with sudden realizations of one's own nature, which may be used for self-improvement. A talent, never before suspected, may be discovered. Qualities not evident before in friends and marriage partners are likely to be noticed. As this is a period in which the truth seems to emerge, the discovery of false characteristics is likely to lead to disenchantment or a shift in attachments. However, when qualities are accepted, it should lead to happiness and deeper feeling. Surprise solutions could bob up for old problems. There may be a public announcement of the solving of a crime or mystery. People with secrets may find someone has "guessed" correctly. The secrets of the soul or the inner self also tend to reveal themselves. Religious and philosophical groups may make some interesting discoveries. CAUTION: Not a time for activities that depend on secrecy.

NOTE: When you read your daily forecasts, use the Moon Sign Dates that are provided in the following section of Moon Tables. Then you may want to glance back here for the Moon's influence in a given sign.

MOON TABLES

CORRECTION FOR NEW YORK TIME, FIVE HOURS WEST OF GREENWICH

Atlanta, Boston, Detroit, Miami, Washington, Montreal,
Ottawa, Quebec, Bogota,Havana, Lima, Santiago...... Same time

Chicago, New Orleans, Houston, Winnipeg, Churchill,
Mexico City .... Deduct 1 hour

Albuquerque, Denver, Phoenix, El Paso, Edmonton,
Helena .... Deduct 2 hours

Los Angeles, San Francisco, Reno, Portland,
Seattle, Vancouver .... Deduct 3 hours

Honolulu, Anchorage, Fairbanks, Kodiak .... Deduct 5 hours

Nome, Samoa, Tonga, Midway .... Deduct 6 hours

Halifax, Bermuda, San Juan, Caracas, La Paz,
Barbados .... Add 1 hour

St. John's, Brasilia, Rio de Janeiro, Sao Paulo,
Buenos Aires, Montevideo .... Add 2 hours

Azores, Cape Verde Islands .... Add 3 hours

Canary Islands, Madeira, Reykjavik .... Add 4 hours

London, Paris, Amsterdam, Madrid, Lisbon,
Gibraltar, Belfast, Raba .... Add 5 hours

Frankfurt, Rome, Oslo, Stockholm, Prague,
Belgrade .... Add 6 hours

Bucharest, Beirut, Tel Aviv, Athens, Istanbul, Cairo,
Alexandria, Cape Town, Johannesburg .... Add 7 hours

Moscow, Leningrad, Baghdad, Dhahran,
Addis Ababa, Nairobi, Teheran, Zanzibar .... Add 8 hours

Bombay, Calcutta, Sri Lanka .... Add $10^{1/2}$

Hong Kong, Shanghai, Manila, Peking, Perth............. Add 13 hours

Tokyo, Okinawa, Darwin, Pusan .... Add 14 hours

Sydney, Melbourne, Port Moresby, Guam .... Add 15 hours

Auckland, Wellington, Suva, Wake .... Add 17 hours

2011 MOON SIGN DATES—
NEW YORK TIME

JANUARY		FEBRUARY		MARCH	
Day Moon Enters		**Day Moon Enters**		**Day Moon Enters**	
1. Sagitt.		1. Aquar.	6:22 pm	1. Aquar.	12:15 am
2. Sagitt.		2. Aquar.		2. Aquar.	
3. Capric.	2:40 am	3. Aquar.		3. Pisces	11:48 am
4. Capric.		4. Pisces	6:25 am	4. Pisces	
5. Aquar.	11:09 am	5. Pisces		5. Pisces	
6. Aquar.		6. Aries	5:47 pm	6. Aries	12:15 am
7. Pisces	9:58 pm	7. Aries		7. Aries	
8. Pisces		8. Aries		8. Taurus	12:53 pm
9. Pisces		9. Taurus	6:24 am	9. Taurus	
10. Aries	10:25 am	10. Taurus		10. Taurus	
11. Aries		11. Gemini	5:22 pm	11. Gemini	12:32 am
12. Taurus	10:38 pm	12. Gemini		12. Gemini	
13. Taurus		13. Gemini		13. Cancer	9:31 am
14. Taurus		14. Cancer	12:50 am	14. Cancer	
15. Gemini	8:24 am	15. Cancer		15. Leo	2:34 pm
16. Gemini		16. Leo	4:15 am	16. Leo	
17. Cancer	2:30 pm	17. Leo		17. Virgo	3:54 pm
18. Cancer		18. Virgo	4:40 am	18. Virgo	
19. Leo	5:17 pm	19. Virgo		19. Libra	3:04 pm
20. Leo		20. Libra	4:02 am	20. Libra	
21. Virgo	6:11 pm	21. Libra		21. Scorp.	2:18 pm
22. Virgo		22. Scorp.	4:30 am	22. Scorp.	
23. Libra	7:00 pm	23. Scorp.		23. Sagitt.	3:48 pm
24. Libra		24. Sagitt.	7:47 am	24. Sagitt.	
25. Scorp.	9:17 pm	25. Sagitt.		25. Capric.	8:58 pm
26. Scorp.		26. Capric.	2:33 pm	26. Capric.	
27. Scorp.		27. Capric.		27. Capric.	
28. Sagitt.	1:56 am	28. Capric.		28. Aquar.	6:01 am
29. Sagitt.				29. Aquar.	
30. Capric.	9:05 am			30. Pisces	5:39 pm
31. Capric.				31. Pisces	

Daylight saving time to be considered where applicable.

2011 MOON SIGN DATES—
NEW YORK TIME

APRIL		MAY		JUNE	
Day Moon Enters		**Day Moon Enters**		**Day Moon Enters**	
1. Pisces		1. Aries		1. Gemini	
2. Aries	6:17 pm	2. Taurus	12:59 am	2. Gemini	
3. Aries		3. Taurus		3. Cancer	3:37 am
4. Taurus	6:47 pm	4. Gemini	12:10 pm	4. Cancer	
5. Taurus		5. Gemini		5. Leo	10:04 am
6. Taurus		6. Cancer	9:33 pm	6. Leo	
7. Gemini	6:23 am	7. Cancer		7. Virgo	2:34 pm
8. Gemini		8. Cancer		8. Virgo	
9. Cancer	4:03 pm	9. Leo	4:36 am	9. Libra	5:32 pm
10. Cancer		10. Leo		10. Libra	
11. Leo	10:38 pm	11. Virgo	9:00 am	11. Scorp.	7:34 pm
12. Leo		12. Virgo		12. Scorp.	
13. Leo		13. Libra	10:58 am	13. Sagitt.	9:39 pm
14. Virgo	1:41 am	14. Libra		14. Sagitt.	
15. Virgo		15. Scorp.	11:33 am	15. Sagitt.	
16. Libra	2:00 am	16. Scorp.		16. Capric.	1:00 am
17. Libra		17. Sagitt.	12:24 pm	17. Capric.	
18. Scorp.	1:20 am	18. Sagitt.		18. Aquar.	5:48 am
19. Scorp.		19. Capric.	3:17 pm	19. Aquar.	
20. Sagitt.	1:51 am	20. Capric.		20. Pisces	3:46 pm
21. Sagitt.		21. Aquar.	9:33 pm	21. Pisces	
22. Capric.	5:25 am	22. Aquar.		22. Pisces	
23. Capric.		23. Aquar.		23. Aries	3:25 am
24. Aquar.	1:00 pm	24. Pisces	7:25 am	24. Aries	
25. Aquar.		25. Pisces		25. Taurus	3:54 pm
26. Pisces	11:59 pm	26. Aries	7:37 pm	26. Taurus	
27. Pisces		27. Aries		27. Taurus	
28. Pisces		28. Aries		28. Gemini	2:57 am
29. Aries	12:34 pm	29. Taurus	8:03 am	29. Gemini	
30. Aries		30. Taurus		30. Cancer	11:14 am
		31. Gemini	6:57 pm		

Daylight saving time to be considered where applicable.

2011 MOON SIGN DATES—
NEW YORK TIME

JULY Day Moon Enters		AUGUST Day Moon Enters		SEPTEMBER Day Moon Enters	
1. Cancer		1. Virgo	3:43 am	1. Scorp.	1:49 pm
2. Leo	4:44 pm	2. Virgo		2. Scorp.	
3. Leo		3. Libra	5:05 am	3. Sagitt.	4:05 am
4. Virgo	8:16 pm	4. Libra		4. Sagitt.	
5. Virgo		5. Scorp.	6:58 am	5. Capric.	9:05 pm
6. Libra	10:55 pm	6. Scorp.		6. Capric.	
7. Libra		7. Sagitt.	10:22 am	7. Capric.	
8. Libra		8. Sagitt.		8. Aquar.	4:43 am
9. Scorp.	1:32 am	9. Capric.	3:39 pm	9. Aquar.	
10. Scorp.		10. Capric.		10. Pisces	2:28 pm
11. Sagitt.	4:48 am	11. Aquar.	10:49 pm	11. Pisces	
12. Sagitt.		12. Aquar.		12. Pisces	
13. Capric.	9:14 am	13. Aquar.		13. Aries	1:50 am
14. Capric.		14. Pisces	7:55 am	14. Aries	
15. Aquar.	3:31 pm	15. Pisces		15. Taurus	2:26 pm
16. Aquar.		16. Aries	7:03 pm	16. Taurus	
17. Aquar.		17. Aries		17. Taurus	
18. Pisces	12:14 am	18. Aries		18. Gemini	3:07 am
19. Pisces		19. Taurus	7:37 am	19. Gemini	
20. Aries	11:26 am	20. Taurus		20. Cancer	1:55 pm
21. Aries		21. Gemini	7:54 am	21. Cancer	
22. Taurus	11:59 pm	22. Gemini		22. Leo	8:56 pm
23. Taurus		23. Gemini		23. Leo	
24. Taurus		24. Cancer	5:32 am	24. Virgo	11:50 pm
25. Gemini	11:35 am	25. Cancer		25. Virgo	
26. Gemini		26. Leo	11:10 am	26. Libra	11:52 pm
27. Cancer	8:13 pm	27. Leo		27. Libra	
28. Cancer		28. Virgo	1:14 pm	28. Scorp.	11:06 pm
29. Cancer		29. Virgo		29. Scorp.	
30. Leo	1:17 am	30. Libra	1:26 pm	30. Sagitt.	11:42 pm
31. Leo		31. Libra			

Daylight saving time to be considered where applicable.

2011 MOON SIGN DATES— NEW YORK TIME

OCTOBER Day Moon Enters		NOVEMBER Day Moon Enters		DECEMBER Day Moon Enters	
1. Sagitt.		1. Aquar.	5:09 pm	1. Pisces	9:46 pm
2. Sagitt.		2. Aquar.		2. Pisces	
3. Capric.	3:17 am	3. Aquar.		3. Aries	8:52 pm
4. Capric.		4. Pisces	2:19 am	4. Aries	
5. Aquar.	10:19 am	5. Pisces		5. Aries	
6. Aquar.		6. Aries	2:03 pm	6. Taurus	9:36 am
7. Pisces	8:14 pm	7. Aries		7. Taurus	
8. Pisces		8. Aries		8. Gemini	9:53 pm
9. Pisces		9. Taurus	2:46 am	9. Gemini	
10. Aries	7:58 am	10. Taurus		10. Gemini	
11. Aries		11. Gemini	3:11 pm	11. Cancer	8:27 am
12. Taurus	8:36 pm	12. Gemini		12. Cancer	
13. Taurus		13. Gemini		13. Leo	4:49 pm
14. Taurus		14. Cancer	2:20 am	14. Leo	
15. Gemini	9:16 am	15. Cancer		15. Virgo	11:00 pm
16. Gemini		16. Leo	11:18 am	16. Virgo	
17. Cancer	8:39 pm	17. Leo		17. Virgo	
18. Cancer		18. Virgo	5:20 pm	18. Libra	3:07 am
19. Cancer		19. Virgo		19. Libra	
20. Leo	5:07 am	20. Libra	8:17 pm	20. Scorp.	5:34 am
21. Leo		21. Libra		21. Scorp.	
22. Virgo	9:42 am	22. Scorp.	8:59 pm	22. Sagitt.	7:04 am
23. Virgo		23. Scorp.		23. Sagitt.	
24. Libra	10:50 am	24. Sagitt.	8:58 pm	24. Capric.	8:58 am
25. Libra		25. Sagitt.		25. Capric.	
26. Scorp.	10:09 am	26. Capric.	10:06 pm	26. Aquar.	12:15 pm
27. Scorp.		27. Capric.		27. Aquar.	
28. Sagitt.	9:46 am	28. Capric.		28. Pisces	6:46 pm
29. Sagitt.		29. Aquar.	2:03 am	29. Pisces	
30. Capric.	11:40 am	30. Aquar.		30. Pisces	
31. Capric.				31. Aries	4:49 am

Daylight saving time to be considered where applicable.

2011 PHASES OF THE MOON—
NEW YORK TIME

New Moon	First Quarter	Full Moon	Last Quarter
Jan. 4	Jan. 12	Jan. 19	Jan. 26
Feb. 2	Feb. 11	Feb. 18	Feb. 24
March 4	March 12	March 19	March 26
April 3	April 11	April 17	April 24
May 3	May 10	May 17	May 24
June 1	June 8	June 15	June 23
July 1	July 8	July 15	July 23
July 30	August 6	August 13	August 21
August 28	Sept. 4	Sept. 12	Sept. 20
Sept. 27	Oct. 3	Oct. 11	Oct. 19
Oct. 26	Nov. 2	Nov. 10	Nov. 18
Nov. 25	Dec. 2	Dec. 10	Dec. 17
Dec. 24	Jan. 1 ('12)	Jan. 9 ('12)	Jan. 16 ('12)

Each phase of the Moon lasts approximately seven to eight days, during which the Moon's shape gradually changes as it comes out of one phase and goes into the next.

There will be a solar eclipse during the New Moon phase on January 4, on June 1, on July 1, and on November 25.

There will be a lunar eclipse during the Full Moon phase on June 15 and on December 10.

2011 FISHING GUIDE

	Good	Best
January	3-4-6-9-14-20-28-31	2-8-18-27
February	2-10-14-19-24-28	5-15-23
March	5-7-12-14-20-25-27	4-13-22-31
April	1-6-10-11-13-21-25-27	2-10-19-28
May	3-5-11-12-18-21-26	8-16-25
June	1-18-12-17-20-22	4-12-21
July	6-11-21-22-26-28-31	1-2-10-19-29
August	2-5-10-18-26-28-30	6-15-25
September	1-6-9-17-23-24-25	2-11-21-29
October	6-16-20-22-24-28	8-18-27
November	5-10-15-19-25	4-14-23
December	3-8-13-17-20-22-23-35	2-12-21-29

2011 PLANTING GUIDE

	Aboveground Crops	Root Crops
January	1-4-8-9-10-18-19	24-25-26-31
February	5-6-15-16	1-21-22-28
March	5-6-14-15-18	1-20-21-27-28-29
April	10-11-12-15-16	18-22-23-24
May	8-9-12-13-16-17	20-21-30-31
June	4-5-8-9-12-13-14	17-18-19-27-38
July	18-19-20-29-30	14-15-23-24-25
August	15-16-25-26-29	20-21
September	12-22-23-26-27	17-18-27-28
October	19-20-23-24	13-14-15-25
November	15-16-19-20-23	10-11-21-22-23
December	12-13-17-18-21-22	19-20

	Pruning	Weeds and Pests
January	11-12	20-21
February	13-14	17-18
March	13-16-17	29-30
April	13-14	25-26-27
May	10-11	24
June	15-16	29-30
July	12-13	13-14-15
August	8-9-10	12-13
September	4-5	9-10
October	11-12	6-7
November	8-9	2-3-4
December	4-5-6	1-10-11

MOON'S INFLUENCE OVER PLANTS

Centuries ago it was established that seeds planted when the Moon is in signs and phases called Fruitful will produce more growth than seeds planted when the Moon is in a Barren sign.

Fruitful Signs: Taurus, Cancer, Libra, Scorpio, Capricorn, Pisces
Barren Signs: Aries, Gemini, Leo, Virgo, Sagittarius, Aquarius
Dry Signs: Aries, Gemini, Sagittarius, Aquarius

Activity	Moon In
Mow lawn, trim plants	**Fruitful sign:** 1st & 2nd quarter
Plant flowers	**Fruitful sign:** 2nd quarter; best in Cancer and Libra
Prune	**Fruitful sign:** 3rd & 4th quarter
Destroy pests; spray	**Barren sign:** 4th quarter
Harvest potatoes, root crops	**Dry sign:** 3rd & 4th quarter; Taurus, Leo, and Aquarius

MOON'S INFLUENCE OVER YOUR HEALTH

ARIES	Head, brain, face, upper jaw
TAURUS	Throat, neck, lower jaw
GEMINI	Hands, arms, lungs, shoulders, ner vous system
CANCER	Esophagus, stomach, breasts, womb, liver
LEO	Heart, spine
VIRGO	Intestines, liver
LIBRA	Kidneys, lower back
SCORPIO	Sex and eliminative organs
SAGITTARIUS	Hips, thighs, liver
CAPRICORN	Skin, bones, teeth, knees
AQUARIUS	Circulatory system, lower legs
PISCES	Feet, tone of being

Try to avoid work being done on that part of the body when the Moon is in the sign governing that part.

MOON'S INFLUENCE OVER DAILY AFFAIRS

The Moon makes a complete transit of the Zodiac every 27 days 7 hours and 43 minutes. In making this transit the Moon forms different aspects with the planets and consequently has favorable or unfavorable bearings on affairs and events for persons according to the sign of the Zodiac under which they were born.

When the Moon is in conjunction with the Sun it is called a New Moon; when the Moon and Sun are in opposition it is called a Full Moon. From New Moon to Full Moon, first and second quarter— which takes about two weeks—the Moon is increasing or waxing. From Full Moon to New Moon, third and fourth quarter, the Moon is decreasing or waning.

Activity	Moon In
Business: buying and selling new, requiring public support	Sagittarius, Aries, Gemini, Virgo 1st and 2nd quarter
meant to be kept quiet	3rd and 4th quarter
Investigation	3rd and 4th quarter
Signing documents	1st & 2nd quarter, Cancer, Scorpio, Pisces
Advertising	2nd quarter, Sagittarius
Journeys and trips	1st & 2nd quarter, Gemini, Virgo
Renting offices, etc.	Taurus, Leo, Scorpio, Aquarius
Painting of house/apartment	3rd & 4th quarter, Taurus, Scorpio, Aquarius
Decorating	Gemini, Libra, Aquarius
Buying clothes and accessories	Taurus, Virgo
Beauty salon or barber shop visit	1st & 2nd quarter, Taurus, Leo, Libra, Scorpio, Aquarius
Weddings	1st & 2nd quarter

Capricorn

CAPRICORN

Character Analysis

People born under Capricorn, the tenth sign of the Zodiac, are generally strong-willed and goal-directed. They seldom do anything without a purpose. They tend to be quite ambitious. They hammer away at something until they have made their point. Capricorns know what they want out of life. Through perseverance and patience, they generally achieve it. There is almost nothing they cannot attain once they make up their minds. They are interested in progress, in making things better. When Capricorns believe in something, they put themselves behind it totally. They do not believe in acting in a halfhearted fashion.

The Goat is the zodiacal symbol of Capricorn. The Goat climbs, always slowly and surely, keeping balance even under unstable circumstances and on difficult terrain. At times, in order to get ahead, Capricorn will make use of people. But these people are also likely to gain through such manipulation.

Capricorns, because of their steady nature, inspire confidence and trust. They do not sit idly by watching the action. And they openly admire qualities they lack. Overall, Capricorn is an excellent manager and very shrewd in their quiet way.

When Capricorns like or believe in someone, they will stick by that person for the rest of their life. They are loyal and constant. They seldom waver once they have committed themselves to an ideal or a person. They can always be depended on to speak up for something or someone they believe in. At times Capricorn is utterly charming, at other times aloof and proud.

Capricorn men and women are in possession of clear, uncluttered minds. They are not necessarily brilliant, but they are capable of concentrating on what interests them in an effective manner. They believe in doing things right, never halfway. Generally, Capricorns are exact and accurate. They pride themselves on doing their work correctly. They are conscientious and careful. They can always be counted on to hold up their end of a bargain. They tend to be stiff when it comes to making judgments. They are more interested in justice than forgiveness. In spite of this, one could never accuse them of not being fair-minded in most things. They make a point of it.

Capricorns could hardly be called softhearted. They can be quite harsh at times in the way they handle someone, especially if they think they're right. People are likely to find Capricorn cold and callous. Honor and pride are important, and Capricorn is bound to have some intellectual pretensions.

Capricorns who are weak in character are apt to feel they are a cut above others and will do what they can to let this be felt. Often they suffer from a feeling of inadequacy. They may not know how to rid themselves of this complex that has an adverse effect on their disposition. They are often depressed and insecure. For these reasons, people may find Capricorn difficult to get along with. If Capricorn men and women are too conscious of the qualities they lack, they may ruin their chances of attaining the ends they desire.

Some Capricorns of this caliber find it difficult to settle down. They roam from one thing to another, never satisfied. Their cleverness may become mean and cutting. They may be destructive rather than constructive and positive. They may be afraid to forge ahead. The future frightens them and increases their feelings of insecurity. The frightened Goat may strike out at people he suspects are laughing at him behind his back.

The weak Capricorn man or woman is not an easy person to get along with. Others may be afraid to be truthful with them. This Capricorn is likely to be narrow-minded and conservative. They cling desperately to the past, afraid of moving on. They think more of themselves than of others and may abuse friends and acquaintances.

Some Capricorns may be lacking in a healthy sense of humor. A harmless joke may make them suspicious and aggressive if they think it was secretly directed at them. They cannot easily laugh at themselves when they pull a boner.

Some Capricorns are exceedingly careful with their money. As a rule, however, they tend to be on the generous side. They would never refuse someone in need. They will, at times, go out of their way to help someone in trouble. They do not expect or insist that the favor be returned; a word of thanks is good enough for them.

Capricorn men and women are very grateful when someone offers to lend them a helping hand. They never forget a favor. Although they may find it difficult to express thanks at times, they do appreciate any help that is given to them.

Health

During childhood, Capricorns may not be too strong or sturdy. Often they are subject to a series of childhood diseases. As they grow older, however, they become stronger. An adult Capricorn often has a strong resistance to diseases. The Goat is a fighter. They never want to lose in anything, not even illness. Many people born under this sign live a long life. They are generally very active people and have a store of energy at their disposal.

The weak areas of a Capricorn person's body are the knees and joints. When they have an accident, these areas are often involved. Some Capricorns have poor teeth; this may be the result of insufficient calcium in the system. Skin troubles often plague them. In later life they may become the victim of an arthritic disease.

Being a practical sort of person, Capricorn generally sees to it that they eat sensibly. A balanced diet is essential. They need plenty of fresh fruits and vegetables in order to remain fit. Hard work and exercise help them to maintain their good constitution. As they mature, Capricorns become stronger and their strength is seldom undermined.

Moods, however, may have an unsettling effect on the health in general. Capricorn is given to dark, somber moods. Gloomy thoughts and depressed feelings can be hard to dispel. Melancholy can persist longer than is wise or desirable. Capricorn men and women can easily fall into the bad habit of worrying about small things. Such worries can drain them of energy and may make them prey to a variety of illnesses.

Plenty of fresh air, sunshine, and exercise will help Capricorn keep a healthy disposition and a happy frame of mind. Companions and associates will also play a great role in Capricorn's health. They get along best with people who are youthful, positive, and energetic.

Occupation

The Capricorn man or woman is very much interested in being successful in life. They will work hard to win at whatever it is they do. Reputation means a lot to them. They will fight to advance and to hold their position. They like a job that carries a bit of prestige with it. Having people respect them is very important. Capricorn enjoys being in a position of authority.

Money, of course, has a great attraction for the man or woman born under the sign of the Goat. When accepting a job, salary usually plays an important part. They would not take a job just for the glory or prestige alone. It has to have its financial advantages.

There are Capricorns who believe that the only way to win is to stick to something that is regular, or routine. They don't mind plodding along if they are sure that they will get that pot of gold at the end of the rainbow. Still and all, the strong Capricorn, while seeing the advantages of routine work, will never become a robot or slave to a humdrum work schedule. Capricorn men and women try to move along with the times. They keep abreast of new developments in the field, applying new techniques to their work wherever they see fit.

Hard work does not frighten Capricorn. They are willing to put in long and hard hours, if they feel the benefits they are to receive are indeed worth their efforts. They are usually conscientious and loyal in their work. Many of them start at the bottom and slowly work their way up.

There are seldom any complaints about Capricorn's work. These men and women are very good at what they do. They are determined, methodical, thorough. They have a fine grasp of details while keeping sight of the big idea. They are supremely focused and fixed in their purpose—to do an excellent job. Any employer of Capricorn men and women are usually satisfied with their job performance because they are accurate and professional.

Although they are interested in being successful, some Capricorns tend to become a bit depressed if it seems to take them longer than it does for other people. But Capricorns are willing to bide their time. They hold no rosy view of the future. They know that they will really have to apply themselves to their tasks in order to attain their goals.

It is the idea of winning that keeps Capricorn on the go. They never falter once they have made up their mind to get ahead in the world. Some of them never attain what they're after until very late in life. But they are not afraid of pushing ahead, making small gains here and there, as long as they seem to be on the right road.

Once on the road to any fame or fortune, the success-oriented Capricorn man or woman is sure to steer steadily ahead. He or she will let no one stand in the way. At times, Capricorn can be quite brutal and heartless in their methods for getting to the top. So the climb to the summit can be agonizing indeed—at least for the person who the Goat is pushing out of the way.

Needless to say, the pushy sort of Goat has no trouble becoming unpopular with teammates and associates. Obsessed with success, he or she is always on the lookout for an opportunity to get ahead. If necessary, they will step on another's toes in order to make a gain, no matter how small it is.

Politics is an area where someone born under the sign of the Goat usually excels. Capricorn has a diplomatic way and a tactful demeanor. They are interested in justice and being fair. Some Capricorns make good researchers. They are not afraid to put in long hours when involved in investigation. They are reliable and steady. In a position that gives them a chance to organize or arrange things, they could do very well.

Authoritarian positions hold a particular attraction for Capricorn men and women. They enjoy the challenge of this sort of position, also the respect it generally commands. Having people under their control sometimes makes them respect themselves more. It makes them more sure of their own worth. In crafts and sciences, they often do well, too.

Money is important to the Capricorn man and woman. They'll work hard to build up their financial resources. If they wind up rich, it's not because of luck, generally, but because they have earned it. Capricorn is an open opportunist, and will not try to disguise this. He or she is no hypocrite. They are direct in actions, even if they do not talk about them.

Of all the signs, Capricorn is the most interested in gain and profit. Security is something the Goat must have. It drives them on; it motivates them. During difficult moments, they may feel a bit discouraged or depressed. Still, there is that interest in the ultimate goal that keeps Capricorn going.

Capricorn individuals are generally thrifty. They believe in saving. Waste disgusts them. For the most part they are quite conservative in the way they handle their finances. Although they may be given to moods in which they feel very expansive or generous, on the whole they manage to keep tight control of their money. They can be trusted with other people's money, too.

During their youth, Capricorn may impress others as being rather penny-pinching. They are cautious in the way they manage finances. Generally, they can account for every cent they spend.

With an eye always on the future, they think about that inevitable rainy day, and prepare themselves for it. However, once they have gained quite a bit and feel financially secure, their attitudes are likely to change. They become generous and charitable. They are very helpful to those in need, especially if a person's background is similar to their own.

Home and Family

The average Capricorn enjoys the security of home life. Still, it generally does not appeal to them in the same way as it does others. They may not marry for love or companionship alone. They may think of marriage and domesticity as a practical means for realizing their material goals.

The person born under this sign sometimes marries for position or money. Not that they are all that coldhearted and calculating. But Capricorn finds it just as easy to fall in love with a socially prominent and wealthy person as it is to become romantically involved with a poor person.

The occupation or career of a Capricorn man or woman is apt to play the central role in their life. Family comes in second, playing a supporting role. Many Capricorns are not fond of large families, that is, one with many children.

Parenthood can be something of a burden for the average Capricorn. They take their responsibilities toward the family very seriously. Family ties are strong, but the Goat may seem a bit distant even to loved ones. Capricorn is capable of great affection, but is apt to be more demonstrative when managing or organizing household affairs. The goal is that everything connected with home life should run smoothly.

Capricorns sometimes feel lacking in some quality or characteristic. It is this feeling of inadequacy that drives them in romance. They want to find someone who has what they lack. A loving mate and a harmonious family give Capricorn the feeling of being needed, of being a complete person. Once settled, then he or she is interested in improving or expanding home life in various ways.

The Capricorn husband or wife will often do what he or she can to make the home harmonious and tasteful. They generally have a great interest in all that is beautiful and cultural. Some Capricorns are fond of music, and a piano in the home is a must. The home of a Capricorn person generally radiates good taste and beauty. It may be a bit on the luxurious side—if they can afford it—but never in an ostentatious way.

The home is usually peaceful and harmonious. Capricorn feels that everything in the household should run on some regular basis: a special time for meals, for sleeping, for entertaining. The home is a comfortable place, and it is usually easy for someone to feel at ease while visiting a Capricorn friend.

Capricorns are proud of their home and property. They are responsible members of the community and will do what is necessary to fulfill their duties as a neighbor. However, they like to keep their home life to themselves. They value their privacy.

Capricorn's home is usually well kept and attractive. They like to be respected and highly thought of because of their possessions. Prestige in the community is important to them. A materialistic duel with the Joneses is not beneath the Goat. They will always try to do the neighbors one better if they can afford it.

Children bring joy into the Goat's life. Still, Capricorn men and women may not be very fond of a large family. But they will give the necessary love and attention to the few children they do have. Capricorn parents are interested in the youngsters as distinct individuals and enjoy seeing them grow up. The hope, of course, is that the children will be a credit to the parents and will reflect the good upbringing Capricorn has given them.

At times, the Capricorn parent may seem a bit unsympathetic, especially if the youngsters misbehave. But as they mature, they will respect and love their Capricorn parent for the security he or she has given them while they were growing up.

Social Relationships

The Capricorn personality projected onto the social scene is marked by reserve and dignity. At first it may appear that these men and women are hanging back, waiting to be drawn into the thick of things. Capricorns may seem unapproachable and cold to someone newly introduced. But the one who does win a Goat's friendship is rewarded by kindness, loyalty, and fidelity.

Capricorns have many acquaintainces but true few friends. Among strangers the Goat may feel scrutinized and judged, so there is a tendency to wait in the wings, to hide from imagined harsh criticism. The fear of criticism also gives rise to a tendency to be secretive. Capricorns are unwilling to broadcast their intentions, except to the chosen few.

Capricorn men and women seldom, if ever, gossip or talk behind someone's back. Friends can always count on them to guard a confidence. Even though the Goat is wary of revealing his or her own secrets, the secrets of other people are kept under wraps.

Capricorn sometimes picks the wrong people as companions. In youth and early adulthood the Goat may be tempted to run with a bad crowd, and unfortunately is likely to gain a bad reputation because of it. The troublemakers and freeloaders take advantage and often blame the innocent Goat. Such disappointments and betrayals are all too common. But Capricorns learn from their mistakes. For that reason, as they mature they become more cautious and discriminating in their choice of friends.

Capricorn men and women are prominent in the life of their community. They play an active role in neighborhood groups and civic organizations. Where there is a club or association formed to promote the general good, you will find a Capricorn and often in a leadership position.

To true friends, Capricorn is a pillar of strength, a rock. He or she is capable of making great sacrifices in order to help a friend. That is why solid friendships last a lifetime and provide much support and comfort all around.

Love and Marriage

The Capricorn man or woman is not what one could accurately describe as being romantic. But they are emotional, and their feelings run deep. Their respect for intellect and convention may prevent them from expressing themselves in a demonstrative way, vigorously exhibiting their love and affection.

Capricorn is a considerate lover, a well-mannered dating partner. Their approach to courtship and romance is conventional. They would never do anything that might injure the feelings or sensibilities of their mate or date. Doing the right thing at the right time is important.

Capricorns do not let their affections run rampant. Their mind reigns over their emotions. Flirting has little or no appeal. When in love, the Goat is serious. Even if a love relationship does not end in a permanent union, the Goat takes it seriously. Capricorn men and women will not run from one love affair to another—or enjoy several romances at the same time. Capricorn is constant.

Still, Capricorn will not give his or her heart away immediately. They like to begin a romance by being friends. If the love interest is encouraging and indicates reciprocal feelings, Capricorn will then allow the relationship to enter a more intimate phase. He or she does not want to be deceived or made a fool of. Ever protective, the Goat will take steps to guard against betrayal.

Driven by ambition, Capricorn in love is apt to direct his or her affections toward someone who can help them get ahead in their career. In love, they do not totally lose their heads. They know what they want. That does not mean Capricorn is insincere in love—just practical.

The person who falls under Capricorn's charm—and there is plenty of it—may find it difficult to understand the dark and pessimistic moods that emerge from nowhere. The inhibition and hesitation and secretiveness seem to be without reason. Although Capricorns build a love affair slowly, they will end it quickly if they feel it is a waste of time. When disappointed, they are direct and to the point.

The cultivated, strong Capricorn tries to be open in love so that the relationship will be a lasting one. They admit their faults readily and do what they can to be more affectionate and demonstrative. An exciting, impulsive person is sometimes the ideal mate for a Capricorn man or woman.

Romance and the Capricorn Woman

The Capricorn woman is very serious when it comes to love and courtship. She is correct. When her loved one offends her sensibilities, she lets him know in short order. She can be quite affectionate with the right man. On the whole, however, she is rather inhibited. A warm and understanding man can teach her how to be more demonstrative in her affection.

She is not fond of flirting. A man who tries to win her with his charm may not have much of a chance. She is interested in someone who is serious on whom she can depend. Respect also plays an important part when she selects a lover or partner. A man who abuses her affections is quickly dismissed. She will never take the lead in a love affair, yet she is not fond of people who move fast. She likes to take her time getting to know someone. Whirlwind romance has very little appeal to a Capricorn woman.

She is a perfectionist to some extent. She wants a man she can look up to and respect. Someone who is in a position to provide a good home and the necessary security is more important and interesting to her than someone who is amorous and charming.

The Capricorn woman needs someone who is warm and affectionate even though she may not show or indicate it. She needs someone who is what she is not. She may spend a great deal of time looking for the right person. She is not someone who will settle for something short of her ideals. Some female Goats marry late in life as a result. The cultivated Capricorn woman, however, knows how to take the bitter with the sweet. If she meets someone who basically lines up with her ideals but is not perfect, she will settle for him and try to make the most of it.

The Capricorn wife runs her home in a very efficient manner. She is faithful and systematic. She enjoys taking care of her family and sees to it that everything runs smoothly. She may not be very romantic, even after marriage. However, the right man can help her to develop a deeper interest in love and companionship as the marriage grows.

She is a correct mother. Her children never want. She may not be too loving or sympathetic, but she is responsible and protective. Children's love for her grows as they grow older.

Romance and the Capricorn Man

The Capricorn man is no Lothario. He will never be swept off his feet by romance. He's more intellectual than romantic. He is fond of affection but may find it difficult to express affection toward the one he is interested in.

He is capable of great passion—yet passion that is lacking in affection. His loved one is apt to find him difficult to understand at times. He is honest in his love relationships. He would never lead a woman astray. Flirting has no interest for him. He believes in steady, gradual relationships. He likes to know his partner well as a person before going on to romance or love. He may seem casual at first in the way he demonstrates his interest. As he wins the woman's trust, however, he will begin to unwind and reveal his feelings for what they are.

A woman who can help him gain those things in life that interest him holds a great attraction for him. He is not a fortune hunter. But if the woman he is interested in has some money or social background, so much the better. He can be practical, even when in love.

He is an idealist. He has a dream woman running around in his head, and he won't give up his search until he has found her—or someone like her. He is faithful in marriage. He does what he can to provide well for his family. He can be depended on to fulfill his role as father and husband to the letter.

He always tries to do what is best for his children. He may not be the most affectionate father, but he is dutiful and responsible. The feelings a Capricorn father has for his youngsters generally intensify as they grow up.

Woman—Man

CAPRICORN WOMAN
ARIES MAN

In some ways, the Aries man is the black sheep in the family, always seeking adventure. He has an insatiable thirst for knowledge. He's ambitious and is apt to have his finger in many pies. He can do with a woman like you—someone attractive, quick-witted, and smart.

He is not interested in a clinging vine kind of wife. He wants someone who is there when he needs her, someone who can give advice if he should ever need it, which is not likely to be often. The Aries man wants a woman who will look good on his arm without hanging on it too heavily. He is looking for a woman who has both feet on the ground and yet is mysterious and enticing, a kind of domestic Helen of Troy whose face can launch a thousand business deals if need be.

That woman he's in search of sounds a little like you, doesn't she? If the shoe fits, put it on. You won't regret it. The Aries man makes a good husband. He is faithful and attentive. He is an affectionate man. He'll make you feel needed and loved.

Love is a serious matter for the Aries man. He does not believe in flirting or playing the field—especially after he's found the woman of his dreams. He'll expect you to be as constant in your affection as he is in his. He'll expect you to be one hundred percent his. He won't put up with any nonsense while romancing you.

The Aries man may be pretty progressive and modern about many things. However, when it comes to pants wearing, he's the boss and that's that. Once you have learned to accept that, you'll find the going easy.

The Aries man, with his endless energy and drive, likes to relax in the comfort of his home at the end of the day. The good homemaker can be sure of holding his love. He likes to watch the news from his favorite chair. If you see to it that everything in the house is where he expects to find it, you'll have no difficulty keeping the relationship on an even keel.

Life and love with an Aries man may be just the medicine you need. He'll be a good provider. He'll spoil you if he's financially able.

The Aries father is young at heart and will spoil the children every chance he gets. His quick mind and energetic behavior appeal to the young. His ability to jump from one thing to another keeps the kids hopping. You must introduce some focus into the children's activities. Always emphasize the practical in order to prepare the kids for success.

CAPRICORN WOMAN
TAURUS MAN

Some Taurus men are strong and silent. They do all they can to protect and provide for the women they love. The Taurus man will never let you down. He's steady, sturdy, and reliable. He's pretty honest and practical, too. He says what he means and means what he says. He never indulges in deceit and will always put his cards on the table.

Taurus is affectionate. Being loved, appreciated, understood is important for his well-being. Like you, he is also looking for peace and security in his life. If you both work toward these goals together, you'll find that they are easily attained.

If you should marry a Taurus man, you can be sure that the wolf will never darken your door. Bulls are notoriously good providers and do everything they can to make their families comfortable and happy.

He'll appreciate the way you have of making a home warm and inviting. Soft lights and the evening papers are essential ingredients in making your Taurus husband happy at the end of the workday. Although he may be a big lug of a guy, you'll find that he's fond of gentleness and soft things. If you puff up his pillow and tuck him in at night, he'll eat it up and ask for more.

You probably won't complain about his friends. Taurus tends to seek out friends who are successful or prominent. You admire people, too, who work hard and achieve what they set out for.

The Taurus man doesn't care too much for change. He's the original stay-at-home. Chances are that the house you move into after you're married will be the house you'll live in for the rest of your life.

You'll find that the man born under the sign of the Bull is easy to get along with. It's unlikely that you'll have many quarrels or arguments that last more than a short time.

Although he'll be gentle and tender with you, your Taurus man is far from being a sensitive type. He's a man's man. Chances are he loves sports from fishing to football. He can be earthy as well as down to earth.

Taurus, born under an earth sign as you are, has much affection for the children and has no trouble demonstrating his love and warmth. Yet the Taurus father does not believe in spoiling the kids, so you and he will share the challenge of disciplining them. Both of you want your youngsters to succeed in the world. The Taurus father especially sees to it they grow up knowing their place in society.

CAPRICORN WOMAN
GEMINI MAN

Gemini men, in spite of their charm and dashing manner, may leave you cold. They seem to lack the sort of common sense you set so much store in. Their tendency to start something, then out of boredom never finish it, may exasperate you.

You may interpret a Gemini's jumping around from here to there as childish, if not downright neurotic. A man born under the sign of the Twins will seldom stay put. If you should take it upon yourself to try and make him sit still, he will resent it strongly.

On the other hand, the Gemini man may think you're a slowpoke—someone far too interested in security and material things. He's attracted to things that sparkle and dazzle. You, with your practical way of looking at things most of the time, are likely to seem a little dull and uninteresting to this gadabout. If you're looking for a life of security and permanence, you'd better look elsewhere for your Mr. Right.

Chances are you'll be taken by his charming ways and facile wit. Few women can resist Gemini magic. But after you've seen through his live-for-today, gossamer facade, you'll most likely be very happy to turn your attention to someone more stable, even if he is not as interesting.

You want a man who is there when you need him. You need someone on whom you can fully rely. Keeping track of a Gemini's movements will make you dizzy. Still, if you are patient, you should be able to put up with someone contrary—especially if you feel the experience is worth the effort.

A successful and serious Gemini could make you a very happy woman, if you gave him half a chance. He generally has a good brain and can make good use of it when he wants. Some Geminis who have learned the importance of being consistent have risen to great heights professionally. Once you can convince yourself that not all people born under the sign of the Twins are witless grasshoppers, you'll find that you've come a long way in trying to understand them.

Life with a Gemini man can be more fun than a barrel of clowns. You'll never have a chance to experience a dull moment. He's always the life of the party. He's a little scatterbrained when it comes to handling money most of the time. You'd better handle the budgeting and bookkeeping.

The Gemini father is in some ways like a child himself, and perhaps that is why he gets along so well with the younger generation. He usually lets the children do what they want until they are running the household. You will put a stop to this nonsense without suppressing the sense of humor the youngsters have picked up from their Gemini father.

CAPRICORN WOMAN
CANCER MAN

The Cancer-Capricorn combination is astrologically linked. You two are zodiacal mates, as well as zodiacal opposites, so chances are you will hit if off in love. But Cancer is very sensitive—thin-skinned and moody. You've got to keep on your toes not to step on his.

Cancer may be lacking in some of the qualities you seek in a man. But when it comes to being faithful and being a good provider, he's hard to beat.

True to his sign, the Crab can be fairly cranky and crabby when handled the wrong way. If you want to catch him and keep him, you will learn to understand and flow with his moods.

The perceptive woman will not mistake the Crab's quietness for sullenness or his thriftiness for penny-pinching. In some respects, he is like that wise old owl out on a limb. He may look like he's dozing, but actually he hasn't missed a thing.

Cancers often possess a well of knowledge about human behavior. They can come up with helpful advice to those in trouble or in need. He can certainly guide you in making investments both in time and money. He may not say much, but he's always got his wits about him.

If you're smarter than your Cancer friend, be smart enough not to let him know. Never give him the idea that you think he's a little short on brainpower. It would send him scurrying back into his shell, and all that lost ground will never be recovered.

The Crab is most comfortable at home. Settled down for the night or the weekend, wild horses couldn't drag him any further than the gatepost, unless those wild horses were dispatched by his mother. The Crab is sometimes a Mama's boy. If his mate does not put her foot down, he will see to it that his mother always comes first.

No self-respecting Capricorn wife would ever allow herself to play second fiddle to her mother-in-law. With a little bit of tact, you'll slip into that number-one position as easy as pie.

Cancers make proud, patient, and protective fathers. But they can be a little too protective. Their sheltering instincts can interfere with a youngster's natural inclination to test the waters outside the home. Still, the Cancer father doesn't want to see his kids learning about life the hard way from the streets. The fact that you are Cancer's zodiacal opposite, as well as mate, helps to balance how your children will view life and cope with a variety of challenging situations.

CAPRICORN WOMAN
LEO MAN

To know a man born under the sign of the Lion is not necessarily to love him—even though the temptation may be great. When he fixes most girls with his leonine double-whammy, it causes their hearts to pitter-pat and their minds to cloud over.

You are a little too sensible to allow yourself to be bowled over by a regal strut and a roar. Still, there's no denying that Leo has a way with women—even sensible women like yourself. Once he's swept a woman off her feet, it may be hard for her to scramble upright again. Still, you are no pushover for romantic charm—especially if you feel it's all show.

He'll wine you and dine you in the fanciest places. He'll croon to you under the moon and shower you with diamonds if he can get a hold of them. Still, it would be wise to find out just how long that shower is going to last before consenting to be his wife.

Lions in love are hard to ignore, let alone brush off. Your reserve will have a way of nudging him on until he feels he has you completely under his spell. Once mesmerized by this romantic powerhouse, you will most likely find yourself doing things you never dreamed of.

Leos can be vain pussycats when involved romantically. They like to be cuddled and petted. This may not be your cup of tea exactly. Still, you'll do everything to make him purr.

Although he may be big and magnanimous while trying to win you, he'll whine if he thinks he's not getting the tender love and care he feels is his due. If you keep him well supplied with affection, you can be sure his eyes will never look for someone else and his heart will never wander.

Leo men often tend to be authoritarian. They are bound to lord it over others in one way or another it seems. If he is the top banana at his firm, he'll most likely do everything he can to stay on top. If he's not number one, he's most likely working on it and will be sitting on the throne before long.

You'll have more security than you can use if he is in a position to support you in the manner to which he feels you should be accustomed. He is apt to be too lavish, though, at least by your standards.

You'll always have plenty of friends when you have a Leo for a mate. He's a natural-born friend-maker and entertainer. He loves parties, and he will help you let your hair down and have a good time.

Leo fathers have a tendency to spoil the children—up to a point. That point is reached when the children become the center of attention, and Leo feels neglected. Then he becomes strict and insists that his rules be followed. You will have your hands full pampering both your Leo mate and the children. As long as he comes first in your affections, the family will be happy.

CAPRICORN WOMAN
VIRGO MAN

Although the Virgo man may be a bit of a fussbudget at times, his seriousness and dedication to common sense may help you to overlook his tendency to sometimes be overcritical about minor things.

Virgo men are often quiet, respectable types who set great store in conservative behavior and levelheadedness. He'll admire you for your practicality and tenacity, perhaps even more than for your good looks. He's seldom bowled over by a glamor-puss.

When he gets his courage up, he turns to a serious and reliable woman for romance. He'll be far from a Valentino while dating. In fact, you may wind up making all the passes. Once he does get his motor running, however, he can be a warm and wonderful fellow—to the right woman.

He's gradual about love. Chances are your romance with him will most likely start out looking like an ordinary friendship. Once he's sure you're no fly-by-night flirt and have no plans of taking him for a ride, he'll open up and rain sunshine all over your heart.

Virgo men tend to marry late in life. He believes in holding out until he's met the right partner. He may not have many names in his little black book. In fact, he may not even have a black book. He's not interested in playing the field; leave that to men of the more flamboyant signs. The Virgo man is so particular that he may remain romantically inactive for a long period. His lover has to be perfect or it's no go.

If you find yourself feeling weak-kneed for a Virgo, do your best to convince him that perfect is not so important when it comes to love. Help him realize that he's missing out on a great deal by not considering the near-perfect or whatever it is you consider yourself to be. With your surefire perseverance, you will make him listen to reason and he'll wind up reciprocating your romantic interests.

The Virgo man is no block of ice. He'll respond to what he feels to be the right flame. Once your love life with a Virgo man starts to bubble, don't give it a chance to fall flat. You may never have a second chance at winning his heart.

If you should ever break up with him, forget about patching up. He'd prefer to let the pieces lie scattered. Once married, though, he'll stay that way—even if it hurts. He's too conscientious to try to back out of a legal deal of any sort.

The Virgo man is as neat as a pin. He's thumbs down on sloppy housekeeping. Keep everything bright, neat, and shiny. And that goes for the children, too, at least by the time he gets home.

The Virgo father appreciates courtesy, good manners, and family honor as much as you do. He will instill a sense of order in the household, and he expects the children to respect his wishes. He is very concerned with the health and hygiene of the youngsters, so he may try to restrict their freedom, especially at play. Although you are an earth sign like your Virgo mate, you will be less fearful and will prepare the children always to be poised and practical.

CAPRICORN WOMAN
LIBRA MAN

If there's a Libra in your life, you are most likely a very happy woman. Men born under this sign have a way with women. You'll always feel at ease in a Libra's company. You can be yourself when you're with him.

The Libra man can be moody at times. His moodiness is often puzzling. One moment he comes on hard and strong with declarations of his love. The next moment you find that he's left you like yesterday's mashed potatoes. He'll come back, though; don't worry. Libras are like that. Deep down inside he really knows what he wants even though he may not appear to.

You'll appreciate his admiration of beauty and harmony. If you're dressed to the teeth and never looked lovelier, you'll get a ready compliment—and one that's really deserved. Libras don't indulge in idle flattery. If they don't like something, however, they are tactful enough to remain silent.

Libras will go to great lengths to preserve peace and harmony, even tell a fat lie if necessary. They don't like showdowns or disagreeable confrontations. The frank woman is all for getting whatever is bothering her off her chest and out into the open, even if it comes out all wrong. To Libra, making a clean breast of everything seems like sheer folly sometimes.

You may lose your patience while waiting for your Libra friend to make up his mind. It takes him ages sometimes to make a decision. He weighs both sides carefully before committing himself to anything. You seldom dillydally—at least about small things—and so it's likely that you will find it difficult to see eye-to-eye with a hesitating Libra when it comes to decision-making methods.

All in all, though, he is kind, considerate, and fair. He is interested in the real truth. He'll try to balance everything out until he has all the correct answers. It's not difficult for him to see both sides of a story.

Libras are not show-offs. Generally, they are well-balanced, modest people. Honest, wholesome, and affectionate, they are serious about every love encounter they have. If he should find that the woman he's dating is not really suited to him, he will end the relationship in such a tactful manner that no hard feelings will come about.

The Libra father is patient and fair. He can be firm without exercising undue strictness or discipline. Although he can be a harsh judge at times, he will radiate sweetness and light with the youngsters in the hope that they will grow up to follow his gentle, charming manner.

CAPRICORN WOMAN
SCORPIO MAN

Some people have a hard time understanding the man born under the sign of Scorpio. Few, however, are able to resist his fiery charm. When angered, he can act like an overturned wasps' nest. His sting can leave an almost permanent mark. If you find yourself interested in the Scorpio man, you'd better learn how to keep on his good side.

Scorpio men are straight to the point. They can be as sharp as a razor blade and just as cutting to anyone who crosses them. In fact, Scorpio prides himself on his bluntness. But at times he may seem rather hard-hearted. He can be touchy every now and then, which is apt to get on your nerves after a while. When you feel like you can't take it anymore, you'd better tiptoe away from the scene rather than chance an explosive confrontation.

If he finds fault with you, he'll let you know. He might misinterpret your patience as indifference. Still, you can adapt to almost any sort of relationship or circumstance if you put your heart and mind to it.

Scorpio men are all quite perceptive and intelligent. In some respects, they know how to use their brains more effectively than most. They believe in winning at whatever they do. Second place holds no interest for them. In business, they usually achieve the position they want through drive and use of intellect.

Your interest in home life is not likely to be shared by him. No matter how comfortable you've managed to make the house, it will have very little influence on him or make him aware of his family responsibilities. He does not like to be tied down, and would rather be out on the battlefield of life, belting away at some just and worthy cause. Don't try to keep the home fires burning too brightly while you wait for him to come home.

The Scorpio man is passionate in all things—including love. Most women are easily attracted to him, and you are perhaps no exception. Those who allow themselves to be swept off their feet by a Scorpio man soon find that they're dealing with a carton of romantic fireworks. The Scorpio man is passionate with a capital P, make no mistake about that. Some women may find that he's too intensely sexual and too intent on sex.

Scorpio likes fathering large families. That may not suit your desire to have a small, close-knit family, especially as Scorpio often fails to live up to his responsibilities as a parent. But when he takes his fatherly duties seriously, he is a proud and patient parent. He is wonderful with difficult youngsters because he knows how to tap the best in each child. Like you, he believes in preparing the children for the hard knocks life sometimes delivers.

CAPRICORN WOMAN
SAGITTARIUS MAN

Sagittarius men are not easy to catch. They get cold feet whenever visions of the altar enter the romance. You'll most likely be attracted to Sagittarius because of his sunny nature. He's lots of laughs and easy to get along with. But as soon as the relationship begins to take on a serious hue, you may find yourself a little let down.

Sagittarius are full of bounce, perhaps too much bounce to suit you. They are often hard to pin down; they dislike staying put. If he ever has a chance to be on the move, he'll latch onto it without so much as a how-do-you-do. Sagittarius are quick people both in mind and spirit. If ever they do make mistakes, it's because of their zip. They leap before they look.

If you offer him good advice, he most likely won't follow it. Sagittarius like to rely on their own wits and ways whenever possible.

His up-and-at-'em manner about most things is likely to drive you up the wall at times. He's likely to find you a little too slow and deliberate. He may tease and nudge you when you're accompanying him on a stroll or jogging through the park. He can't abide a slowpoke.

At times you'll find him too much like a kid—too breezy and casual. Don't mistake his youthful zest for premature senility. Sagittarius are equipped with first-class brainpower and know how to use it. They are often full of good ideas and drive. Generally, they are very broad-minded people and very much concerned with fair play and equality.

In romance he's quite capable of loving you wholeheartedly while treating you like a good pal. His hail-fellow-well-met manner in the arena of love is likely to scare off a dainty damsel. However, a woman who knows that his heart is in the right place won't mind it too much if backpatting takes the place of a gentle embrace.

He's not much of a homebody. He's got ants in his pants and enjoys being on the move. Humdrum routine, especially at home, bores him silly. At the drop of a hat, he may ask you to travel away for a night out. He's a past master in the instant surprise department. He'll love to keep you guessing. His friendly, candid nature will win him many friends. He'll expect his friends to be yours, and vice versa.

The Sagittarius father can be all thumbs when it comes to tiny tots. He will dote on any infant son or daughter from a distance. As soon as the children are old enough to walk and talk, Sagittarius feels comfortable enough to play with them. He will encourage all their talents and skills, and he will see to it that they get a well-rounded education.

CAPRICORN WOMAN
CAPRICORN MAN

The Capricorn man may be more inhibited and cautious than the Capricorn woman. So it may be up to you to thaw his romantic reserve and warm his sensual interest in you. He is capable of giving his heart completely once he has found the right lover. As you know, Capricorn is thorough and deliberate in all that he does. He is slow and steady and sure.

He doesn't believe in flirting and would never lead a heart on a merry chase just for the game. If you win his trust, he'll give you his heart on a platter. Quite often, the woman has to take the lead when romance is in the air. As long as he knows you're making the advances in earnest, he won't mind—in fact, he'll probably be grateful.

Although some Capricorns are indeed quite capable of expressing passion, others often have difficulty in trying to display affection. He should have no trouble in this area, however, as long as you are patient and understanding.

The Capricorn man is very interested in getting ahead. He's quite ambitious and usually knows how to apply himself well to whatever task he undertakes. He's far from being a spendthrift. Like you, he knows how to handle money with extreme care. Both of you have a knack for putting away pennies for that rainy day. The Capricorn man thinks in terms of future security. He wants to make sure that he and his wife have something to fall back on when they reach retirement age. There's nothing wrong with that; in fact, it's a plus quality.

The Capricorn man will want to handle household matters efficiently. Most Capricorn women will have no trouble in doing this. If he should check up on you from time to time, don't let it irritate you. Once you assure him that you can handle it all to his liking, he'll leave you alone.

Although he's a hard man to catch when it comes to marriage, once he's made that serious step, he's quite likely to become possessive. Capricorns need to know that they have the support of their wives in whatever they do—every step of the way.

The Capricorn man needs to be liked. He may seem dull to some, but underneath his reserve there is sometimes an adventurous streak that has never had a chance to express itself. He may be a real daredevil in his heart of hearts. The right woman—the affectionate, adoring woman—can bring out that hidden zest in his nature.

A Capricorn father is dutiful and steady, although he may not understand the children as well as you do. He can be cold and aloof at times, and the youngsters may confide to you that they secretly dislike him. However, as they get older and wiser, they realize that the Capricorn father always acted in their best interests.

CAPRICORN WOMAN
AQUARIUS MAN

You will find the Aquarius man the most broad-minded man you have ever met. On the other hand, you will find him the most impractical. Oftentimes, he's more of a dreamer than a doer. If you don't mind putting up with a man whose heart and mind are as wide as the universe but whose head is almost always up in the clouds, then start dating that Aquarius who has somehow captured your fancy. Maybe you, with your good sense, can bring him back down to earth when he gets too starry-eyed.

He can be busy making some very complicated and idealistic plans when he's got that out-to-lunch look in his eyes. But more than likely he'll never execute them. After he's shared one or two of his progressive ideas with you, you may think he's crazy. But don't go jumping to conclusions. There's a saying that Aquarius are a half-century ahead of everybody else in the thinking department.

If you decide to marry him, you'll find out how right his zany whims are on or about your 50th anniversary. Maybe the wait will be worth it. Could be that you have an Einstein on your hands—and heart.

Life with an Aquarius won't be one of total despair if you can learn to temper his airiness with your down-to-earth practicality. He won't gripe if you do. Aquarius always maintains an open mind. He'll entertain the ideas and opinions of everybody. He may not agree with all of them.

Don't go tearing your hair out when you find that it's almost impossible to hold a normal conversation with your Aquarius friend at times. No matter what he says, keep in mind that he means well.

His broad-mindedness doesn't stop when it comes to you and your personal freedom. You won't have to give up any of your hobbies or projects after you're married. He'll encourage you to continue in your interests.

He'll be a kind and generous husband. He'll never quibble over petty things. Keep track of the money you both spend. He can't. Money burns a hole in his pocket.

At times, you may feel like calling it quits. Chances are, though, that you'll always give him another chance.

The Aquarius father is a good family man. He understands children as much as he loves them. He sees them as individuals in their own right. Aquarius can talk to the kids on a variety of subjects, and his knowledge can be awe-inspiring. You will often have to bring the youngsters back down to earth.

CAPRICORN WOMAN
PISCES MAN

Pisces could be the man you've looked for high and low and thought never existed. He's terribly sensitive and terribly romantic. Still, he has a very strong individual character and is well aware that the moon is not made of green cheese. He'll be very considerate of your every wish and will do his best to see to it that your relationship is a happy one.

The Pisces man is great for showering the object of his affection with all kinds of little gifts and tokens of his love.

He's just the right mixture of dreamer and realist; he's capable of pleasing most women. When it comes to earning bread and butter, the strong Pisces will do all right in the world. Quite often they are capable of rising to the very top. Some do extremely well as writers or psychiatrists.

He'll be as patient and understanding with you as you undoubtedly will be with him. One thing a Pisces man dislikes is pettiness. Anyone who delights in running another into the ground is almost immediately crossed off his list of possible mates. If you have any small grievances with your friends, don't tell him. He couldn't care less and will think less of you if you do.

If you fall in love with a weak kind of Pisces, don't give up your job at the office before you get married. Better hang onto it until a good time after the honeymoon; you may still need it. A Pisces man can be content almost anywhere. This is perhaps because he is quite inner-directed and places little value on material things. In a shack or a palace, the Pisces man is capable of making the best of all possible adjustments. He won't kick up a fuss if the roof leaks and if the fence is in sad need of repair.

At this point, you'll most likely feel like giving him a piece of your mind. Still and all, the Pisces man is not shiftless or aimless. It is important to understand that material gain is never a direct goal for someone born under this sign.

Pisces men have a way with the sick and troubled. He can listen to one hard-luck story after another without seeming to tire. He often knows what's bothering someone before that someone knows it himself.

As a lover, he'll be quite attentive. You'll never have cause to doubt his intentions or sincerity. Everything will be aboveboard in his romantic dealings with you.

The Pisces father, always permissive and understanding, is immensely popular with children. He plays the double role of confidant and playmate for the kids. It will never enter his mind to discpline a child, no matter how spoiled or incorrigible that youngster becomes.

Man—Woman

CAPRICORN MAN
ARIES WOMAN

The Aries woman may be a little too bossy and busy for you. Generally, Aries are ambitious creatures. They tend to lose their patience with thorough and deliberate people who take a lot of time to complete something. The Aries woman is a fast worker. Sometimes she's so fast she forgets to look where she's going.

When she stumbles or falls, it would be nice if you were there to grab her. But Aries are proud. They don't like to be chided when they err. Scolding can turn them into blocks of ice. However, don't begin to think that the Aries woman frequently gets tripped up in her plans. Quite often she is capable of taking aim and hitting the bull's-eye. You'll be flabbergasted at times by her accuracy as well as by her ambition.

You are perhaps somewhat slower than Aries in attaining your goals. Still, you are not apt to make mistakes along the way; you're seldom ill-prepared.

The Aries woman is quite sensitive at times. She likes to be handled with gentleness and respect. Let her know that you love her for her brains as well as for her good looks. Never give her cause to become jealous. When your Aries woman sees green, you'd better forget about sharing a rosy future together. Handle her with tender love and care and she's yours.

The Aries woman can be giving if she feels her partner is deserving. She is no iceberg; she responds to the proper masculine flame. She needs a man she can look up to and feel proud of. If the shoe fits, put it on. If not, better put your sneakers back on and quietly tiptoe out of her sight. She can cause you plenty of heartache if you've made up your mind about her and she hasn't made up hers about you.

Aries women are very demanding at times. Some of them tend to be high-strung. They can be difficult if they feel their independence is being hampered.

The cultivated Aries woman makes a wonderful homemaker and hostess. You'll find that she's very clever in decorating; she knows how to use colors. Your house will be tastefully furnished. She'll see to it that it radiates harmony. Friends and acquaintances will love your Aries wife. She knows how to make everyone feel at home and welcome.

The Aries woman makes a fine, affectionate mother. Because she is not keen on burdensome responsibilities, like you she prefers a small family with a few children. She is skilled at juggling both career and motherhood, so the kids will never feel she is an absentee parent. You can help prepare the youngsters for their roles as young adults.

CAPRICORN MAN
TAURUS WOMAN

A Taurus woman, an earth sign like you, could perhaps understand you better than most women. She is very considerate and loving. She is thorough and methodical in whatever she does. She knows how to take her time in doing things; she is anxious to avoid mistakes. She is a careful person. She never skips over things that may seem unimportant; she goes over everything with a fine-tooth comb.

Home is very important to the Taurus woman. She is an excellent homemaker. Although your home may not be a palace, it will become, under her care, a comfortable and happy abode. She'll love it when friends drop by for the evening. She is a good cook and enjoys feeding people well. No one will ever go away from your house with an empty stomach.

The Taurus woman is serious about love and affection. When she has taken a tumble for someone, she'll stay by him—for good, if possible. She will try to be practical in romance, to some extent. When she sets her cap for a man, she keeps after him until he's won her. The Taurus woman is a passionate lover, even though she may appear otherwise at first glance. She is on the lookout for someone who can return her affection fully. Taurus are sometimes given to fits of jealousy and possessiveness. They expect fair play in the area of marriage. When it doesn't come about, they can be bitingly sarcastic and mean.

But the Taurus woman is generally easygoing. She's fond of keeping peace. She won't argue unless she has to. She'll do her best to maintain your love relationship on an even keel.

Marriage is generally a one-time thing for Taurus. Once they've made the serious step, they seldom try to back out of it. Marriage is for keeps. They are fond of love and warmth. With the right man, they turn out to be ideal wives.

The Taurus woman will respect you for your steady ways. She'll have confidence in your common sense.

The Taurus mother will share with you the joys, the burdens, and the challenges of parenthood. She seldom puts up with any nonsense from the youngsters. She can wield an iron fist in a velvet glove. She may have some difficult times when they reach adolescence. But in later life the teenagers are often thankful they were brought up in such a conscientious fashion.

CAPRICORN MAN
GEMINI WOMAN

The Gemini woman may be too much of a flirt for you. Then again, it depends on what kind of mood she's in. Gemini women can change from hot to cold quicker than a cat can wink its eye. Chances are her fluctuations will tire you after a time, and you'll pick up your heart—if it's not already broken into small pieces—and go elsewhere. Women born under the sign of the Twins have the talent of being able to change their moods and attitudes as frequently as they change their party dresses.

Sometimes, Gemini gals like to whoop it up. Some of them are good-time gals who love burning the candle to the wick. You'll see them at parties and gatherings, surrounded by men of all types, laughing gaily or kicking up their heels at every opportunity. The next day you may bump into this creature at the neighborhood library and you'll hardly recognize her for her sensible attire. She'll probably have five or six books under her arm—on five or six different subjects. In fact, she may even work there.

You'll probably find her a dazzling and fascinating creature—for a time, at any rate. Most men do. But when it comes to being serious about love you may find that this sparkling Eve leaves quite a bit to be desired. It's not that she has anything against being serious, it's just that she might find it difficult trying to be serious with you.

At one moment, she'll be capable of praising you for your steadfast and patient ways. The next moment she'll tell you in a cutting way that you're an impossible stick in the mud.

Don't even begin to fathom the depths of her mercurial soul—it's full of false bottoms. She'll resent close investigation, anyway, and will make you rue the day you ever took it into your head to try to learn more about her than she feels is necessary. Better keep the relationship full of fun and fancy-free until she gives you the go-ahead sign. Take as much of her as she is willing to give; don't ask for more until she takes a serious interest in you.

There will come a time when the Gemini woman will realize that she can't spend her entire life at the ball. The security and warmth you have to offer is just what she needs to be a happy, complete woman.

A Gemini mother, like her children, is often restless, adventurous, and easily bored. She will never complain about their fleeting interests because she understands the changes they will go through as they mature. She has a youthful streak that guides her in bringing up the kids through the various stages of infancy through young adulthood. Better make sure she doesn't spoil the children.

CAPRICORN MAN
CANCER WOMAN

A Capricorn-Cancer union can be a match made in heaven, at least in the astrological scheme of things. You are, after all, zodiacal opposites as well as zodiacal mates. If you fall in love with a Cancer woman, though, be prepared for anything. In one hour she can unravel a whole gamut of emotions; it will leave you in a tizzy. She'll always keep you guessing, that's for sure.

You may find her a little too uncertain and sensitive for your liking. You'll most likely spend a good deal of time encouraging her—helping her to erase her foolish fears.

Don't chide her about her personal interests, or her family. If you do, you'll most likely reduce her to tears. She can't stand being made fun of. It will take bushels of roses and tons of chocolates—not to mention the apologies—to get her to come back out of her shell.

In matters of money managing, she may not be as generous as you are. You may get the notion that your Cancer sweetheart or mate is a direct descendant of Scrooge. If she has her way, she'll hang onto that first dollar you earned. She's not only that way with money, but with everything right on up from bakery string to jelly jars. She's a saver; she never throws anything away, no matter how trivial.

Once she loves you, she will be an affectionate, self-sacrificing, and devoted woman. Her love for you will never alter unless you want it to. She'll put you up on a high pedestal and will do everything—even if it's against your will—to keep you there.

Cancer women love home life. For them, marriage is an easy step to make. They're domestic with a capital D. She'll do her best to make your home comfortable and cozy. The Cancer woman is happiest in her own home. She makes an excellent hostess. The best in her comes out when she's in her own environment, one in which she can be a nurturer and caregiver.

Of all the signs of the Zodiac, Cancer women make the best mothers. She'll treat every complaint of her child as a major catastrophe. With her, children come first. If you're lucky, you'll run a close second. You may think she's too devoted to the children. You may have a hard time convincing her to cut her apron strings. Still, the Cancer-Capricorn parent combination is one of the best in terms of devotion and discipline for the youngsters.

CAPRICORN MAN
LEO WOMAN
The Leo woman can make most men roar like lions. If any woman in the Zodiac has that indefinable something that can make men lose their heads and find their hearts, it's the Leo woman.

She's got more than a fair share of charm and glamour. And she knows how to make the most of her assets, especially when she's in the company of the opposite sex. Jealous men are apt to lose their cool or their sanity when trying to woo a woman born under the sign of the Lion.

She likes to kick up her heels quite often and doesn't care who knows it. She often makes heads turn and tongues wag. You don't necessarily have to believe any of what you hear—it's most likely jealous gossip or wishful thinking. Needless to say, other women in her vicinity turn green with envy and will try anything to put her out of the running.

This Leo vamp makes the blood rush to your head and makes you momentarily forget all the things you thought were important and necessary in your life. You may feel differently when you come back down to earth and the stars are out of your eyes.

You may feel that she isn't the kind of woman you planned to bring home to Mother. Not that your mother might disapprove of your choice—but you might after the shoes and rice are a thing of the past. Although the Leo woman may do her best to be a good wife for you, chances are she'll fall short of your idea of what a good wife should be like.

If you're planning on not going as far as the altar with that Leo woman who has you flipping your lid, you'd better be financially equipped for some very expensive dating. Be prepared to shower her with expensive gifts and to take her dining and dancing in the smartest spots in town. Promise her the moon if you're in a position to deliver. Luxury and glamour are two things that are bound to lower a Leo's resistance. She's got expensive tastes, and you'd better cater to them if you expect to get to first base with this lady.

If you've got an important business deal to clinch and you have doubts as to whether you can swing it or not, bring your Leo partner along to the luncheon. Chances are that with her on your arm, you'll be able to win any business battle. She won't have to say or do anything—just be there at your side. The grouchiest oil magnate can be transformed into a gushing, obedient schoolboy if there's a charming Leo woman in the room.

A Leo mother can be so proud of her children that she is sometimes blind to their faults. Yet when she wants them to learn and take their rightful place in the social scheme of things, the Leo mother can be strict. She is a patient teacher, lovingly explaining the rules the youngsters are expected to follow. Easygoing and friendly, she loves to pal around with the kids and show them off on every occasion.

CAPRICORN MAN
VIRGO WOMAN

The Virgo woman may be a little too difficult for you to understand at first. Her waters run deep. Even when you think you know her, don't take any bets on it. She's capable of keeping things hidden in the deep recesses of her womanly soul—things she'll only release when she's sure that you're the man she's been looking for.

It may take her some time to come around to this decision. Virgo women are finicky about almost everything. Everything has to be letter-perfect before they're satisfied. Many of them have the idea that the only people who can do things right are Virgos.

Nothing offends a Virgo woman more than slovenly dress, sloppy character, or a careless display of affection. Make sure your tie is not crooked and your shoes sport a bright shine before you go calling on this lady. Take her arm when crossing the street.

CAPRICORN—LOVE AND MARRIAGE / **121**

Don't rush the romance. Trying to corner her in the back of a cab may be the one way of striking out. Never criticize the way she looks. In fact, the best policy would be to agree with her as much as possible. Still, there's just so much a man can take; all those dos and don'ts you'll have to observe if you want to get to first base with a Virgo may be just a little too much to ask of you.

After a few dates, you may come to the conclusion that she just isn't worth all that trouble. However, the Virgo woman is mysterious enough generally speaking to keep her men running back for more. Chances are you'll be intrigued by her airs and graces.

If lovemaking means a lot to you, you'll be disappointed at first in the cool ways of your Virgo friend. However, under her glacial facade there lies a hot cauldron of seething excitement. If you're patient and artful in your romantic approach, you'll find that all that caution was well worth the trouble. When Virgos love, they don't stint. It's all or nothing as far as they're concerned. Once they're convinced that they love you, they toss all cares to the wind.

One thing a Virgo woman can't stand in love is hypocrisy. They don't give a hoot about what the neighbors say if their hearts tell them to go ahead. They're very concerned with human truths. So if their hearts stumble upon another fancy, they will be true to the new heartthrob and leave you standing in the rain. She's honest to her heart and will be as true to you as you are with her. Do her wrong once, however, and it's farewell.

The Virgo mother has high expectations for her children, and she will strive to bring out the very best in them. The children usually turn out just as she hoped, despite her anxiety about their health and hygiene, their safety and good sense. Like her, you are an earth sign and can understand her fears for the children both in school and at play. Both of you will see the need for discipline. But the Virgo mother is more tender than strict.

CAPRICORN MAN
LIBRA WOMAN
The Libra woman's changeability, in spite of its undeniable charm, could actually drive even a man of your patience up the wall. She's capable of smothering you with love and kisses one day, and on the next avoid you like the plague. If you're a man of steel nerves, then perhaps you can tolerate her sometime-ness without suffering too much. However, if you're only a mere mortal who can only take so much, then you'd better fasten your attention on a partner who's somewhat more constant.

But don't get the wrong idea. A love affair with a Libra is not bad at all. In fact, it can have an awful lot of pluses to it. Libra women are soft, very feminine, and warm. She doesn't have to vamp all over the place in order to gain a man's attention. Her delicate presence is enough to warm any man's heart. One smile and you're a piece of putty in the palm of her hand.

She can be fluffy and affectionate, which you like. On the other hand, her indecision about which dress to wear, what to cook for dinner, or what to decorate could make you tear your hair out. What will perhaps be more exasperating is her flat denial of the accusation that she cannot make even the simplest decision. The trouble is that she wants to be fair or just in all matters. She'll spend hours weighing pros and cons. Don't make her rush into a decision; that will only irritate her.

The Libra woman likes to be surrounded by beautiful things. Money is no object when beauty is concerned. There will always be plenty of flowers in the house. She'll know how to arrange them tastefully, too. Libras adore beautiful clothes and furnishings. These women will run up bills without batting an eye—if given the chance.

Once she's cottoned to you, the Libra woman will do everything in her power to make you happy. She'll wait on you hand and foot when you're sick and bring you breakfast in bed Sundays. She'll be very thoughtful and devoted. If anyone dares suggest you're not the grandest man in the world, your Libra wife will tell that person where to get off in no uncertain terms.

The Libra mother is moderate and even-tempered, like you, so together you will create a balanced family life in which the children can grow up to be equal partners in terms of responsibilities and privileges. She knows that youngsters need both guidance and encouragement in a harmonious environment. The children will never lack for anything that could make their lives easier and richer.

CAPRICORN MAN
SCORPIO WOMAN

When the Scorpio woman chooses to be sweet, she's apt to give the impression that butter wouldn't melt in her mouth. But, of course, it would. When her temper flies, so will everything else that isn't bolted down. She can be as hot as a tamale or as cool as a cucumber when she wants. Whatever mood she's in, you can be sure it's for real. She doesn't believe in poses or hypocrisy.

The Scorpio woman is often seductive and sultry. Her femme fatale charm can pierce the hardest heart like a laser beam. She doesn't have to look like Mata Hari (many of them resemble the tomboy next door). But once you've looked into those tantalizing eyes, you're a goner.

The Scorpio woman can be a whirlwind of passion. Life with her will not be all smiles and smooth sailing. If you think you can handle her tempestuous moods, then try your luck.

The stable and steady Capricorn man will most likely have a calming effect on her. You're the kind of man she can trust and rely on. But never cross her—even in the smallest things. If you do, you'd better tell Fido to make room for you in the doghouse; you'll be his guest for the next couple of days.

The Scorpio woman will keep family battles within the walls of your home. When company visits, she'll give the impression that married life with you is one big joyride. It's just her way of expressing her loyalty to you, at least in front of others. She believes that family matters are and should stay private. She'll certainly see to it that others have a high opinion of you both. She'll be right behind you in whatever it is you want to do.

Although she's an individualist, after she has married, she'll put her own interests aside for those of the man she loves. With a woman like this backing you up, you can't help but go far. She'll never try to take over your role as boss of the family. She'll give you all the support you need in order to fulfill that role. She won't complain if the going gets rough. She is a courageous woman. She's as anxious as you to find that place in the sun for you both. She's as determined a person as you are.

Although the Scorpio mother loves her children, she will not put them on a pedestal. She is devoted to developing her youngsters' talents. The Scorpio mother is protective yet encouraging. Under her skillful guidance, the children will learn how to cope with extremes. She will teach her young ones to be courageous and steadfast.

CAPRICORN MAN
SAGITTARIUS WOMAN

The Sagittarius woman is hard to keep track of. First she's here, then she's there. She's a woman with a severe case of itchy feet. She's got to keep on the move.

People generally like her because of her hail-fellow-well-met manner and breezy charm. She is constantly good-natured and almost never cross. She is the kind of gal you're likely to strike up a palsy-walsy relationship with. You might not be interested in letting it go any farther. She probably won't sulk if you leave it on a friendly basis, either. Treat her like a kid sister and she'll eat it up like candy.

She'll probably be attracted to you because of your steady self-assured manner. She'll need a friend like you to help her over the rough spots in her life. She'll most likely turn to you for advice on money and investments.

There is nothing malicious about the female Archer. She is full of bounce and good cheer. Her sunshiny disposition can be relied upon even on the rainiest of days. No matter what she says or does, you'll always know that she means well.

Sagittarius are sometimes short on tact. Some of them say anything that comes into their heads no matter what the occasion. Sometimes the words that tumble out of their mouths seem cutting and cruel. They mean well, but often everything they say comes out wrong. She's quite capable of losing her friends—and perhaps even yours—through a careless slip of the lip. Always remember that she is full of good intentions. Stick with her if you like her and try to help her mend her ways.

She's not a woman you'd most likely be interested in marrying, but she'll certainly be lots of fun to pal around with. Quite often, Sagittarius women are outdoor types. They're crazy about hiking, fishing, camping, and mountain climbing. They love the wide open spaces. They are fond of all kinds of animals. Make no mistake about it—this busy little lady is no slouch. She's full of get-up-and-go.

She's great company most of the time. She's more fun than a three-ring circus when she's in the right company. You'll like her for her candid and direct manner. On the whole, Sagittarius are very kind and sympathetic women.

If you do wind up marrying this girl-next-door type, you'd better see to it that you handle all of the financial matters. Sagittarius often let money run through their fingers like sand.

The Sagittarius mother is a wonderful friend to her children. She'll shower them with love and give them all the freedom they think they need. She is not afraid if a youngster learns some street smarts. But she might preach too much for the kids. You must switch the focus to the practical in order to prepare the youngsters for wordly success.

CAPRICORN MAN
CAPRICORN WOMAN

The Capricorn woman shares with you the same approach to romance. A Capricorn mate may be the right man for her. She believes in true love. She doesn't appreciate getting involved in flings. To her, they're just a waste of time.

She's looking for a man who means business—in life as well as in love. Although she can be very affectionate with her boyfriend or mate, she tends to let her head govern her heart. That is not to say she is cool or calculating. On the contrary, she just feels she can be more honest about love if she consults her brains first. She wants to size up the situation before throwing her heart in the ring. She wants to make sure it won't get stepped on.

The Capricorn woman is faithful, dependable, and systematic in just about everything she undertakes. She is quite concerned with security and sees to it that every penny she spends is spent wisely. She is very economical about using her time, too. She does not believe in whittling away her energy on a scheme that is bound not to pay off.

Ambitious themselves, they are quite often attracted to ambitious men—men who are interested in getting somewhere in life. If you win her heart, she'll stick by you and do all she can to help you get to the top.

The Capricorn woman is almost always diplomatic. She makes an excellent hostess. She can be very influential when your business acquaintances come to dinner.

The Capricorn woman is very concerned, if not downright proud, about her family tree. Relatives are important to her, particularly if they're socially prominent.

She's generally thorough in whatever she does. Capricorn women are well-mannered and gracious, no matter what their backgrounds. They seem to have it in their natures to always behave properly.

If you should marry a a female Goat, you need never worry about her going on a wild shopping spree. She understands the value of money better than most women. If you turn over your paycheck to her at the end of the week, you can be sure that a good hunk of it will wind up in the bank.

The Capricorn mother is very ambitious for her children, just as you are. She wants them to have every advantage and to benefit from things she perhaps lacked as a child. She will train the youngsters to be polite and kind, and to honor traditional codes of conduct. Together, Capricorn parents can be correct to a fault. But the children will have an edge in the world.

CAPRICORN MAN
AQUARIUS WOMAN

If you find that you've fallen head over heels for a woman born under the sign of the Water Bearer, you'd better fasten your safety belt. It may take you quite a while to actually discover what this woman is like. Even then you may have nothing to go on but a string of vague hunches.

Aquarius is like a rainbow, full of bright and shining hues. She's like no other female you've ever known. There is something elusive about her, something difficult to put your finger on.

The Aquarius woman can be odd and eccentric at times. Some say this is the source of her mysterious charm. You may think she's just a plain screwball, and you may be half right.

Aquarius women often have their heads full of dreams. By nature, they're unconventional. They have their own ideas about how the world should be run. Sometimes their ideas may seem pretty weird. Chances are they're just a little bit too progressive. They say that Aquarius is about fifty years ahead of the rest of the world in her thinking. She'll most likely be the most tolerant and open-minded woman you've ever encountered.

If you find that she's too much mystery and charm for you to handle, just talk it out with her and say that you think it would be better to call it quits. She'll most likely want to remain friends. Aquarius women are like that. Perhaps you'll both find it easier to get along in a friendship than in a romance.

It is not difficult for her to remain buddy-buddy with an ex-lover. For many Aquarius, the line between friendship and romance is a fuzzy one.

She is not a jealous person. And while you're romancing her, she won't expect you to be, either. You'll find her a free spirit most of the time. Just when you think you know her inside out, you'll dis- cover that you don't really know her at all.

She's a very sympathetic and warm person. She is often helpful to those in need of assistance and advice.

She'll seldom be suspicious even when she has every right to be. If the man she loves makes a little slip, she's will forgive and forget up to a point. Don't test her limits.

The Aquarius mother is generous and seldom refuses her chil- dren anything. You may feel the youngsters need a bit more disci- pline and practicality. But you will appreciate your Aquarius mate's worldly views, which prepares the youngsters to get along in life. They will grow up to be tolerant young people who fit in and feel at ease in any situation.

CAPRICORN MAN
PISCES WOMAN

The Pisces woman places great value on love and romance. She's gentle, kind, and receptive. She has very high ideals. She will only give her heart to a man who she feels can live up to her expectations.

Many a man dreams of an alluring Pisces woman. You're per- haps no exception. She's soft and cuddly and very domestic. She'll let you be the brains of the family; she's contented to play a behind-the-scenes role in order to help you achieve your goals. The illusion that you are the master of the household is the kind of magic that the Pisces woman is adept at creating.

She can be very ladylike and proper. Your business associates and friends will be dazzled by her warmth and femininity. Although she's a charmer, there is a lot more to her than just a pretty exterior. There is a brain ticking away behind that soft, womanly facade. You may never become aware of it—that is, until you're married to her. It's no cause for alarm, however; she'll most likely never use it against you, only to help you and possibly set you on a more successful path.

If she feels you're botching up your married life through careless behavior or if she feels you could be earning more money than you do, she'll tell you about it. But any wife would, really. She will never try to usurp your position as head and breadwinner of the family.

She can do wonders with a house. She is very fond of dramatic and beautiful things. There will always be plenty of fresh-cut flowers around the house. She will choose charming artwork and antiques, if they are affordable. She'll see to it that the house is decorated in a dazzling yet welcoming style.

She'll have an extra special dinner prepared for you when you come home from an important business meeting. Don't dwell on the boring details of the meeting, though. But if you need that grand vision, the big idea, to seal a contract or make a conquest, your Pisces woman is sure to confide a secret that will guarantee your success. She is canny and shrewd with money, and once you are on her wavelength you can manage the intricacies on your own.

If you are patient and kind, you can keep a Pisces woman happy for a lifetime. She is not without her faults. Her sensitivity may get on your nerves. You may find her lacking in practicality and good old-fashioned stoicism. You may even feel that she uses her tears as a method of getting her own way.

The Pisces mother has a strong bond with her children. Self-sacrificing, she can deny herself in order to fulfill their needs. She will teach her youngsters the value of service to the community while not letting them lose their individuality. She will see to it that her children earn honors.

CAPRICORN
LUCKY NUMBERS 2011

Lucky numbers and astrology can be linked through the movements of the Moon. Each phase of the thirteen Moon cycles vibrates with a sequence of numbers for your Sign of the Zodiac over the course of the year. Using your lucky numbers is a fun system that connects you with tradition.

New Moon	First Quarter	Full Moon	Last Quarter
Jan. 4	Jan. 12	Jan. 19	Jan. 26
1610	1358	0236	6495
Feb. 2	Feb. 11	Feb. 18	Feb. 24
7668	8107	7397	3859
March 4	March 12	March 19	March 26
2924	4016	6951	0722
April 3	April 11	April 17	April 24
2460	9382	2957	4880
May 3	May 10	May 17	May 24
4309	9586	6273	3792
June 1	June 8	June 15	July 23
6084	4751	0637	7468
July 1	July 8	July 15	July 23
0510	4273	3944	6704
July 30	August 6	August 13	August 21
3931	1062	8833	5708
August 28	Sept. 4	Sept. 12	Sept. 20
8751	0637	7792	2085
Sept. 27	Oct. 3	Oct. 11	Oct. 19
5262	7748	8130	6952
Oct. 26	Nov. 2	Nov. 10	Nov. 18
2951	7224	4603	3823
Nov. 25	Dec. 2	Dec. 10	Dec. 17
5419	9557	9372	2534
Dec. 24	Jan. 1 ('12)	Jan. 9 ('12)	Jan. 16 ('12)
1960	1035	6101	9161

CAPRICORN
YEARLY FORECAST 2011

Forecast for 2011 Concerning Business
and Financial Affairs, Job Prospects,
Travel, Health, Romance and Marriage
for Persons Born with the Sun
in the Zodiacal Sign of Capricorn.
December 21–January 19

For those born under the influence of the Sun in the zodiacal sign of Capricorn, ruled by Saturn, the planet of discipline and structure, 2011 promises to be one of continual change, movement, and action in the area of career and business matters. With Saturn, the taskmaster of the zodiac as your lifetime ruler, trials and tribulations are an integral part of the life of Capricorn folks. You are very aware that your challenge is to keep progressing toward the achievement of your ultimate goals. Even if the road is long and hard, you continue the climb to receive and enjoy the rewards of your labor.

As the year begins, the Sun, Mars, and Pluto are all in your sign and impacting your first house of personality and self. Capricorn confidence and self-assurance will be greatly enhanced. Most of you will feel more energized, empowered, and ready to climb over whatever obstacle is placed along your path. With Pluto remaining in your Capricorn first house for many years, a metamorphosis will take place. Many of you may experience the need to express yourself in ways entirely different from your patterns in the past.

Your ruler Saturn all year transits Libra, your house of vocation, business, and how you are seen by others. Libra is an elevated position for Saturn and can indicate that you have reached a pinnacle in your life. Rewards for your dedication, service, and effort may be received. Achievements and honors should be part of the scene in 2011. Many of you could be presented with interesting professional opportunities to move higher up the ladder of success.

Career challenges will test your courage to experiment with new ideas and options. Self-growth and success shouldn't be difficult. An honorable and ethical approach is essential, because success and failure can become public knowledge. In many ways your life will be about constant change. If you can embrace the transition and go with the flow, your life will be enhanced. Originality and expertise will be aided by a disciplined approach. Capricorn artists, writers, musicians, and other creative Goats can move steadily toward your cherished hopes and produce works that are appreciated by others.

Accolades should be more frequent as manuscripts are published and paintings sold at higher prices than in the past. Even those of you who are not employed in artistic fields should find release from the self-imposed pressure and strain of long hours on the job by pursuing a creative hobby or pastime. Developing a life outside your vocation is important for the career-minded Goat this year. For some of you this might be creating a beautiful, welcoming home, large or small, that is an oasis, a sanctuary, and a showcase. Your friendship circle will widen as you expand your field of interests and join various groups and clubs, both social and professional.

With your ruler Saturn moving through Libra all year, problems in relationships can come to light. Some Capricorns may have already ended a love affair, separated from a partner, or are currently experiencing a rocky patch in a committed union. Your innate workaholic tendencies could continue to wreck havoc with your social and emotional life unless some leisure time is set aside for play.

Romantic interludes should be abundant for both the solo and partnered Capricorn. It will be essential to cub an overly ambitious attitude so you can focus on your nearest and dearest. Make sure that continual neglect doesn't further alienate an intimate partnership or spoil a budding affair. An associate or longtime friend could suddenly be seen through romantic eyes. An older or more stable partner might appeal to those of you looking for security as well as love. There is also a possibility that Capricorn singles could begin dating a boss or superior. A marriage or permanent relationship is foreseen with a partner who is in the public eye or who belongs to a wealthy family.

Establishing your own family unit can be a strong desire. Jupiter, the planet of good fortune, visits three zodiac signs this year. Jupiter begins the year in Pisces, your house of communication. From late January to early June, Jupiter visits Aries, your house of home and family. Then Jupiter finishes 2011 in Taurus, your house of leisure, pleasure, and treasure. This can be a year when many happy occasions, celebrations, and special events take place. A summer wedding and honeymoon may be the highlight of 2011 for some Capricorn folks. For others, the birth of a child is foreseen.

There should be plenty of action taking place in the area of home and family. More harmony and happiness on the domestic scene can be expected. Improved relations with immediate and extended family appear likely. If tension or feuds exist, this can be the year to hold out the olive branch and resolve old grievances and issues. Being hospitable and inviting others into your home should come more naturally, which in turn creates emotional satisfaction and increases the happiness and harmony.

Many Capricorn movers and shakers could place importance on changing the home environment. Renovating, expanding, or moving to an upmarket location is foreseen. Arranging for contractors, architects, or real estate agents can be successful, especially from January through May. Although it will be important to improve your living quarters to create a harmonious environment, even the most frugal Goats will need to be prudent spending money. You may be inclined to spend too much on home comforts and entertainment. Relocating could also be for the purpose of taking up new employment or a study grant. Now and over the next few years Capricorn individuals should define and set professional and business goals to ensure that effort is focused properly. Returning to study on a part-time basis is an option for some of you.

Dreamy Neptune moving through Aquarius will be impacting your house of personal money and possessions. So you can expect some chaos to continue to affect money management and the generation of income. Neptune doesn't have to be an adverse influence. Focusing on what you need rather than what you want could find you receiving assistance in unexpected ways. There is a good chance that a well-connected ally or benefactor can advance your cause this year, which in turn will add more money to your coffers. As long as your usual frugal attitude and conservative approach to all financial dealings are maintained, there shouldn't be too many problems to overcome. It is never good to be rash with your cash, but there are times when a calculated risk can be beneficial.

A desire to enter the field of real estate could pay dividends over the next few years. But you will need to do your homework and to conduct the appropriate research. Expanding your own property portfolio can be an excellent means of investing. Capricorns who are savvy and know current property values should find a number of good real estate options from January through May. Avoid impulsive purchases unless you have conducted the research from March onward. On March 11 Uranus, planet of the unexpected, moves into your Aries house of family and home, bringing more movement and chaos around domestic and property matters.

On April 4 a major celestial transit occurs. Dreamy Neptune prepares to enter Pisces, the sign that Neptune rules, giving Capricorns a sample of what can be expected for many years to come. Those of you with talent or who have dreamed of pursuing a creative field can now take action and use imagination and inspiration in an artistic manner. Take the plunge. Begin to write, draw, or design. Learn constructive uses of self-expression. Enroll in courses or classes that can teach you how to organize ideas into a cohesive form. Under

Neptune's transit deception can occur for those of you who are native. Be careful shopping for a new car or expensive electronic equipment. Memory lapses could occur. If you have problems with finding locations, purchase an up-to-date navigation system to avoid becoming lost.

Capricorn well-being and energy level remain stable throughout the year. Powerful Pluto in your first house of the physical body positively affects your vim and vitality. Most ailments or seasonal sniffles should disappear fairly quickly, as your power to recuperate remains strong. Guard against your typical workaholic tendencies. Prevention is better than cure. Your ruler Saturn governs the skeletal structure and bones, so calcium and vitamin supplements can help to ensure strong and healthy bones.

The Sun visiting your opposite sign of Cancer from June 21 through July 22 is an opportune period to be more alert to signals from your body. Adopt a healthy diet. Guard against overeating and consuming junk food. Spending less time on the job and more time with those you love can also have a beneficial effect on physical and emotional well-being. Capricorn folks should actively pursue hobbies and favored pastimes as a way to relax and unwind. Meditate to slow down the constant flow of thoughts. A gentle exercise program could be advantageous if you do not want a heavy round of weights, bikes, and treadmills.

Planet Mercury rules the thought process, communication and all forms of expression, and transport. In 2011 Mercury has three retrograde periods: March 30 through April 22, August 3 through 26, and November 24 through December 13. During these retrograde periods it is to your advantage to defer signing important documents and to postpone buying major items such as a car or electronic equipment. However, these are wonderful periods to re-organize, review, and reflect so you can make positive changes and decisions.

The phases of the Moon can provide Capricorn people with valuable information that will also assist decision making. Beginning new projects during the New Moon phase will give a nice boost to advance the enterprise. There is more chance of completing outstanding tasks or ongoing ventures successfully during Full Moon phase.

Capricorn is one of the most capable of all the zodiac signs. If you put your mind to a task, you can resolve issues and turn problems around so that the best results are achieved. Have faith in your creativity and expertise. The year 2011 will flow smoothly and successfully, bringing well-deserved rewards and recognition your way.

CAPRICORN DAILY FORECAST

January–December 2011

JANUARY

1. SATURDAY. Happy New Year! Many Goats may prefer to remain in bed or lounge around rather than face any more socializing today, especially if celebrations were long and noisy last night. The Moon is now moving through your Sagittarius twelfth house of solitude and secrets. So this is the time of the month when your body signals you to slow down, rest, and relax in order to ensure that you are revitalized. Don't be afraid to ask for space if you need a respite from family and friends over the next couple of days. Now is the perfect period to review and reassess situations and events that occurred over the past twelve months. It is an ideal period for making plans and setting goals for the year ahead.

2. SUNDAY. Fair. Another day dawns when you could be more comfortable in your own company. If social plans are arranged, put on a happy face and break through any moodiness. Then enjoyment of the day will be your reward. Self-deception could be an issue. Or you may be judging a situation incorrectly. Talk to a trusted relative if a personal problem is causing concern. Someone objective will take a different approach to resolving a problem. Capricorn folks are not usually free and easy with your cash. But right now you might be too easygoing about money and resources. Deceptive trends abound, warning Goats to beware flattery. The motives of others might not be totally honest and aboveboard.

3. MONDAY. Vital. With the Moon in your own sign, motivation and enthusiasm should be restored. Whether you are back at work or still resting at home, it is time to question if now is the appropriate period to make a few significant changes in your life. If there is a feeling of being in a rut and not enough excitement to look forward to, then perhaps you should implement some alterations and put variety into your routine. Over the next few days romance will be enticing. It could lead into something different from what you have experienced in the past. Capricorn singles should move carefully. Your expectations about a new lover could be totally unrealistic right now.

4. TUESDAY. Lively. The cosmic heavens are bouncing today with a number of planetary links brightening up your day. However, confusing trends also surround Capricorns, which could make it difficult to deal with some folks. If you ease into the day and allow situations to flow freely, things should happen in the manner that brings pleasure. With the Sun and the Moon in your own sign, this is the time of the year when you can shine by taking your place in the spotlight. With a New Moon culminating in Capricorn, you might come across new circumstances or ideas that will enhance your life. Making a good impression and putting your best foot forward will take on greater importance now.

5. WEDNESDAY. Active. A busy and stimulating day ahead seems likely. With the Moon continuing through your sign and your first house of Capricorn, this should be a fruitful period. People are bound to want your company. So try to make time to be available and to be ready to socialize. The Capricorn Moon also helps you to feel emotionally strong and self-confident. You should be feeling full of energy as your vim and vitally peak. Make sure that increased physical resources are used constructively. A message from a friend or an associate will make your day. There might be very good news regarding a travel opportunity, money matters, or a romantic relationship.

6. THURSDAY. Helpful. Personal finances are to the fore now as the Moon slips through your Aquarius house of financial resources. Check to see if your bank account is showing any signs of strain. Lifestyle changes may have occurred that are increasing your expenditure so some of you may be depleting your savings and spending your income just as fast as you make it. A plethora of ideas should also come to mind on how improvements can be made to generate more income and to ease concerns regarding your cash flow. Those of you who are looking for a new job and haven't heard of any potential new career opportunities should remain optimistic. Keep searching, as the cosmos is looking out for your interests now.

7. FRIDAY. Testing. Deep breathing and mild exercise might be what many of you need today. If you are filled with nervous anxiety and continual worries, consider implementing stress-relief strategies to ensure that you remain focused and on track. The Sun in Capricorn is conflicting with your ruler Saturn in Libra. So some of you are likely to encounter an edginess to the day. If you are on the job, there are bound to be problems to confront and even tension, possibly with a boss or an authority figure. Stick to your own duties. Make sure that someone doesn't take credit for your efforts. Spend time with friends this evening. Let them know that they are very special.

8. SATURDAY. Renewing. Venus, the planet of love, beauty, and money, has now entered into the deep, dark realms of your Sagittarius twelfth house. Take the opportunity over the next few weeks to reassess and reestablish links with your inner self and desires. Goats who are not in a permanent union, and even those who are, need to be careful that you don't become involved in a secret or clandestine relationship. Over the next few days feverishness could be bothersome, and might reduce your energy and enthusiasm. Endeavor to get out and about. Mix and mingle, and you should feel better. Those of you who are scheduled to host a special event or speak in public should relax. Chances are you will excel in these activities now.

9. SUNDAY. Surprising. Morning trends are not as helpful as later in the day. Over the next few days the planet Uranus, master of surprises, reins. Fortunately, your sign of Capricorn is not noted for impulsiveness or rash behavior. However, even the most staid among you could be tempted to break out of your normal routine and try something different now. If you do have trouble finding equilibrium in your emotional life, just remember that these feelings will disappear fairly quickly. Listen to and learn from someone close to you. Words of wisdom spoken by another may contain a lesson that you don't need to repeat. Afternoon or evening pleasures promise good times.

10. MONDAY. Edgy. For many Goats this might be your first day back to work after the holiday break. You can expect to have sharp intuition but also a restless attitude. Some Capricorn folks could be unusually impulsive or quick to react negatively to the slightest provocation. Control this impulse. Creating upsets will not be the best way to begin the new working week. The visual and graphic arts and crafts should be of special interest. Those of you who love to design, sew, or draw should have a productive day. An exhibition by a favorite painter or sculptor will inspire. A visit to the local bookshop or library will also provide ideas that could be reproduced in interior design or handmade goods.

11. TUESDAY. Busy. It is a day to go after what you want as long as it isn't unrealistic. However, a sense of joviality is likely to be missing today. Take care with words spoken. It may be easy to offend others even if this isn't your intention. Fine-tune your communication skills. Be on guard with others. They may have a tendency to exaggerate, miscalculate, and promise more than can be delivered. An empty pledge given by another could leave you feeling a little miserable. Over the next few days those of you involved in any electronics or technology business should have a chance to increase profits. Make sure goods are marketed and displayed professionally, then reap the rewards.

12. WEDNESDAY. Energetic. Capricorn enthusiasm should be heightened now. Although when you realize how much work awaits you today, your spirits could become slightly dampened. Your attitude is likely to play a large part in your ability to complete tasks and to move forward. The desire to make things happen quickly could bring frustration unless a flexible approach is maintained. Get serious and seek to discover the causes of family disunity and disharmony. This is an excellent period to purchase new electronic equipment to enhance efficiency. If you need a new mobile phone or computer, start researching online for the best prices available.

13. THURSDAY. Happy. A favorable day dawns for Capricorn. The Moon is in the sensual sign of Taurus, your house of pleasure. The focus turns to romance, children, physical activities, and creative pursuits. An involvement in competitive sports can be a positive release for those of you in high-stress positions or situations. Athletes should excel in your chosen field of play. Talkative Mercury moves into your sign and your first house of personality, encouraging many of you to express, share viewpoints, and discuss ideas with people in close proximity. Finding an audience eager to listen to your opinions shouldn't be difficult. Make sure that others are given a chance to communicate their beliefs and viewpoints.

14. FRIDAY. Favorable. Postiive cosmic forces continue to beam down on Capricorn. There may be a few hiccups along the way that will require your attention. A scenario that has been annoying should begin to sort itself out now. Tackling problems head-on may bring the hoped-for results. Physical activity continues to be the best source of reducing pressure and stress. Capricorn parents should find time to play with children. Games will be relaxing and therapeutic for those of you who have had a hard week at work. This is also a positive period to tell a significant other what you want, how you are feeling, and how much you care. Prepare for a romantic evening ahead.

15. SATURDAY. Forceful. The good times continue to roll, especially through the morning hours. If you are usually shy and unassuming, opportunities to assert your intentions are likely to appear and should be eagerly grasped. Mighty Mars enters your Aquarius solar house of financial rewards, material possessions, and value systems. So from now until February 22, energy applied to supplementing your income, negotiating a pay increase, or looking for a better-paying position can pay dividends. You may need to curb impulse buys and any overspending if you are required to stay within a set budget. An important financial undertaking should be researched thoroughly before you move too far ahead.

16. SUNDAY. Mixed. Those of you who are working today could find that differences of opinion with coworkers are likely to upset your day. Refrain from taking things too personally. Then the discord should melt away fairly rapidly later on. Spend your spare time in a practical way. If your health needs attention, start to implement methods that can improve overall well-being and vitality. Straightening out domestic plans might take patience and diplomacy but will be worth the effort to ensure that family harmony remains intact. Workaholic Capricorn folks may find that stress is building in your life right now. So allow yourself plenty of relaxation time to unwind mentally and emotionally.

17. MONDAY. Pressured. Disgruntled colleagues could create issues on the employment scene for some Capricorns. Lessen the chances of disruption by refusing to enter into arguments with teammates. Then the tension should remain minor. Increased obligations are foreseen. Someone moving a deadline forward could upset your agenda and cause a few problems that will need to be dealt with. Do justice to your commitments. But take care that you don't work so hard and long that the point of physical exhaustion is reached. Make sure that you also adopt a diet that supplies your body with the proper nutrition to keep your strength high. Friends should be a great source of encouragement. Take advantage, and socialize tonight.

18. TUESDAY. Animated. Emotional needs might not be met today as lunar trends are not looking very bright. However, talkative Mercury makes a good link to passionate Pluto. So there should be a boost of power to verbal conversations that will raise Capricorn self-confidence and self-assurance. Those of you who need to sell, lecture, or persuade others should find that the right words roll off your tongue without any difficulty. This is a good time to make changes or adjustments to methods and routines that are not working, especially in the area of personal and professional relationships. An open and honest discussion with a loved one might be required to clear the air and to establish or reaffirm mutual goals.

19. WEDNESDAY. Sensitive. Harness the positive power of the day. Good luck looms on the horizon. Many of you could be in party mode. Other people, especially your Cancer friends or relatives, might not share your exuberance. A Full Moon in your own sign of Capricorn could touch off intense emotions. Someone close may be a little touchy and overly sensitive. This can be a positive period to take stock of what is happening at home, in your emotional life, and with a personal or professional partnership. It would be timely now to assess and address any problems that are currently occurring in a relationship in order to ensure that you are moving toward achieving mutual goals.

20. THURSDAY. Promising. Another good day dawns for Capricorn folks. You are about to enter a very positive money period. Today the golden Sun moves into your Aquarius second house of personal possessions and financial resources. What you own and what you intend to buy come into focus. If you have been living beyond your means, this is the time to reassess your income and expenditure so that your budget can be brought into line. If professional assistance is required regarding finances, seek such help. You will then have a method to ease your mind and to return to a positive cash flow. Business matters should prosper over the next four weeks. A boost of energy and motivation should help to increase your income.

21. FRIDAY. Strategic. Confusion might create chaos this morning for many of you. Something that didn't work out in the past could reappear as feasible now, as the timing appears to have improved. This should be a blessing for those of you who are prepared to take action. Putting new money strategies into place can help stabilize your financial future. Errors may have been made in financial records. So take the time to compare your checks and bills against bank and credit statements. Mistakes could be found in your favor. If a situation becomes overwhelming, count to ten and take deep breaths. That will help to restore peace and calm. Refrain from revealing personal secrets.

22. SATURDAY. Pleasant. Participate in a recreational pursuit on this leisure day. Quality time with loved ones should be on top of today's agenda. Word from overseas or news regarding a long-distance journey could bring a smile to the face of many Capricorn folks. However, there is the possibility that you may have to do a couple of things that you are not keen on. If that is the case, get to these tasks early so they are out of the way and you can move on to more pleasurable activities. Avoid gossiping; otherwise, it might rebound on you. Enrolling in a class on a subject of interest can be the first step toward improving your employment qualifications or steering you into a satisfying hobby.

23. SUNDAY. Decisive. A decision regarding a long-term commitment to the one you love might be required now. This doesn't mean that you will accept or decline a marriage proposal. But a choice to begin living together on a trial period could be under consideration. Some Capricorn folk need a quiet, romantic evening for two to discuss your future intentions. Bring mutual goals into the light for an open and honest discussion. Jupiter, the planet of abundance, has now entered your Aries fourth house of home, family, and property, and visits Aries until June 4. This long period offers a perfect chance to upgrade the family home and to make the necessary changes in order to improve current living conditions.

24. MONDAY. Varied. The morning hours look to be more helpful, than later in the afternoon. Career or business opportunities that you wouldn't normally consider could become more appealing now. If the financial figures add up to support a new venture, don't hold back because of fear or insecurities. This may be a positive chance to move on to something more exciting or different. Concern regarding your reputation could find many of you Goats making a concerted effort to retain your public standing or position as the top salesperson in your company. An early night is one way to avoid potential disharmony around home base this evening.

25. TUESDAY. Profitable. The self-employed Capricorn should find that your business interests are fruitful and profitable today. Those of you employed by others should pay special attention to small details, move at a steady pace, and aim to complete all tasks ahead of schedule. Goats who have a deadline or target to meet will more than likely reach required results as long as you don't become too caught up in daydreaming or fantasy. The talented and artistic Capricorn should find that your innate creative skills will be admired and rewarded now. Spending time with a colleague or associate could strengthen ties. For some of you this may be the blossoming of a new friendship.

26. WEDNESDAY. Tricky. The positive trends prevailing are outnumbered by the negative influences. Messenger Mercury challenging serious Saturn, your lifetime ruler, could cast a somber and pessimistic tinge over proceedings. Disappointment could come if you or others don't measure up to your high standards. But don't be too hard on yourself or on those around you. Capricorn individuals in a new job or at school could find studies, processes, and concepts very confusing, especially if prerequisites were glossed over earlier on. This isn't a good time to come to significant decisions or to hold important meetings, especially if business or commercial interests are involved.

27. THURSDAY. Frustrating. Your ruler, stubborn Saturn, has moved into retrograde motion, bringing focus to your career and status. You can expect delays to occur in business dealings. A promised promotion may be put on hold. Those of you looking for satisfactory employment might need to wait a little longer. Many of you might feel that you are overworked and underpaid. Right now some Capricorn folks could be loaded with more responsibility but without adequate remuneration for extra efforts. From now until June, try to refrain from worrying about your performance on the job. Do the best you can, and results should be favorable.

28. FRIDAY. Quiet. A dreamy period develops, remaining this way for the next couple of days. The Moon is moving through your twelfth house of Sagittarius, conferring an independent attitude. This Moon phase heralds a time when you need to slow down, rest, relax, and recharge run-down batteries as much as you can. Your intuition should be stronger. So listen to that little voice inside your head. That way you will instinctively know what others are thinking and will find the best method to solve a problem without being asked. Be careful with any tasks you undertake. Leave the heavy lifting and labor-intensive chores until next week when your vim and vitality should be at a peak.

29. SATURDAY. Tranquil. Another quiet day appears on the horizon. This is a good period to check facts and figures, tie up loose ends, and complete unfinished business. There may be a few emotional issues that you need to handle or come to terms with. Individuals typical of your sign of Capricorn are not known to be overtly affectionate or sentimental. However, it isn't wise to bury your feelings all of the time. Sometimes, it is essential that feelings are displayed and that other people are allowed to take part in this process. Social activities look promising this evening. Venture out even if you would rather stay home, and you are bound to find enjoyment.

30. SUNDAY. Fulfilling. By mid-morning the Moon will have entered your own sign of Capricorn, emphasizing your first house of personality. The tempo of life increases. Fortunately, your energy should also be fully restored, providing you with the vim and vitality to keep on top of whatever activity is planned for the day. Tasks that require a practical approach or that need concentration to complete can be undertaken, as your efficiency should be at a peak. Minor arguments could blossom into a nasty battle of words unless care is taken. Listen without passing judgment or giving an opinion until a friend or a loved one finishes stating their personal point of view.

31. MONDAY. Renewing. Excellent progress with significant tasks or projects can be made today. Take action and make your move, then increased benefits can be your reward. You should be feeling great, ready to tackle whatever obstacles come your way. Capricorn charm and social graces are at a peak. So dress to impress. Influencing people and getting others on your side should be easily accomplished. If unresolved problems are causing issues at home, it would be preferable to face facts and to confront matters rather than allowing them to boil beneath the surface. Once concerns are brought out into the open, it shouldn't take long to find satisfactory solutions.

FEBRUARY

1. TUESDAY. Fine. Morning and afternoon hours see the Moon still transiting your sign in your first house of personality. Any problems or recent troubles could seem to slip quietly away. Or you may be more inclined to respond in a favorable manner. Ease into the relaxed tone of the day and don't try to push along too quickly. Otherwise, things might not go exactly to plan. The Sun transits Aquarius in your personal finance sector, generating smart ideas on how to improve your current level of income. Before setting out on a long journey, Capricorn drivers should check tires and gas. Once you are on the road, it is essential to keep within the speed limit and obey the rules. Do not risk getting pulled over.

2. WEDNESDAY. Spirited. This is a day when you may be more chatty than usual. However, do yourself a favor and don't blindly accept or believe everything you hear or are told, especially if money, children, or love is involved. A family discussion that includes exciting plans could be the trigger for the emergence of old grievances. A tactful approach will be needed to avoid opening wounds from the past. Romantic influences should bubble along nicely. You can make the most of the dreamy vibes as long as a realistic attitude is maintained. For Capricorn singles, an encounter within the next few days holds promise. Dress to impress whenever venturing out to socialize. Be alert for romance.

3. THURSDAY. Helpful. Many Goats are entering the last phase of wanting to spend most of your time alone. Venus is preparing to move into your sign and your first house. So the tempo of life should gradually increase. Today Mercury joins the Sun, Mars, and Neptune already residing in Aquarius, your second house of personal money. Now starts an excellent period to look at your accounts, household budget, and bank balance to ensure that the ledger is on the upside and not sliding into the red. It should be easier to manage your finances, to be thrifty, and to keep cash flow under control. This ability is an innate quality of Capricorn, and is highlighted now. A unique leisure activity may whet your appetite for more of the same.

4. FRIDAY. Satisfying. Positive trends continue to make life very interesting. In the unlikely event that your finances are not in good order, consider setting time aside to make constructive changes. Venus, the goddess of love and money, is now moving into your sign and your first house of personality and self. Venus here signals the beginning of a new cycle that gives you the chance to embark on fresh experiences and activities. Platonic and love relationships will benefit. It should be easier even for the shy Capricorn to display affection and to let feelings flow more freely. If personal tasks have been neglected recently, such as updating your wardrobe, take action now while your sense of style is enhanced.

5. SATURDAY. Promising. News that you have been waiting for should begin to filter through now. The day ahead appears to be pleasant. Capricorn individuals will most probably be in a happy mood. Follow the urge to go out and have fun socializing with friends, visiting landmark sites, or shopping for a special outfit. Even those of you classified as workaholics might feel like having a day off for a change. Goats who prefer to remain close to home can expect a few visitors to drop in. Or you may find visiting others an enjoyable experience. You will obtain a positive reaction from people you hope to impress because you will say the right thing at the right time.

6. SUNDAY. Structured. Even on this leisure day you can put concerted effort into practical applications. The fruits of hard work should be realized, and you will be very happy with your productive output. Financially, a large domestic outlay that has been delayed for a while might be up for consideration again now. Run the money figures first before proceeding. Don't get carried away just because your cash flow is now improving. Moderation is the name of the game over the next few days. A tendency to overindulge could affect even the practical and thrifty Goat. Stick to preset plans. All bases should be covered if you move one step at a time.

7. MONDAY. Focused. There may be plenty of work required to complete an important project. But remaining focused is easy for the tenacious Capricorn. You are not usually inclined to scatter your resources. So make sure you don't do this now, and once again productivity should be high. There may be a special power behind words spoken today, and this should also considerably raise self-confidence and self-assurance. A meeting might set the scene for an important development. For some of you the outcome could include a promotion or a salary increase. However, beware spending more money on home improvements than you have allotted in your original plan.

8. TUESDAY. Serene. Early morning vibes bring delays. But once most Capricorn folks get into the swing of things, positive trends arrive. Expect the remainder of the day to slip by without too many problems or issues to stop progress. For home owners lots of effort can be poured into an improvement project with planned renovations. Creative inspiration remains accentuated. Your fondness for quality items over inferior products can lead to your doing the finishing touches that will successfully complete this design venture. Pay special attention to personal appearance and grooming so that you will look your best for a special occasion. Add a few bright colors to your attire if grays, browns, and other earthy colors are your usual choice.

9. WEDNESDAY. Passionate. Romance is a highlight today as lovely Venus merges with passionate Pluto. Many of you have spent a lot of time thinking about your lover or a special person of interest. This is a wonderful period to get together with your partner. Consider arranging a candlelight dinner or, even better, a weekend retreat just for two. Those of you in a permanent relationship could receive a marriage proposal or make a decision to move in with your lover. Creative Capricorns will crave stimulation as your desire to produce and to utilize your talents emerges in full force. Solo Goats should guard against falling for flattery. Refrain from becoming too involved with someone new right now.

10. THURSDAY. Stimulating. Intense passions continue again today. An old flame could reignite for those of you currently without a partner. Injecting extra zest into a stale relationship is easier now for Goats keen to reinvigorate or strengthen loving bonds. A calm and practical approach is required to ensure that good results are obtained. If you're creative, you are inspired to throw extra energy into a project that holds special appeal. Capricorn parents could find that children are a little more annoying, disruptive, or stubborn than usual. A firm but loving approach is the best way to bring youngsters back into line fairly quickly. A relaxing hobby could keep you happily occupied this evening.

11. FRIDAY. Varied. Mixed planetary trends prevail today. Influences this morning are not as helpful as later in the day. So, if possible, defer important tasks until later on. Those of you with a lot of routine duties to fulfill should clarify priorities. Perform jobs in a systematic method so that important contributions and progress can be made. If you have a romantic evening in mind, make the arrangements by mid-afternoon so that you can share happy experiences with your lover or spouse and not be interrupted. Honoring a promise can show a loved one how much you care. Capricorns who have been under pressure at work or school should let off steam in a positive manner in order to maintain good health.

12. SATURDAY. Edgy. Although your sign is not noted for restless or rash behavior, this inclination could possibly emerge today. Focusing on practical and mundane chores and activities may be difficult. It might be wiser to consider deferring routine tasks for a day or two. Some of you might need to pay attention to health and well-being. You do not want to come down with a sore throat or mild cold symptoms. That might affect your ability to fulfill your home and employment obligations. If you are feeling under the weather, consider visiting the doctor's office sooner rather than later. Then you should be on the right track to a speedy recovery.

13. SUNDAY. Great. Lunar trends look positive all day, so make plans to relax and enjoy activities of interest. The Moon continues to move through Gemini, your sixth house of health and service to others. So this is a positive period to implement a new fitness regime or eating plan. Signing up for a yoga or tai chi class can assist the connection between the body and mind as well as help to reduce built-up stress. Those of you working in the hospitality or retail fields should cultivate amicable relations with coworkers. Helping others can be beneficial and productive for all concerned. An early night is recommended, especially if you are recovering from a cold or sore throat.

14. MONDAY. Fulfilling. Capricorn folks involved in marketing should receive a boost from the positive aspect between Mercury and your life ruler, stable Saturn. Clinching a special deal or signing a significant document could also bring a smile to your face. If a pay raise or promotion is overdue, consider approaching the boss in the next few days. A favorable response should be forthcoming. Differences in style or personal taste could emerge with an intimate or professional partner. This will convey a need to compromise in order to reach the middle ground. The efficient Capricorn shouldn't experience any difficulty arranging a romantic evening with your lover to celebrate Valentine's Day.

15. TUESDAY. Tricky. A difficult day looms ahead for many Goats. Intimate and professional relationships could be strained, calling for cooperation and conciliation to reduce pressure and stress. Over the next few days, students could find some of the topics and concepts confusing, so perhaps you might need to ask a tutor or a learned friend for assistance. Expressing feelings verbally to loved ones might be a little difficult. It may be better to display your affections rather than attempting to put thoughts into words. Monitor family expenses carefully. Unbeknown to you, your mate could be spending more than the budget allows.

16. WEDNESDAY. Strategic. Today's events will tap your ingenuity and facility managing money. The Moon is now in Leo, your eighth house. So joint finances and shared assets could attract more attention than usual. Recent hard work and effort should begin to pay dividends. For some Capricorns money could come through the successful tendering of a lucrative contract, a tax refund, or a small inheritance. However, if you are about to make some type of financial commitment, be sure that every word written in a lease or binding agreement is read thoroughly before you sign on the dotted line. Power plays might bring upsets this evening if manipulation or emotional blackmail gets out of hand.

17. THURSDAY. Fruitful. It might be time to find out about a tax or insurance matter. Regardless of what you are working on, be sure to double-check facts and figures and tie up loose ends. There may be unfinished emotional business that has to be dealt with. Capricorn is ingenious enough to cope with any matters that arrive on your doorstep. Financially, there could be a need to renegotiate a deal or to change the ground rules in an important arrangement. But this, too, should only require a little give-and-take to bring about a swift resolution. Your imagination may be working overtime. Use renewed inspiration to finish an important creative project.

18. FRIDAY. Sensitive. A rather unsettling day appears likely. A Full Moon in Leo could bring money issues to a head, which in turn might signal a rise in your stress level. If you do find your temper rising, take time out and go for a walk outdoors or around the office. Taking this action will provide a little breathing space so that you can think through various options. Capricorn money managers and debt collectors should tread carefully when contacting late-paying customers. If there is any chance of alienating a debtor, it will be even harder to recoup the money owed. Romance and affairs of the heart are not looking rosy tonight and over the weekend.

19. SATURDAY. Mixed. Much to your frustration most plans and activities are likely to flow easier only through the early part of the day. Take advantage and complete routine obligations and tasks as soon as possible. That way you lessen the chance of annoyance and even anger occurring. Defer making long-term commitments. While socializing, Capricorn singles should plan on having a good time rather than hoping for a permanent lover to appear. The Sun is now residing in Pisces, your third house of transportation, movement, close relatives, and the local community. If the purchase of a new car is on your wish list, carrying out research and checking prices now should be fruitful.

20. SUNDAY. Hectic. A very busy day dawns in the cosmic heavens. It is definitely a period when going with the flow is recommended. It might be a challenge dealing with people close by. Confusion and lack of logic could be contagious. Wherever possible, defer important business. Focus on tasks that can be performed without too much concentration. Tension between your private life and public persona could surface, with both family and career matters needing attention. Perhaps taking a more spontaneous approach rather than constantly trying to organize and control every situation would help reduce the disharmony. Do what you can to ease the pressure.

21. MONDAY. Interesting. The Moon's presence in Libra, your house of career, business, and reputation, calls for tact and diplomacy when dealing with others. And today Mercury, the planet of the mind, moves into Pisces, your house of concepts and communications. So these areas are likely to become focal points for the next few weeks. Persuading others to do your bidding should be successful. During this Mercury transit you should find that conversation and discussion will include more spiritual, creative, or glamorous subjects. Although members of your sign are usually extremely discreet, some of you may be guilty of saying just a little bit more than is wise. So tread carefully, Capricorn.

22. TUESDAY. Trying. Today you may require a helping hand. Just ask, and support should be quickly forthcoming. A new field of interest could require much of your concentration over the next few weeks. Capricorn students preparing for exams should hit the books for hours to provide the best possibility of obtaining top results. If neighbors or siblings seem as though they are not being as cooperative as usual, it might not be personal. Perhaps they have their own worries to think about. This is not a day to make a major decision. Your thoughts could tend to a pessimistic nature, which will hinder your ability to be logical and practical.

23. WEDNESDAY. Vibrant. Your solar house of communication is further accentuated now. Energetic planet Mars has joined the Sun, Mercury, and Uranus in the sign of Pisces. You can expect to be more assertive when in discussions with others. But there will be a need to ensure that an overly assertive attitude is not displayed too frequently. Try to avoid situations throughout the day when you are required to sit still for long periods. A fidgety and restless demeanor could make it more difficult to focus. Helping out a friend brings positive rewards. Your evening plans for a romantic escapade or for a game of chance will eventuate and make you smile.

24. THURSDAY. Uncertain. Expect a drop in energy level over the next few days. This morning the Moon is preparing to change signs, leaving Scorpio and slipping into Sagittarius. Sagittarius represents the twelfth house of your solar horoscope, signaling a time to obey body indicators calling for rest and relaxation. Fiery Mars is also conflicting with Saturn, your ruler, and further depleting your vim and vitality. If you are waiting for answers regarding something important, delays are more than likely right now. If possible go with the flow and take things in your stride. Some things cannot be hurried. Loved ones or folks who mean a lot will be your choice for companionship tonight.

25. FRIDAY. Reassuring. A busy and intriguing day ahead appears certain to challenge your need for peace and tranquillity. Even with the Sagittarius Moon urging time out while sliding through your twelfth house of secrets and solitude, this is unlikely to happen. People will be vying for your attention. An insightful discussion or some soul-searching could reveal a difficult situation or bring closure to a problem that has up until now been very elusive. Accomplishing a personal goal could open the door to more achievements. Sharing values and cherished desires with friends or relatives will give you the support or the encouragement you are seeking.

26. SATURDAY. Pleasant. There is a possibility of running into someone or something from your past today. A secret divulged could raise a few questions, but you might need to be patient before receiving answers. If you are worried about a problem or issue, confide in a trustworthy friend or sibling. Sharing a concern can bring a measure of relief and sometimes a resolution. Relaxing could be on your mind this morning. However, as the hours slip by, the urge to socialize and have fun with friends or loved ones will return. Plan to go out this evening. Dancing or just listening to live music can be a great way to spend leisure hours.

27. SUNDAY. Bright. With the Moon continuing to move through your own sign of Capricorn, your energy and enthusiasm remain high. Ingenuity combined with practicality can lead you to new methods of accomplishing your goals. You will probably want to get out and mix and mingle with stimulating or interesting people. A lighthearted encounter could make for a fun day. Assistance from a friend or relative could really put a smile on your face. There is a strong likelihood of a favorite visitor arriving, increasing your pleasure even more. Later this evening an awkward issue with an authority figure could be touchy. But you can handle the matter in a positive manner as long as anger is kept under control.

28. MONDAY. Ideal. This is a good day to give yourself a fresh image or to explore different methods of doing things. Dressing to impress can often provide the career-minded Goat with an advantage over the competition. Acquiring a couple of stylish outfits will go a long way to substantially raise self-confidence and self-assurance. Enhanced creativity and inspired imagination can help the talented Capricorn increase productivity over the next couple of days. Romance is also in the air. Those of you coupled happily share love and companionship. Singles could find that an interesting encounter leaves you feeling dreamy and hopeful.

MARCH

1. TUESDAY. Expressive. With the Sun shining in Pisces, your communication sector remains an important focus for Capricorn folks as the new month begins. The positive link between lover Venus and unpredictable Uranus should also increase pleasure and excitement over the coming days, with lots of surprises in store. A lunchtime shopping expedition with a friend or loved one by your side should be fun as long as the urge to splurge doesn't become too overwhelming. Seeking a second opinion on a financial decision may provide a broader selection of options to choose from. Success purchasing real estate is more likely now. Just keep emotions out of the equation.

2. WEDNESDAY. Beneficial. Stylish Venus is now settling into your Aquarius solar sector of money and remains there until March 27. Personal finances and income will come into the frame. Your handling of monies as well as people should improve. However, your taste for the good things in life could also rise. Remember to smile more often now, even at people you don't know. New friendships could be formed spontaneously. Having friends on the job helps to break up your regular routine. A financial adviser may hold the answers for setting up a successful investment plan. If possible, take a brief power nap during the day. It can be a valuable rest period that enables you to plow ahead with greater steam.

3. THURSDAY. Complicated. Today is a positive period to perform duties that require attention to detail and focus. Determined and committed may be an apt description of your attitude and demeanor. However, impatience could arise if other people are unwilling to perform a job thoroughly and to completion. Expansive Jupiter in Aries is now moving to oppose structured Saturn in Libra, possibly bringing feelings of restriction and limitations. Over the next few weeks, frustration may be felt more keenly. Obstacles may suddenly appear in your pathway to block your progress. Delays involving home or business plans are likely, creating a need to rearrange ideas and readjust strategies.

4. FRIDAY. Positive. Favorable trends are forming now with the culmination of a New Moon in your Pisces zone of transportation and communication. Expressing your thoughts and your feelings about other people should be a lot easier now. Take advantage of this wonderful new cycle to promote your ideas and to begin new activities. Capricorn folks keen to purchase a new computer and any type of transportation or electronic equipment can start investigating your options and obtaining prices. You should come out with a good deal. Go out dancing tonight. It can be a wonderful way to let off steam, to have fun, and to retain physical fitness.

5. SATURDAY. Adaptable. Try not to stress too much if prearranged plans become unstuck and have to be changed. An adaptable approach can see you accomplishing a lot more than if you are trapped in a rigid way of thinking. Keep your running shoes on. There may be a number of little jaunts and errands to attend to around town. A change of scenery may be an ideal way to break your regular routine. The sound of the waves lapping on the shore could be relaxing. Consider taking a boat ride or sightseeing trip; it will smooth ruffled feathers. Capricorn creative urges are to the fore. If you have thought about enrolling in an art or interior design course, take the plunge now and do it now.

6. SUNDAY. Testing. Keeping emotions under control could challenge many Goats today. You are known for your cool head. Taking the time to explain how you are feeling shouldn't be seen as a weakness. It certainly is preferable to the other option of exploding. Intense energies abound, and can be used constructively to relieve tension by engaging in physical activities. Preparing meals and cooking might not be as pleasurable as usual. So make sure you have handy the phone numbers of favored restaurants nearby as a good alternative. Old habits may have a way of pushing through your defenses. Now would be a good time to seek help in breaking unwanted patterns of behavior.

7. MONDAY. Demanding. Pace yourself throughout the morning hours and try to stay steady. Waiting until later in the day to reorganize your office desk or work space for improved efficiency will bring better results than attempting to do this chore earlier in the day. Cracks could appear in the foundations of relationships that up until now you thought were solid. Experiencing increased strained relations with coworkers appears likely. Issues on the job could create misunderstandings and errors. Remember that humility shows great strength of character. So an apology would go a long way to mend bridges if an overreaction upsets the people around you.

8. TUESDAY. Satisfactory. It is a day when any failures should be viewed as another lesson learned as you make your way up the ladder of success. Focus on completing all work tasks early to ensure that there is plenty of time to relax this evening. Romance is in the air. Tonight a favorable link between the Taurus Moon and seductive Pluto in your sign of Capricorn creates the perfect setting for loving vibes. Soft background music is wonderful for generating inspiration and motivation. Play your favorites at work or at home. Those of you on a diet should stay away from the pantry and refrigerator. For your health's sake, curb the temptation to indulge in rich and sweet foods.

9. WEDNESDAY. Favorable. A quick wit and enhanced originality to your thinking are the gifts provided by today's cosmic influences. Capricorn writers, lecturers, teachers, and public speakers should be shown appreciation by your audience. Goats who sell for a living should experience a lucrative period. Relationships take on a deeper and more powerful flavor. Your ability to speak your mind and to express clearly is at a peak, helping you to strengthen loving ties with a partner or relative. There is, however, an edginess to the day that may be released in a rash or impulsive manner. This kind of erratic behavior doesn't usually sit well with conservative Capricorn. Tread warily without stifling spontaneous urges.

10. THURSDAY. Harmonious. Keep the romantic flames alive. Reaffirm loving vibes to your partner before heading off to tackle daily activities. Messenger Mercury has now entered the sign of Aries, providing a sharper edge to your thought patterns and communication. Applying yourself to problem solving should be easier if you can think outside the box. There is nothing wrong with a little bit of healthy competitiveness while working in a team effort. Friendly rivalry can be what helps you stay on the right track. Showcasing your wit and charm while entertaining at home can be enjoyable with those of you eager to display hospitality. Other Goats might prefer unwinding alone with an interesting novel as your companion.

11. FRIDAY. Guarded. Ensure that you breathe in plenty of fresh air today. Keep a window open, take a walk during your lunch period, or go on a pleasant drive to reduce boredom or anxiety. Don't believe everything you hear around the office as well as throughout the neighborhood. Take a prudent approach to your diet, especially any of you who suffer from digestive ailments. Care should also be taken while driving. Today the tendency for impulsive behavior increases, so perhaps you should rely on a steady companion to guide your actions. Over the next week financial negotiations and business deals should be easier to resolve.

12. SATURDAY. Interesting. Unpredictable Uranus has moved forward into Aries, your solar sector of home, family, and tradition.

You have already experienced a small sample of what this planetary influence can bring. Over the next seven years while Uranus transits Aries, you can expect things to change in your home life. Many of you are likely to relocate, renovate, or welcome a new addition to your home. In the long run replacing household goods might not be as expensive as repairing faulty goods, especially if you look around for the best deal. Try to keep a healthy balance between work and play so as to avoid becoming too obsessive in one area. Information shared during an impromptu meeting with neighbors or friends could be enlightening.

13. SUNDAY. Erratic. Relaxing in the comfort of your own home would be a good choice today. As stable and practical as you Capricorn folks usually are, today you may have a few ups and downs as you try to gain balance and harmony. Avoiding harsh verbal expression and intense emotionality could be a challenge. There is a chance that you will hurt people's feelings by your insensitive manner of speech. When it comes to sharing the housework, it may be necessary to let go of perfection. Just accept whatever assistance is offered. Going out to the movies or a concert is a wonderful way to lose yourself for a few hours in a world of fantasy and make-believe.

14. MONDAY. Mixed. Difficult planetary influences cast a shadow over today's proceedings. Whatever is thrown at you, just believing in your abilities will help you to climb over obstacles. A physical outlet should alleviate tension. So pack a pair of comfortable shoes, and engage in a fitness program. Your enhanced leadership skills may help to guide people in a team or group endeavor. Be assertive without any display of aggression. Displaying plants or fresh flowers should brighten up your work space. Tonight let a loved one cook a favorite meal. Enjoy a little comfort from somebody who cares.

15. TUESDAY. Fair. An ex may resurface out of the blue. If conversation is kept light, the experience should be pleasant and amicable. Harmonious patterns make it easy for those of you wishing to enter into a business partnership. This could be a very lucrative step to take if you have carried out appropriate checks and balances. Quarrels between coworkers could place you in the middle as a mediator endeavoring to restore the peace. Just listen to all points of view and don't take sides. Honesty with a large dose of tact and diplomacy would be the best policy to bid farewell to unexpected guests who have outstayed their welcome.

16. WEDNESDAY. Heartening. Support from others will be forth-coming if you display a warm and amicable demeanor. To combat waste, use your inventive powers. Think up new ways to recycle at work and at home. If you have been putting off making changes around the home, consider taking a good look now at what could be easily accomplished to improve living conditions. Capricorn cre-ative urges are at a peak. Scouring secondhand shops can be a great alternative to purchasing expensive antiques. A wonderful find that only needs a little work to restore back to original glory could be your reward. The Internet can also be a valuable resource for snar-ing quality goods at bargain prices.

17. THURSDAY. Uneasy. Thoroughly read financial documents or important paperwork to avoid misinterpretations. Confusion with insurance policies can be cleared up if you ask searching ques-tions before you sign on the dotted line. Self-analysis can lead to self-deception now. So it would be wise to obtain an opinion from someone objective, someone who will tell you the truth. Take a re-alistic approach toward organizing the household budget. Ensure that there is money available to save as well as to spend. Clarify the difference between a loan and a gift when dealing with friends or family. Take care when discarding rubbish; you could accidently throw away important receipts needed for your tax return.

18. FRIDAY. Varied. Tasks that involve adventure might be ap-pealing today. You don't need to be a visitor to take a tour around your hometown and gain more local knowledge. With talkative Mercury opposing Saturn, your life ruler, the urge to withdraw increases. Although your thinking should be practical and logical, many of you could also become more pessimistic and gloomy. Mer-cury's influence can be used constructively by engaging in pursuits that require concentration and attention to detail. This is a good period for Capricorn students, teachers, and writers. Defer for a few more days any important decisions that involve career, busi-ness, home, or family.

19. SATURDAY. Bumpy. Capricorn tolerance and patience toward the actions and behavior of other people could be at a low level throughout the day. Today's Virgo Full Moon increases tension. But it would be wise to remember that everyone is suffering to some degree under this lunar influence, not just you. Be careful when driving or when participating in any adventurous activities. Be sure to observe all safety precautions. Sibling rivalry could creep into relationships, regardless of how old you are, so try to keep competition within a healthy balance. Late evening is the time when you are more likely to give in to sudden urges or impulses.

20. SUNDAY. Variable. Mixed trends prevail throughout the day. An exciting domestic undertaking could run into problems. You may need to slow down a little in order to ensure that a job is completed professionally. Conflict between family responsibilities and work duties may create issues for the Goat intent on moving quickly up the career ladder. Many of you do fit the workaholic mold, but everyone needs to have some fun and pleasure. So make sure you take some time out to spend with loved ones. Pleasure in leisure pursuits is likely for all concerned. If your parents live at a distance, traveling halfway to meet them would be a good compromise.

21. MONDAY. Stimulating. A busy and exciting day awaits. The Sun has now moved into fiery Aries, joining a number of other planets there in your house of family, traditions, emotional roots, and origins. Expect plenty of action within the home. There may also be a bit of chaos and disruptions. Whatever plans have been arranged, introduce plenty of variety into your schedule. Mundane chores and routine activities are unlikely to hold your interest for very long. An unusual social scene should be fun. Participating in a variety of experiences could introduce you to new hobbies and leisure pursuits that could provide a new method of increasing income and enjoyment.

22. TUESDAY. Rewarding. Restlessness is on the rise. Your urge to move out of your comfort zone and to break new ground continues today. Capricorn folks seeking to buy property could unexpectedly find what you are seeking. Those of you selling may receive a higher than anticipated offer. Joining a group or an organization that has similar values to you will be a rewarding experience and can put you on the path to finding new friends with common interests. Working within a team environment should be productive. Hopes and dreams that may have been put on the back burner could rise to the surface, bringing a timely reminder of what is really important to you.

23. WEDNESDAY. Tricky. Transportation delays are likely to cause frustration and angst today. Remember to pack an interesting novel or a small laptop computer to help pass the time while you are in transit. Team and staff meetings are unlikely to bring instant results. However, if ideas are consolidated, the development of a unified plan could begin. Some Capricorns might achieve a lot more by working alone or at home over the next few days. As the warmer months arrive, remember to keep your fluid intake at a healthy level. Sharing a secret with a friend could help ease your burden and may bring a solution that you hadn't even considered.

24. THURSDAY. Cloistered. Taking time out to be by yourself and to restore inner balance will be important today and over the next day or two. A flexible approach may be the best method of remaining calm and relaxed. Your home should be a safe haven, a place to revitalize run-down batteries. Clear away objects that are no longer functional. Hanging on to old and worn-out items will just take up valuable space. Be mindful of self-imposed limits that are caused by secret fears and worries. Mystical things may hold fascination. Get into books or studies that satisfy your quest for knowledge. Skin dryness may be a problem for some Capricorns now, so keep a moisturizer handy at all times.

25. FRIDAY. Good. Writing or studying should be easier today. Find the time to escape for a little while and shut yourself away in your own world. Answers to problems are available, but you might need to do a little digging to discover the truth. An act of kindness toward someone in need will bring rewards. If meditating is difficult, try playing soft music to help relax and unwind after a busy week. It would be wise to take off the rose-colored glasses before becoming too involved in a secret love affair. Letting go of past mistakes can help you move forward. You may have a great loyalty to a cause. But be wary when it comes to handing over hard-earned cash; ask questions to clear up any gray areas.

26. SATURDAY. Meaningful. Venus, goddess of love and money, strongly stimulates your solar horoscope throughout the next week, conveying a mixture of positive and negative influences. The areas that are likely to be affected relate to personal finances, career, and family matters. Defer purchasing expensive pieces of art or investing money in property. Your heart is likely to rule your head, and unrealistic thinking is stronger now. Personal magnetism should be harnessed to your advantage now while the Moon travels through your own sign of Capricorn. People will notice your appearance and grooming, so dress to impress and reap the rewards.

27. SUNDAY. Active. Venus continues to create waves in your life. Today the saucy planet moves into Pisces, the communication sector of your solar chart. Venus here expands your intuition and powers of perception. Electronic equipment, a new phone, or a car could be on your wish list. Conducting research now could find many of you coming up with a great price for quality goods. Frugal Capricorns always seek to shop within your means. A picnic in the park or brunch at a local restaurant would be a wonderful way to meet friends if home entertaining is out of the question. Home renovations may be taking their toll on your finances and health, especially if things are not going to plan.

28. MONDAY. Productive. A home or commercial real estate property that you have had your eye on could suddenly come on the market. If you can afford to finance the purchase, this should be a lucrative long-term investment. A positive message that you send might be just what is needed to cheer up a sick friend. Keep a check on the Internet for any items that you are collecting. Something that you hope to own might be unexpectedly discovered. A scrapbook filled with personal memorabilia may be the perfect gift for a loved one. Be prudent with your money if shopping at an upscale department store is part of today's plans. A day away from the office would be the perfect antidote to reduce work-related stress.

29. TUESDAY. Unsettling. A trying day looms in the celestial sphere, so tackle important duties as early as possible to get the most out of the day. Avoid taking on too many tasks, or you will end up frazzled and tired. Patience is required now. Many Capricorns could suffer from frustration and anxiety. Feelings of being held back might strain your resolve. An annoying domestic incident could tip the balance, causing emotions to go into overwhelm. Someone in authority might overlook one of your achievements, and a promise to you could be broken. However, most things that develop now should have positive results at a later time, so don't fret too much.

30. WEDNESDAY. Uncertain. If financial freedom is at the top of your list of priorities, keep your ears open for strategies that can be put into practice. However, plans will need to be researched before you implement them. Communicative Mercury moves into retreat in Aries, your house of domestic and family concerns. Retrograde Mercury here will cause confusion when it comes to home renovations, signing mortgages, or purchasing real estate. If there isn't a choice, and you need to make a large purchase over the next three weeks, be vigilant. The same applies if a watertight agreement needs to be signed. Put in a safe place all receipts for goods you are buying in case there are flaws and breakdowns.

31. THURSDAY. Positive. Studying online can be a good alternative for learning if your time is limited and you are unable to complete a short course at a school. Inner tension could develop because of a persistent bad habit. Try to let go of these old patterns so that new and positive habits can be implemented. Putting your best foot forward socially can increase self-confidence and give you the assertiveness you need to handle a challenging situation. There may be a financial agreement that satisfies you and your landlord if it is necessary to break a lease. Having coffee and a chat with a neighbor may be a good way to unwind this evening.

APRIL

1. FRIDAY. Compelling. Concentration may be more difficult if you forgot to eat a healthy breakfast before leaving home. Capricorn folks are known as hard workers with a strong dedication to duty. So make sure you look after your body by supplying the right fuel. With the Moon passing through Pisces, your communication sector, even the most reserved among you could be more talkative than usual. Engaging in gossip is fine as long as unkind remarks are not part of the scenario and if discretion is applied. A quick e-mail could be all that's needed to keep in touch with siblings and friends. A favored magazine may provide the inspiration for do-it-yourself work around the home.

2. SATURDAY. Busy. Prepare for increased action around the home base. Energetic Mars enters Aries, your sector of home and family, and joins five other planets currently in residence there. Under this influence all types of renovation work would prove to be a satisfying challenge, especially because Uranus urges change and Pluto calls for transformation. But it is also a time to be careful while working around the home. If haste is the rule, then care may be thrown out the window. Keeping yourself active could forestall domestic arguments. Try not to intervene when household members keep stepping on one another's toes. If you are single, harmless flirting could be a fun way to connect with a potential romantic interest.

3. SUNDAY. Renewing. With the arrival of the Aries New Moon today, a new cycle begins. Over the next week you have a terrific period to begin new projects and to implement fresh ideas. With the Aries elevated energy impacting your solar sector of home and family, success is more than likely in this area. Disciplined Saturn is your ruler. And no one understands more than a practical Capricorn that strategies need to be well thought out before implementation, especially under the current planetary patterns. So do the homework and preparation first. Dinner out at a favored restaurant with family or close friends in attendance could be a lovely way to end the weekend.

4. MONDAY. Inspired. A major celestial influence occurs today. Dreamy Neptune prepares to enter into its own sign of Pisces, giving Capricorn folks a taste of what can be expected over the next few years. Those of you with talent who have dreamed of writing or some other form of creative expression could experience the urge to begin now. Take the plunge. Enroll in a course that sparks your interest. Soon you will be on the road to a wonderful relaxing hobby or a profitable second income. You may be more easily deceived when it comes to purchasing a car, so bring along a friend or shop around first. Allow yourself time to daydream because an inspired vision may eventually become a reality.

5. TUESDAY. Sensuous. Food may be a way to win the heart of a love interest, compliments of today's Taurus Moon. Senses are heightened. Walking in a garden smelling the sweet scent of the flowers or watching the visual display of the Sun sinking on the horizon can set the scene for a romantic evening. Keeping track of meetings and engagements might be necessary. If you forget or are unable to keep an appointment, a courtesy call to explain would be appreciated. Speak to a teacher if your child is experiencing difficulties at school. Relaying your concerns earlier rather than later can be the first step to finding a resolution.

6. WEDNESDAY. Fortunate. Your sign of Capricorn is well known as the worker of the zodiac. However, you should also remember to slow down at times and give yourself a treat. With lucky trends in force courtesy of the vibrant Sun and abundant Jupiter merging in Taurus, you should not pass up the chance to put yourself in a winning position. Purchase raffle tickets, buy a lottery ticket, and consider any propositions that could increase your bank balance. Introduce some fun into your exercise routine so that your motivation to improve health and well-being remains strong. This shouldn't cost much money. The great outdoors can provide a number of free resources.

7. THURSDAY. Variable. Enjoy the camaraderie and the gossip of colleagues, friends, and children. But keep in mind that not everything spoken will be the honest truth. Apply caution when it comes to job openings on offer now. Employers may be inclined to exaggerate or promise more than is feasible. So the saying that the grass is greener on the other side of the pasture may not be apt. Don't attempt to cover up mistakes made at work. It would be wiser to own up if you are at fault, then put energy into rectifying any errors. Romance isn't well starred for singles or for couples. It might be a night for television as your sole companion.

8. FRIDAY. Beneficial. The capacity to make others believe in your ideas and strategies is enhanced. Promotions and plans presented at a sales or staff meeting should be well received, and can have an added benefit of raising your profile. A humorous, dry wit is a renowned characteristic of your sign of Capricorn. This along with a charming demeanor can bring support from others and assist your cause. Stretching the truth is not something many Goats are guilty of. But these tactics could be employed now and might trip you up later. Take heed and stick to the facts. Relaxing techniques such as meditation or yoga might be of assistance if you are suffering from anxiety and tension.

9. SATURDAY. Buoyant. Capricorn confidence and optimism are at a peak today. The current cosmic forces aid any Goats who are scheduled to present a lecture, write an assignment, or complete a literary piece. Those of you involved in selling home products should excel. Organizing competent contractors to complete a renovation or an extension may be easier than expected. Those of you seeking a new home to rent or buy will more than likely find a number of residences that will suit your budget and family requirements. If socializing appeals, either your own dining table or a fancy restaurant could be the place to catch up on the news and gossip.

10. SUNDAY. Uncertain. Today doesn't provide the best influences to get what you want. Logic might be in short supply. Although there is a mild lucky streak running through your solar chart, power struggles between business or love partners could arise and force your hand to the point that you cannot stall or procrastinate any longer. Rather than losing your cool, it would be wiser to watch, observe, weigh your options and then act when you are of a calmer demeanor. Keep your home and valuables secure. Make sure broken windows or locks are promptly repaired. Ask a neighbor to keep watch on your home if you are planning to stay away for any length of time.

11. MONDAY. Tense. Tricky planetary patterns are forming, so be prepared to confront a few challenges and obstacles. Tension within the home front could erupt. But if problems can be discussed in calm and rational manner, resolutions should be found that are satisfactory to all concerned. Issues that have been buried, hidden, or just not brought out into the light for discussion could surface now. Although some unpleasant incidents may occur, this could be a very cathartic period when things are finally straightened out. Security and stability might appear to be under threat for Capricorns who are presented with a prenuptial agreement to sign. If in doubt, delay signing until you feel comfortable with all the terms.

12. TUESDAY. Useful. Don't pass up an opportunity to snare a bargain. Investigate the auctions online, read the newspapers, haunt the secondhand stores. Then you should make considerable savings, as people are constantly cleaning out their closets, garages, or attics. If assistance in any form is required, it might be time to call in some favors. They will most likely be granted. Freezing food in bulk should make a lot of practical sense to the never wasteful Capricorn. Insurance coverage may need to be changed if recent renovations have improved the value of your home or property. Getting a suitable babysitter might be overdue if current child care is proving to be unreliable.

13. WEDNESDAY. Purposeful. Solving problems brings satisfaction today. For many Goats this may be as simple as finding solutions to the daily crossword, or as difficult as negotiating a financial deal worth millions of dollars. Whatever activity you are involved in, continually exercising your capacity to confront and to resolve conundrums will prove to be emotionally gratifying. With Mercury still moving retrograde, this is a great period to look for lost or misplaced items around the house. Food cravings could plague Capricorns keen to diet. Today's Leo Moon intensifies the need for comfort. Keep healthy snacks available to help quell your desires.

14. THURSDAY. Disconcerting. Take a map or navigation device if you are traveling to unfamiliar places today. Becoming lost in an unknown area can be disconcerting and a waste of valuable time. Not all advice given will be on target now. Disappointment could come for some Capricorns involved in a sports activity. But if you have put in your best effort, you should be happy with the results. Young Goats could find that listening to music while trying to study is more of a distraction than a motivator. If you are serious about studies, find a quiet and peaceful place to learn the required knowledge. Sleep may be difficult to achieve for travelers; take advantage of ear plugs and blindfolds if offered.

15. FRIDAY. Challenging. Look beyond whatever is presented today, and you may find answers. Relying on someone else may lead to disillusionment. So be independent, step out of your comfort zone, and expand your consciousness. Enrolling in short courses might satisfy your quest for knowledge for a while. However, the call to greater understanding may be what lures you to seek an advanced degree in your current field of expertise. Everything that you experience can help you to grow, but how you grow is your choice. If returning to full-time or part-time study would forward your career, then it might be time to consider further education as a worthwhile option.

16. SATURDAY. Unsettling. Today's planetary combinations could find some Capricorns firmly in the mold of a rebel without a cause. You may be restless and edgy but not sure why, and certainly not sure what to do about these feelings. Although excitement could come through an interest in a new concept, hold off from impulsively committing to anything new and untried. Embarking too quickly on an idea or vision could find many of you running out of steam or motivation for the project in the not-too-distant future. A shake-up in the family home could see a change of responsibilities. Plan an evening of dancing or skating. Being constantly on the move this way will put your energy to constructive use.

17. SUNDAY. Mixed. Early morning risers might experience a sense of sluggishness, which should wear off as the day progresses. Temptation looms for those of you watching your weight, especially if today's social activity centers around food. Goats who are entertaining at home should accept help from others. Don't feel obligated to carry all of the responsibility associated with catering and cleaning. Use your innate organizing skills to delegate and share so that there is more time available for you to mix and mingle. When handling issues associated with family members, a gentle and diplomatic approach is advised, especially tonight under the Libra Full Moon.

18. MONDAY. Unsteady. The tricky energies linked to any Full Moon linger on today and over the ensuing days. Juggling matters regarding family and work may be difficult. A partner or loved one could accuse you of neglect. Physical energy is bound to be at lower ebb as dynamo Mars crosses swords with restrictive Saturn, your ruler. Keep a strict hold on your emotions, as this isn't a good day to pick an argument or lose your cool. Authority figures or elderly people could create more frustration and angst, mainly due to a severe lack of patience on everyone's part. Concentration and focus should be high, so any project that needs attention to detail can benefit.

19. TUESDAY. Good. Early morning sluggishness might be due to overindulging the night before or staying up later than usual. Nesting instincts could be stronger now as Mercury and Mars blend together in Aries, your solar sector of domestic matters. Moving in with a loved one could keep you busy. Lots of new ideas can come from department store displays. Help from friends could also make the transition easier. Gardening should be on the priority list for Capricorn folk with green thumbs, especially while warmer weather encourages new growth. Consider planting herbs and vegetables along with flowers and shrubs on a patio or in a backyard so you can harvest your own produce.

20. WEDNESDAY. Quiet. As the Moon enters Sagittarius, your twelfth sector, your need for solitude and privacy increases. An Internet café may be the perfect place to cocoon yourself from everyone. Catch up on research and writing there, if you don't have access to the Internet at home. Your levelheadedness and practical nature could draw others to confide in you. Be ready to offer your shoulder to anyone needing comfort. An interesting book could provide well-deserved relaxation this evening. Today the Sun enters the practical and patient sign of Taurus, illuminating your solar sector of creativity, romance, and fun. So it is now time for even the workaholics among you to lighten up.

21. THURSDAY. Promising. An early morning start at work could find the Goat achieving a lot. The peace and tranquillity should aid your concentration. If romance is on your mind, then take things slow and steady to create a solid foundation. Money may be an important factor to consider now. Some of you may want to start budgeting for a romantic, fun-filled vacation with the one you love. Attractive Venus now graces Aries, your fourth sector, encouraging Capricorn home owners to upgrade, beautify, or expand your home. Magazines that are dedicated to home improvements and craft projects will enable you to combine creative talents with money-saving ideas.

22. FRIDAY. Forceful. Diverse cosmic trends prevail today. Harness the powerful positive forces for personal advancement. If you want a promotion soon, present this aspiration to the people in charge. With the Moon in your own sign of Capricorn, appearance and grooming are to the fore. Those of you who dress to impress should reap the rewards of your efforts. Try to release the need for control if possible. It may be easy to boss others around on the job, but family will not be as accommodating. If you prevent disharmony and conflict from arising, romance will follow.

Dinner for two at home would be a wonderful way to strengthen loving bonds.

23. SATURDAY. Favorable. Do-it-yourself repairs or regular household chores could contribute to a few family dramas today, especially if everyone is working in a confined space. When overwhelm begins to threaten, take a brief walk outside by yourself. Chatty Mercury is now moving forward in Aries, signaling a positive time to sell or buy a home, sign a rental agreement, or make a major purchase to improve living conditions. Your creative juices continue to flow, helping you to complete a special labor of love. A meaningful occasion scheduled for this evening should bring delight to everyone. Pat yourself on the back for your contributions to a successful affair.

24. SUNDAY. Enriching. Allow your creative side to shine through. Goats now have a wonderful ability to turn even the most routine situations and events into something unique and exciting. Finances should be on the upswing. However, if you are worried about unexpected bills arriving, go over income and expenditure carefully to ensure that funds are available to cover accounts due. Athletic Capricorns should do well in a sports event, but take care with your back and knees. Have fun at a special celebration tonight. Don't try to claim the spotlight if you are not the center of attention. Competition with a loved one may bring out the worst in you if you feel you are not winning an argument.

25. MONDAY. Reassuring. The day ahead looks promising. Most of you by now should have employment duties and home responsibilities balanced, reducing emotional demands on your time. Financial plans for the future can be made with more assurance that a successful outcome will follow. Bargains could be had for those of you seeking furniture or equipment for a home office. Buying and selling real estate looks profitable. There are encouraging signs for the Capricorn eager to set up in self-employment. Good advice from an older or wiser person who can provide guidance and support with your career moves will save you from various pitfalls.

26. TUESDAY. Steady. Capricorn folks have an innate ability to work hard and to make cherished dreams materialize. Right now the stars are assisting your efforts, so follow up on the opportunities presented. Self-help books will hold your interest. Your ability to work through issues and old patterns of behavior is well within your grasp. Consider enrolling in a course that satisfies your spiritual, mental, and physical needs. It would keep your lifestyle nicely balanced. Working in cooperation with others can provide the chance to practice both your people skills and leadership skills. Swimming would be a good leisure pursuit for fitness as well as fun.

27. WEDNESDAY. Motivating. The planet Pluto in your sign of Capricorn rules the day with a positive link to the Sun in Taurus but an adverse connection to Venus in Aries. These strong influences are giving strength to your ability to focus. With your commanding willpower, nothing will seem impossible. Your capacity to instruct others is formidable. Your enthusiasm and motivation can urge students and teammates to move forward. Your popularity increases. Being the center of attention shouldn't faze you, even though members of your sign are often reserved. Passionate and intense feelings can heat up a committed relationship. But Goats in a new love affair should beware jealous and possessive behavior.

28. THURSDAY. Empowering. Intensity and passion continue unabated. Your need to win remains enhanced, giving you an edge in any form of sports or coaching. There is a strong competitive side to the Capricorn nature. You have endurance and stamina, being able to overcome trials and tribulations that often defeat members of other zodiac signs. Use energy constructively now. Trophies collected along the way should be displayed proudly for all to see. If your partnership needs a little zing, consider putting romantic daydreams into action by planning a fun-filled weekend away with your honey. Single Goats can look forward to interesting love possibilities.

29. FRIDAY. Prosperous. Taking risks with your money is not something the Capricorn person readily succumbs to. But if you have been watching financial trends, then success could come through speculating on the stock market. However, make sure you know what you are doing and don't invest more money than you can afford to lose. Family and domestic matters hold sway over the day. Disruptions at home might be the cause of increased impatience and restlessness. If you stay calm, the storm should quickly pass. Plan a night out on the town. If you are celebrating a special occasion, don't forget to take a photo or purchase a memento of this happy event.

30. SATURDAY. Manageable. Changes in family life may make you feel uncomfortable. The answer is in adapting, something that doesn't always come easily to members of your sign. Practical issues and responsibilities could find some of you more detached and not as warm toward people close to you. However, your understanding of authority will ensure that you can develop good working relationships with people in power. Some Capricorns could worry about a shortage of funds even if there really isn't much to be concerned about. Try to remain optimistic and upbeat. A comedy show will give you a good laugh and can be an excellent tonic for chasing the blues.

MAY

1. SUNDAY. Constructive. Positive vibes herald the start of the new month as Jupiter and Mars are conjunct in Aries. Renovations or any type of repairs that have been put on the back burner around the home base could now be attacked with a new vigor. There may be an urge to hurry through outstanding work. However, rushing could create an environment for accidents to happen. Socializing at home with friends would be an enjoyable pastime as long as touchy subjects are avoided. For the Capricorn sports fanatic, watching a game is a sure way to get your blood pumping. An early night is advisable; otherwise, the ability to concentrate may abandon you tomorrow.

2. MONDAY. Fair. Current planetary energies could exacerbate tension within the family fold. Although these aspects are a passing phase, disagreements occurring now could shake relationship foundations. So try to avoid becoming embroiled in arguments and discord. Spread the love around, Capricorn, with plenty of hugs and kisses to let the ones you love know how you feel. Take a break at lunchtime to visit a park and bask in the radiant warmth of springtime sunshine. A happy evening appears likely for couples as long as you are not critical or bossy. Single Goats may encounter an attractive stranger.

3. TUESDAY. Renewing. A Taurus New Moon culminating well before dawn provides a practical overtone to your creative talents and expertise. Capricorn gardeners and any of you with a green thumb can take advantage of this positive influence and begin planting your seedlings. A favored leisure pursuit could start to show a healthy profit, giving you extra incentive to make use of your creative skills. If there has been any distance between family members, the gentle Taurus energy prevailing all day promotes a time of healing and restoration. Music will be a wonderful way to soothe emotions. If you are eager to learn new dance steps, consider signing up for lessons.

4. WEDNESDAY. Deceptive. You may be deceiving yourself when it comes to love. Listen to family or friends. Their perspective might not be as clouded as yours may be. For Capricorns eager to improve health or to reduce weight, starting a new exercise course or training regime should see good results achieved. If you are on the job, double-check paperwork and messages passed on. There is a likelihood of errors and misunderstandings occurring. Those of you attending an employment interview should ensure that you have the correct address and that you know beforehand what the job entails. Team meetings should bring positive feedback. As long as sensible opinions are voiced, productivity should improve.

5. THURSDAY. Encouraging. Keep the channels of communication open at work. Your positive motivation is what teammates are seeking. Regardless of your daily activities, make sure you are dressed comfortably so that your job performance is not hindered in any way. The Internet is a very valuable source of information. If you have not yet connected at home, perhaps it is time you did. The purchase of a new computer or upgraded software could aid your efficiency. It will not take you long to familiarize yourself. Consider a quick head, neck, or shoulder massage during your lunch break to help alleviate any nervous tension or sore muscles.

6. FRIDAY. Great. The day ahead appears very promising. With positive influences in play, you can zip through your workload. Thoughts of what the weekend holds could also spur you on to complete all tasks on your to-do list. Better results with assignments and essays seem likely now. You could find that listening to background music is an aid to writing or study. Keep luggage light if you are going away for the weekend. With the Moon moving into Cancer late tonight, you will need extra space to hold the many mementos you are bound to pick up in your travels. Capricorns who are one half of a couple should plan a night at home with your honey.

7. SATURDAY. Demanding. Challenging planetary aspects make for a day that will test your character and resolve. The urge to complain or disagree could upset relations between loved ones, and you might need to go for a long walk to use excess energy constructively. This isn't the day to participate in dangerous or daredevil sports. So it would be wise to cancel any potentially risky activities. Splitting up can be hard at the best of times. But if a relationship has come to this point, it would be better to wait for a more advantageous day to divide assets. Otherwise, fresh squabbles may arise. Decision making could also be harder, as many of you are bound to feel as if you are at a deadlock. Look inward for answers.

8. SUNDAY. Varied. Entertaining at home could test your patience today. A diplomatic and tactful stance may be required with guests. So if you have a choice, perhaps going to a restaurant would be more relaxing. Attending a morning wedding should prove to be pleasant and could have some of you daydreaming of the day when you also walk down the aisle. Capricorns who suffer from food allergies should be careful with what you consume now in order to prevent unpleasant episodes. Participation in a sports event could see many of you stretching your abilities to the limit. However, this will bring emotional satisfaction. Sleep should come easily tonight after a long and busy day.

9. MONDAY. Accomplished. With so much fiery energy surrounding Capricorn folks, you would probably burn out if it wasn't for the stable influence of your lifetime ruler Saturn pulling in the reins. Put aside some time for rest and relaxation to ensure that you are in equilibrium. For those of you who love puzzles, you can't beat electronic games for their ability to hook you in. Don't be alarmed if you suddenly have the urge to purge your closet of all unnecessary clothes. This can be useful for making way for the new. This is a good day to work on the pros and cons of an investment. A property settlement should go through without any problems.

10. TUESDAY. Satisfying. Your need for stability and security could test many romances. As charming Venus and abundant Jupiter come together in Aries, your house of home and family, love and endless possibilities greet Capricorn people. Resolving problems within the family circle should be a lot easier now. Courageously offering the first peace offering should see a positive outcome. You should be characteristically prudent if purchasing new appliances or furniture for your living quarters; today's vibes make it easy to blow a hole in the budget. Going out and having fun may also be dangerous for the credit cards, so moderation is the key. Better still, perhaps socializing at home would be a good alternative and save you money.

11. WEDNESDAY. Quiet. Impulsive Mars visits patient Taurus, accentuating your house of treasure, pleasure, and leisure. With Mars in this sign, it can be akin to applying the brakes and slowing down. So now you do have time to stop and smell the roses. If the initial flames of a love affair have sputtered, implement strategies to reintroduce loving vibes. A dinner for two or a weekend retreat could be just what is needed to bring back the zing. Be proud of what you have worked hard for and achieved, but don't be too shy to ask for guidance. Powerful people could be the key to opening doors. Before entering into philosophical discussions, be sure you know what you are talking about.

12. THURSDAY. Purposeful. Use current planetary energies wisely. Your Taurus sector is now under the spotlight. Capricorns who are artistically inclined should not have any trouble receiving guidance or getting a backer to support your work. Ideas and strategies should be well received by people willing to listen to your plans. Don't confine your dreams to just your immediate surrounds. Now you can consider overseas opportunities that become available. Escaping from niggling problems could find many of you planning a trip away to rethink a few of your worries. Reading may be one of the best methods of learning more about a particular subject, so visit the lending library and increase your knowledge.

13. FRIDAY. Manageable. Change is in the air. According to how change is handled, benefits should occur. Prioritize, then consider various adjustments so that you can improve things. The self-employed Goat should be proactive. To be successful in business, there is a need to keep evolving. If this doesn't occur, you might be left behind. Dieting should be easier. This is also a good time to break addictive habits because your willpower is strengthening. The need to be in control could bring power struggles, and a sympathetic shoulder will come in handy as a supportive act. If you enjoy singing, share your talent. A karaoke bar should be the right place to strut your stuff.

14. SATURDAY. Reflective. Seize the time to be by yourself in order to implement plans for your future. Minor setbacks are likely to occur, but you will have a strategy to conquer most obstacles that arise. Capricorns on the job could have a trying day with customer complaints, mix-ups in orders, or slow sales. Taking a disciplined approach to any tasks at hand can ensure that most problems can be avoided or quickly fixed. Movie lovers should read the reviews before heading to the cinema, or you may be disappointed with your film choice. Whether you are going out to paint the town red or staying in with a lover, a scented soak in a hot bath along with relaxing music should work its magic tonight.

15. SUNDAY. Uneven. Be warned if you are a workaholic Capricorn. Discord could develop with loved ones if you are planning to work at home or on the job today. A misunderstanding with a partner may be caused by a problem that you need to face and then to find a resolution. Taurus, your house of leisure pursuits, is becoming crowded now with the entrance of Mercury and Venus into Taurus today. Restoring furniture, artwork, or your home should appeal to the Capricorn renovator. If there is dissatisfaction within your social group, it might be time to initiate change. Trust your instincts and use your persuasive powers to influence others. A little bit of background research would go a long way.

16. MONDAY. Happy. Love, romance, and creativity hold sway today. Capricorn singles could find a potential romantic encounter at work. So be alert, without appearing overly eager. Be positive about your abilities. Inspiration can be found in a number of areas, and your ability to express yourself in an imaginative and artistic manner increases. This is a positive period to discover the child within through painting, drawing, or singing. Those of you who are parents should spend quality time with children or grandchildren. Find a relaxing source of entertainment for tonight. Going to a movie or a play can be a great way to lose yourself in fantasy and fun.

17. TUESDAY. Intense. A powerful Scorpio Full Moon culminates in the sky this morning, bringing out your passionate side. Networking and sharing social activities with friends can be rewarding. However, apply caution and tact to prevent intense emotions from rising quickly to the surface. A special goal or group aim could be moving toward realization. A chance to review current wishes presents itself. You can decide whether your aims remain relevant or are now outmoded and should be discarded. Capricorn members of a professional organization, a social club, or a team sport should also examine whether it still provides emotional satisfaction or if it is time to move on to greener pastures. Unwind before retiring for the night by pursuing a favorite hobby.

18. WEDNESDAY. Subdued. Finding the time for contemplation in your busy life may be difficult. Taking a few days off work and retreating to somewhere that offers peace and tranquillity could be a wonderful pick-me-up, especially for the workaholic Capricorn. If this isn't a feasible option now, consider working only the hours required and resting more than usual. With the Moon in Sagittarius, your twelfth house of solitude, you need a quiet time to recharge body, mind, and spirit. It is very easy for you to neglect your health and well-being. But right now it is vital to relax and be self-nurturing. Put pen to paper or seek solace with your laptop. Writing is a great way to unburden and to release repressed emotions.

19. THURSDAY. Active. Energy lifts as the day progresses and the Moon enters your sign. Spend the travel time to and from work constructively. This can be a positive method of reflecting on what is currently occurring in your life. If you are on the right pathway, methods to build on achievements can be examined. However, if emotional dissatisfaction exists, then look for ways to make changes so you are moving in the right direction. Athletic Capricorn is on fire, and a sports activity could really bring out your competitive side. Enjoyment comes from winning. Goats who are on top of your game might be offered a lucrative sponsorship deal that has the potential to set you up for life. Expect action on the romantic front.

20. FRIDAY. Excellent. Capricorn personal magnetism is at a high level. Current cosmic forces activate a tough and powerful drive, assisting your efforts to advance toward a successful climax. This energy combined with increased sensitivity is the perfect mix for artists of any spectrum. An opportunity to dig deep within and to produce a masterpiece of your best work ever is within your reach, so don't delay. Hiring a literary or theatrical agent could help you with a writing or acting career. A suitable teacher could be found if your interests include any of the performing arts such as dancing or singing. You will find the inspiration to create a romantic setting tonight for the love of your life.

21. SATURDAY. Exciting. Prepare for an active day ahead. The constellation of Gemini now hosts the Sun shining its bright rays into the sixth house of your solar horoscope. With the Sun in Gemini over the next four weeks, the spotlight is directed on your attitude toward work, health, and service to others. Although Capricorn is known for stability, fickle Mercury rules Gemini. So this is a period you may experience restlessness and capriciousness, urging you to seek more variety at work or even to look for a new job. A strong romantic ambience permeates the atmosphere, ready for the eager Goat to take advantage and cement a loving relationship with your partner.

22. SUNDAY. Favorable. Loving vibes continue. Grasp the chance to spend a leisurely breakfast in bed or on the patio. Move slowly through the hours if social plans are flexible. Spending happy companionship with loved ones can relax body and mind, putting you in a good space for any challenges that need to be confronted once the new working week begins. A drive in the countryside or to an area that arouses fond memories could see you falling in love with a property or site. However, don't rush into anything today. Your innate practical and realistic Capricorn nature might be missing in action, with your heart ruling your head when it comes to any type of decision.

23. MONDAY. Good. Adjustments might need to be made today. With intellectual Mercury currently at cross purposes with your life ruler, disciplined Saturn, thinking positively and staying upbeat could be more challenging. By making an exerted effort to remain optimistic, you can take advantage of the happy stars also shining your way. A new romance could blossom. Capricorn singles could see someone close in an attractive light. A social invitation could set a happy tone to the working week. A warm overture from another may help dissolve any barriers built up due to lack of recent contact. Love is in the air, so be ready and willing to take advantage.

24. TUESDAY. Lively. Enthusiasm and restlessness could help allay any lack of physical energy today. Take care if you are lifting heavy objects or carrying out work that requires endurance. An uninhibited attitude needs to be watched. An urge to be free and unencumbered could find many of you engaging in behavior or a scenario that is not usually your style or taste. Originality increases and can be expressed in a unique and dramatic manner. Capricorn involved in a humanitarian cause or group could find that you are suddenly thrust into the spotlight or into a leadership role. Flowers, chocolates, or other meaningful gift will eloquently express your feelings to someone special.

25. WEDNESDAY. Mixed. Stamina could still remain low. However, be patient with yourself and others if this is the case. Friendship is a valuable asset in teamwork. It shouldn't take a lot to let others know the value placed on their efforts. The danger of spreading your energy too thinly can lead to frustration and anxiety, especially if you find that you are slipping behind in your workload. Letting go and delegating duties will display your managerial skills and will send a message that you do consider teammates as capable and responsible. Take notice of office gossip, but don't become overly concerned. Most information will be based on rumors and innuendos.

26. THURSDAY. Challenging. More than likely you will be tested again today. You must learn more about inner flexibility in order to understand yourself and others. You can expect to remain busy again, and your energy should flow to assist your efforts. Accomplishing important projects and meeting deadlines would be aided by writing out a to-do list in order of priorities. Maintain a strong focus. Conversations with friends might prove to be very valuable, and could touch on important issues that help your advancement in some way. Capricorns working with the public might find that being empathic is the quickest method to help calm even the rudest client or customer.

27. FRIDAY. Motivating. Today's planetary influences could be just what you need to initiate changes in your personal or business life. For some Goats this may manifest in an urge to relocate, to purchase a bigger home, or to change jobs. Restlessness could be quelled by refreshing your home with a new paint job or by bringing in new items of furniture to complement the traditional pieces. A team effort might be required to finish a special venture. Don't try to go it alone. Ask for help, and assistance is sure to be given willingly. Do something on the spur of the moment this evening to release stress. Make sure that entertainment is lighthearted and enjoyable.

28. SATURDAY. Guarded. Juggling everything that is going on in your life could be straining your mental and physical limits. If you are working at home, set aside frequent rest breaks. Those of you who are on the job should take time off for morning coffee and lunch. Be wary when signing contracts. Read the fine print thoroughly, as not everyone has your best interests in mind. If you are in doubt, seek a second opinion. Defer updating electronic equipment or computer software unless you are sure of what you want. A super salesperson could be so persuasive that you might buy a product that costs way more than it is worth.

29. SUNDAY. Spirited. Although there is a stable undertone prevailing now, this is a day to forget about work and the daily grind. The practical Taurus Moon is adding strength to your solar house of pleasure, reinforcing the need for relaxation and recreation. A shopping or lunch date with the girls or guys would be a great opportunity to relax, exchange gossip, and catch up on the news. Weather permitting, family gatherings could be held outside in the backyard or at a nearby park. A friendly game of baseball for both adults and children will be fun for all. If you are driving a long distance, take a break to prevent falling victim of fatigue. It would be even better if you have a companion to share the journey.

30. MONDAY. Rebalancing. You might need to seriously consider the current balance between employment duties and home responsibilities. If there aren't enough leisure periods in your life, consider making changes to ensure that there is more recreation introduced into your busy schedule. Conversely, if you are taking things too easy and not making headway at work, perhaps it is time to readjust your thinking. Capricorn folks are very ambitious in a quiet and steady way. If you cannot see the goal ahead or are not sure if you will reach your potential, this can bring on anxiety, even mild depression. Refocus, reclaim your goals. Keep a strong picture in your mind of what you do want to achieve.

31. TUESDAY. Disconcerting. Challenges within the creative sphere could cause difficulties for artistic and imaginative Goats. Writer's block might cause delays with work as you look for alternative ways to be inspired. Jumping to conclusions doesn't always produce the best results. So remember that there are always two sides to every story or situation. Avoid the casino and racetrack. Keep any form of gambling to a minimum. This isn't a good time to invest or to speculate, as the chances of winning are slim. A quiet meal with a loved one can create an opportunity to patiently communicate feelings and to clear up any recent misunderstandings.

JUNE

1. WEDNESDAY. Motivating. It is indeed a rare first day of the month. The Sun and constructive Saturn, your life ruler, are happily linked. This positive planetary influence heralds a productive period when you can make your mark and accomplish a vast array of employment or personal projects. Grasp hold of opportunities and streak ahead, and success should be within sight. Capricorns who have been waiting to hear of a promotion or the outcome of a business merger should be delighted by news received. Today's New Moon culminates in Gemini, your house of daily work, health, and service to others. It is a very beneficial time to look for a new job or to begin a new fitness and exercise regime.

2. THURSDAY. Diverse. A variety of cosmic patterns is forming in the celestial skies today. Relationships with loved ones could take on a more passionate and emotional depth, enabling you to experience heightened intimacy. However, if you are prone to jealousy or possessiveness, love and romance will not flow smoothly. Take care also if you are a Capricorn who loves to flirt. This behavior could create an intense reaction from your current partner or from a close companion. Fitness can be improved if you work off excess energy constructively. Those of you eager to lose weight should consider such simple methods as using the stairs instead of the elevator or walking partway home.

3. FRIDAY. Misleading. The celestial forces are sending a measure of confusion today. Deception has a way of coming out of the shadows at the most inappropriate times. With messenger Mercury, now in Gemini, challenging nebulous Neptune, you can expect tricky issues to surface now. Watch your back. A coworker could shift the blame your way or tell outright lies to cover up errors. Keep a close eye on keys and other small possessions. Place important items in a regular spot. Take notes and put them in visible places to remind you of things you need to do. You will get respect from team members if you encourage and motivate instead of criticize.

4. SATURDAY. Stabilizing. Now you can decide to act on a number of annoying but necessary chores. Your energy and stamina to get started should be in plentiful supply. Relief is sure to come once these tasks are out of the way. Fortunately, Capricorn folks are not prone to boredom, so routine work doesn't usually bother you. However, an edgy tone exists that could increase restlessness. Your mind may be very active right now. This is a good time to share your knowledge and experiences through speaking or writing. Your story may become the inspiration for others to follow. A gathering with a special group of friends can provide stimulating entertainment this evening.

5. SUNDAY. Erratic. Prepare to be active and on the go today. With a number of planetary links occurring, stress could rise as the tempo quickens. Emotionally, many Capricorn folks could be a little scattered and all over the place. Sudden arguments could develop if people find that you are more demanding or difficult to please than usual. Try to step back a bit. You will discover that it isn't too hard to relinquish control and let things just flow. Elderly relatives might require extra care and attention. Some adjustments may be needed around the house to care for an older member of the family. A potluck dinner can create an amicable and easygoing atmosphere at home.

6. MONDAY. Favorable. Today's cosmos heralds a positive period to ensure that finances are under control. Capricorns with expertise and savvy about the stock market could make a few wise investments that should reach expected outcomes over time. For the more conservative Goat, a lottery ticket or a raffle for an expensive prize could yield fruitful results. Winning some kind of contest, perhaps on a game show, could also bring a few pleasant surprises or cash your way. Progress can be made for those of you consulting a broker, a bank manager, or a financial adviser. You, too, can impart wisdom, comfort, and moral support to someone who is in need.

7. TUESDAY. Bumpy. Cosmic tension is high, but the best way to deflect negative energy is by remaining busy and productive. Just keep plowing ahead. You can overcome the bumps and angst that come with the tough times. Taking a cool and calm approach, even if you are under stress, lets others see that you are in their corner and can be relied on when the pressure is on. Continue working on improving your cash flow. Find ingenious ways to cut expenditures so that your bank balance flourishes. If you need to study, this evening is a good time to learn a lot quickly through reading, writing, and listening to recorded lessons.

8. WEDNESDAY. Uplifting. Travel and education are to the fore now. Make sure you have enough money for a trip. There is a bright link between pursuing romance and going on vacation. A holiday romance could develop for some of you. Or you might fall in love with a traveling companion. Capricorns with children who are struggling at school or college could find that hiring a tutor is the answer to helping your child. Capricorn students should seek the advice of a teacher to help you understand the complexities of a specific subject. Be prepared for an emotional good-bye at the airport, train station, or bus depot if you are waving a loved one off on a long journey.

9. THURSDAY. Unsettling. A number of bothersome obstacles will be sent by the cosmos to cause angst today. Rise above petty issues and smile. Then tackle problems one by one. If you retain your balance and good humor, handling interactions with people in authority as well as staff members should be a breeze. Capricorn employees could also discover that working alone might increase rather than decrease productivity. So, if possible, arrange to work at home. Or at least close the office door for a few hours. The saying that a change is as good as a rest has a large measure of truth in it. Dining at a new restaurant tonight could give you a fresh window on the world.

10. FRIDAY. Good. Capricorn creativity in employment tasks moves up a level now that beautiful Venus has settled in Gemini, your solar sector of work. Singles could experience more romantic encounters and opportunities to find love on the job. Resolving problems that require a unique, quick, or artistic solution comes easier. A challenging project might test your resourcefulness now, but it will widen your experience. This isn't the best time to make decisions, particularly if choices relate to a romantic relationship or a change of employment. Your emotions could get in the way of good judgment. Be wary of overcommitting, exaggerating, or promising more than you can deliver.

11. SATURDAY. Tranquil. A fairly relaxed and productive day is ahead. Those of you who are working could find that associates and bosses may be asking you a lot of job-related questions. Your opinion is highly valued, and people know that you supply sensible answers and practical solutions. If you are presented with extra duties or responsibilities, don't fear the challenges. Instead, embrace the chance to gain more knowledge and experience. Some Capricorns may make a strong link with a newcomer introduced to you by a friend. Other Goats could find that a faded friendship gathers strength once again. Entertainment that includes music and dance would be a good choice for tonight.

12. SUNDAY. Exciting. Enthusiastic and energetic could be an apt description of your attitude today. Your ability to turn any negative into a positive can make you a popular companion, and people are bound to seek you out. Unexpected and exciting events will hold a special charm even for the disciplined Capricorn. If you are a slave to routine and the same weekend pattern, consider making a change and introducing a dash of spice and variety into your schedule. A romantic overture could hold a wonderful promise of good times ahead. So take the plunge, but don't expect the relationship to last forever. Take one day at a time, and delight in the ensuing thrills and spills.

13. MONDAY. Useful. A few obstacles are likely to interrupt the smooth flow of the day. However, Capricorn folk are born under the rulership of stern and steady Saturn. So tests and challenges are not something that will halt your progress for any length of time. Productivity can rise when work is carried out in a team or group setting now. By observing others, you could gain a few pointers and skills that will be useful at some other time. Pouring energy into obtaining personal or work-related goals should bring gains. Surround yourself with friends or family tonight if there is a need to socialize. If there isn't, a long swim could aid relaxation and help to reduce stress.

14. TUESDAY. Subdued. The Moon moving through your twelfth house of Sagittarius signals a time to balance work and pleasure. Make sure that you get an equal measure of both. Listen to your instincts. Refuse to be drawn into any situations that don't suit your mood or your needs or that are likely to place an extra burden on your shoulders. Pursue an artistic medium that enables you to express yourself. It can shake off any frustration that you might be experiencing. Time alone to unwind and to reduce the pressure of commitments could also be the perfect method of relaxing. Be wary of becoming involved in a clandestine affair on the job. This could pose hidden dangers.

15. WEDNESDAY. Unsteady. Prepare for a bumpy ride today. Many of you could find it difficult to express your feelings to loved ones. You might not understand why you are so moody. The Sagittarius Full Moon accentuates your twelfth house of solitude. If possible, it would be advisable to find an activity you can do on your own, at least until you are feeling a little more sociable. Working behind the scenes toward a goal you are passionate about will more than likely test your endurance and commitment. But it could bring a positive outcome if your focus is maintained. Old grievances and issues should be left in the past so that you can move on with fewer burdens to carry.

16. THURSDAY. Empowering. With the Moon now in your sign of Capricorn, it is time to focus on personal appeal. Updating your appearance can increase self-confidence and self-assurance. A new cologne or cosmetics could have other people making positive comments on your transformation. However, you don't have to implement dramatic changes if you want to make a good impression. Just smile, be yourself, and add a dash of good humor. Then you are sure to shine. Those of you who are working as a counselor or are receiving counseling should make positive progress. Attend to any health issues now. The sooner a diagnosis is given, the sooner treatment can begin and you can move forward toward a full recovery.

17. FRIDAY. Supportive. Messenger Mercury is now sitting in your opposite sign of Cancer, bringing attention to personal and professional relationships. If there is something that needs to be said to an intimate or business partner, you have the chance to bring issues out into the open any time during the next three weeks. There is bound to be plenty of discussion and planning ahead under the lively planetary influences. Capricorns who are organizing a social event should make the desired headway. Someone could offer a helpful suggestion that may be worth taking further. Use your imagination to introduce sparkle and zing to a special celebration honoring a family occasion.

18. SATURDAY. Satisfying. A rosy glow settles over Goats now. It will be easier to get your own way and to convince others of your point of view, so present your wish list. Love and romance are starred. Those of you who have planned to tie the knot today have a great chance of love remaining secure and stable. Money news is good. A promotion or pay raise could be in the offing. Capricorn employees on the job or working a few hours overtime may hear of improved conditions that will make your life a little easier. An older or more mature romantic partner might appeal to singles seeking a new love affair.

19. SUNDAY. Fidgety. Restless energies mark the day. With Mercury now challenging erratic Uranus and intense Pluto, it will be essential to take a cautious approach. Capricorn drivers should move at a steady pace, obey the road rules, and refrain from becoming entangled in any form of road rage. Rash behavior, sarcasm, and speaking out of turn should also be avoided. You could easily upset people. It isn't the best day to go on a shopping spree if money is a little light. Doing so could create a heated dispute with a partner if he or she finds out that you splashed the cash around or spent big on the credit cards. A lax attitude toward paying household bills on time could also be a trigger for family disharmony.

20. MONDAY. Stressful. As a Capricorn you make it your business to know where the next dollar is coming from. Today could be all about personal finances and material possessions. If you are currently struggling to make ends meet, today's influences are unlikely to bring joy. It would be wise not to pressure your boss for a pay increase or any other favors. Stay away from the stores if you are someone who shops for emotional comfort, which is uncharacteristic of most Goats. Money that is owed to you by a family member could become an arena for challenging and intense discussions, especially if there isn't much chance of your being repaid anytime soon.

21. TUESDAY. Eventful. Communication is the key now as the Moon moves through your Pisces house of thought processes. Other significant cosmic events are also occurring. Most notable for Capricorn is the entrance of the Sun into your opposite sign of Cancer, bringing attention to the other people in your life. And dynamo Mars has just zoomed into your Gemini house of work and service to others. Matters relating to home, family, and relationships could take up lot of your time over the next few weeks. Listening to what your partner has to say could be very beneficial. You may have been so busy lately that you have overlooked important signals, especially hidden emotions about to come to the surface.

22. WEDNESDAY. Challenging. It is a day of ups and downs. Vim and vitality could be at a lower level. Enthusiasm for mundane or routine chores may be in very short supply even for the dedicated and practical Goat. But any project or activity that requires an artistic touch or creative vision should bloom. A story related by another could be the inspiration for Capricorn writers to put pen to paper. A project that hasn't seen the light of day for some time might suddenly seem to be of value once again. Have patience if you are endeavoring to negotiate a pay raise. Seek peaceful entertainment this evening. Steer away from anything that requires effort or energy.

23. THURSDAY. Fair. Physical resources should begin to steadily climb. Still, it would be wiser to pace activities to ensure that you have enough vitality to last throughout the whole day. Progress can be made as the stars are mainly favorable. For some Capricorns a wish could come true. The domestic and family scene is the area under focus now with the Moon wandering through your Aries fourth house. Capricorn folks planning to be the host or hostess who entertains guests should use tried-and-true methods rather than experimenting with something different. Trying out new recipes is better left when you are alone and there isn't any outside pressure.

24. FRIDAY. Wary. Apply caution today when dealing with legal or financial paperwork. Make sure all the i's are dotted and t's crossed. Deception abounds. Someone close could display great cunning, so make sure you are not on the receiving end of any shams or trickery. Difficulties with a personal or business partner or someone with whom you're working closely could cause a breakup. Don't allow yourself to become drawn into other people's disputes. You have enough matters and concerns of your own to deal with. A loved one might be better off working out issues on their own. If you try to solve the problems, it might inhibit a loved one's growth.

25. SATURDAY. Abundant. It can be a delightful lighthearted day if you give yourself time to play. With the Cancer Sun in harmony with lucky Jupiter in Taurus, good fortune can come your way. For older Capricorn people, spending time with youngsters could make you feel young again. Parents should experience joy at the antics and achievements of youngsters. If you have been neglecting work around the home, taking action this morning could bring desired results. An honor could be bestowed on deserving Capricorns. A special social event should be the highlight of the weekend. Purchase a lottery ticket, enter a competition, and have a run at the casino. You could come out on top.

26. SUNDAY. Lively. Positive vibes continue to beam down on Goats. However, you will need to remain active throughout the day to quell a restless attitude. Right now, variety is certainly the spice of life. With the Sun and disruptive Uranus in an unfriendly link, a flexible approach is the best method to manage this energy constructively. Changes and unexpected developments are also likely. For some Capricorns this should manifest in the form of a sudden residential move. Be prepared for social plans to change. There may be a number of encounters with unconventional people, very different from those with whom you normally mix and mingle.

27. MONDAY. Helpful. Agitation and restlessness keep you on the go again today. Minor pressures are likely to occur on the job. But if you can go with the flow, your ability to handle issues will emerge. Use current influences positively by plunging into work that requires an innovative approach. Your original thinking is a plus, and will give you the opening to move ahead with a creative enterprise or a unique venture. Charitable issues hold your interest as well. Capricorns organizing a fund-raising event for people in need should find that plans move along smoothly. Expressing your feelings to a loved one, through spoken or written form, may be easier now.

28. TUESDAY. Intense. Today's trends are mixed. However, problems can be more easily resolved if there is a need for change and you go with this idea rather than remaining stuck and immovable. What it is that you value the most in life could be brought to your attention. Ambitions may be thwarted in some way. But if you stop and think about your life right now, perhaps this is a good thing. An inflated ego and stubbornness could create power struggles with someone in authority, perhaps your boss, partner, or a father figure. Matters could come to a head. Although this may be unpleasant in the short term, it might be long overdue and could be the catalyst for positive change to finally take place.

29. WEDNESDAY. Edgy. Making adjustments to your thinking can make goals and aims more accessible, but a laid-back approach should be displayed. Whenever mighty Mars meets up with passionate Pluto, the drive to win at all costs can become an obsession. Today an unfriendly link occurs between Mars in Gemini and Pluto in your sign of Capricorn. So it is very possible that issues on the job or with a coworker may become heated. If you don't like direct confrontations, you should step back a little. Don't push a point or press the buttons of people near you. Sometimes your intentions are misunderstood by others, and right now the chances of that happening are high.

30. THURSDAY. Interesting. Pleasant cosmic forces prevail during the daylight hours. However, prepare for a possible surprise later in the evening. Keep your eyes open for opportunities. If they do appear, be ready to quickly take advantage. For most of the day Capricorn folk are under a creative influence. You could notice heightened intuition and sensitivity, perfect for writing and speaking. Authors and students of the creative arts should make solid progress. Inspirational words and ideas come easily to mind. Planning a surprise party for a neighbor, sibling, or other relative can be a happy experience. All details of the plan are likely to come together in an organized whole.

JULY

1. FRIDAY. Auspicious. The month of July begins on a very positive note. There should be a fresh and sparkling tone to your demeanor today. A New Moon culminates in Cancer, your seventh house of intimate and business relationships. Many of the issues that have been plaguing you of late should disappear, and you can once again be yourself. This is a time to go beyond the safe and steady route. Now the chance to begin something new arrives. It could be the chance that steers you to a more exciting lifetime journey. Some Capricorns will be cementing a marriage or moving in with a lover. Becoming involved in a public relations venture will be to your advantage.

2. SATURDAY. Mixed. Unsociable could be an apt description for many of you today as the Sun and your ruler Saturn clash. Your energy may be lower, which might make you with feel withdrawn. Out of duty you may attend a social function. Capricorn stability and reliability are wonderful attributes, but make sure you don't take things too seriously all of the time. Slip into your dancing shoes tonight and have fun, without wearing out your vim and vitality. Today communicative Mercury enters the sign of Leo, applying focus to your eighth house of shared resources and assets. Discussions relating to joint business assets, an insurance settlement, or pending legacy are likely to take place over the next four weeks.

3. SUNDAY. Uneven. Vitality might be slightly down as the morning hours begin. Combat lower physical resources by remaining in bed longer or taking it easy with the domestic chores. By mid-morning you should be upbeat and energetic again. However, for some of you a somber mood could prevail. If so, you will have to work hard to appear optimistic and enthusiastic. Spending money may be unavoidable now. Go ahead and invest in a joint venture that will benefit other people as well as yourself. Replacing a household item or upgrading a computer or television might stretch the bank account, but will make a lot of family members very happy.

4. MONDAY. Ideal. Today the waters should be calm, and you can do as your heart desires. Choose a pleasant activity. Spend this special holiday doing whatever brings the most comfort and happiness. Venus is making a bundle of planetary patterns throughout the month. So most Capricorn people should find that recent creative blocks will quickly disappear and that your output begins to rise once again. With Venus now entering your opposite sign of Cancer in your seventh house, all of your partnerships and the other people in your life become more important. This Venus energy provides a fertile period for love, romance, and the opportunity to establish a loving and committed bond with another.

5. TUESDAY. Expressive. With fleet-footed Mercury holding sway over the day's proceedings, life might appear to suddenly speed up. The action doesn't appear to be slowing down anytime soon. Opening yourself up to experience your full desires isn't always the safest approach, so assess the risks first. Refrain from overindulging. Maintain your usual practical and conservative demeanor. Overdoing things can be restricted or totally resisted. Stimulating conversations among friends and family will make this a period of growing knowledge and interest. Even if lunar trends are a little tricky, there are fantastic trends surrounding many areas of your life over the next few weeks.

6. WEDNESDAY. Promising. Great openings and opportunities could be presented for a career or business matter now. Current influences provide extra oomph to Capricorn ambitions. There is an aura of good luck surrounding employment. Work on your professional and commercial aims so that you can quicken your climb up the mountain to the summit of success. A negotiation or deal into which you have put considerable time and energy could now bring favorable results, making the effort well worthwhile. Share your dreams and goals with those higher up the ladder than you. You may get surprising assistance from an unexpected quarter.

7. THURSDAY. Active. A busy day seems likely. But remember, sometimes when you rush around and try to do too many things at once, you end up nowhere or back where you started from. Although this can be a very creative period, you could also experience edginess. So search for the perfect outlet for artistic expression. Luscious Venus now meets up with unpredictable Uranus. So expect the unexpected will most likely be the advice to follow over the next few days. Surprises could come through family members or a partner. Some incidents that occur might not be entirely to your liking. Capricorns looking to sell a home may be upset by the low monetary value placed on your property now.

8. FRIDAY. Tricky. Being prepared for unexpected developments in relationships and finances continues to be the mantra again today. With partnerships of all ilks taking center stage in your life, the complexities of human interaction and attraction could now become more apparent. Sexy Venus is at odds with passionate Pluto now. So it may be necessary to stand back and observe rather than rush headlong into issues relating to love and romance. Capricorn singles could find that the demands of a new lover become overwhelming, especially if there is any hint of possessive behavior about to surface. Beware one-night stands.

9. SATURDAY. Terrific. Right now is an excellent period to spend time with loved ones and to work on relationship issues. Making those you love the most your top priority can ensure that loving bonds strengthen and that support needed by others is freely given. Over the next couple of days, planetary influences are assisting Capricorns who have to set up financial meetings, appointments, and monetary transactions. A healthier bank account and amicable relations with loved ones and partners will remove some of the pressure and strain from your life. Such good tidings contribute to motivation, inspiration, happiness, and well-being. Celebrating a special occasion this evening adds to your joy.

10. SUNDAY. Fine. The good times continue on and by keeping your eye firmly on your goal, success can come. There are refreshing energies surrounding Goats now. Something you were wishing for could finally happen. A friend or associate may make good on a promise, and you could cash in a couple of favors owed to you. Social networks come to the forefront of your attention. The quality of life can take on a wonderful hue when you are favored by good companions. However, ensure that new pals don't take your friendship for granted. Say no to any demands that you feel are unreasonable, given the brief duration of certain acquaintanceships.

11. MONDAY. Lively. Moving forward smoothly and speedily is foreseen now. With intellectual Mercury forming a positive connection with dynamo Mars, most of you are likely to prefer going solo than taking anyone else along for the ride. Compromising is not known to be one of your strong points. But try to keep sharp retorts and comments to yourself, even if someone's ideas and opinions don't jell with your take on a situation or issue. Diplomacy and tact can earn you respect and help you get what you want more than sarcasm can. Work that requires mental facility should be undertaken now. Capricorns who are scheduled to present a motivational speech won't experience any difficulties holding an audience's attention.

12. TUESDAY. Supportive. Even though the Moon is slipping through your house of solitary activities, the tempo of life could still be elevated. However, attempt to slow down a little and seriously think about what you are seeking in your life right now. With careful contemplation and review, you could discover that changes in several areas would make a positive difference. Providing assistance and support to others and working for the common good can be wonderful ways to obtain emotional gratification. But make sure your ultimate goal is to help and not to hinder. Sometimes people in need must be given the chance to stand on their own two feet.

13. WEDNESDAY. Worrisome. Capricorn people may be out of your comfort zone now as saucy Venus glares at your life ruler, stern Saturn. The universe is challenging you to work on relationship issues. You can learn to express your feelings more openly, something that doesn't come naturally to many born under your sign. Unforeseen financial issues, perhaps coupled by less work available for your partner, could be creating a hole in the budget and a need to stretch shared income further. Cutting expenditure and saving money are measures at which you excel. This may be the right time to test your ability and expertise in this regard.

14. THURSDAY. Useful. The Moon is now in your sign of Capricorn. So you can concentrate on personal needs, possibly to the exclusion of everything else currently occurring in your life. Effort and energy expended over the last couple of weeks suggest that you have earned the right to set aside time to focus on your own tasks and activities. Working on your own will guarantee productivity. However, trying to patch up a bumpy relationship or liaison could be futile, especially during the morning hours. It would be wise to wait until you and a partner have plenty of time to get into a discussion that could become heated.

15. FRIDAY. Upsetting. An unsettling day looms as a Full Moon culminates before dawn in your own sign of Capricorn, bringing increased sensitivity to the fore. Personal or business changes might adversely affect you and a partner as a project or relationship comes to an end. Thorny issues with clients may arise. Those of you working in customer service may see an increase in complaints from the general public. Dramas occurring in your friendship circle may be causing waves with your family members. Ideas you propose to placate loved ones' feelings are unlikely to be embraced by them. Those of you chairing a club meeting could question the handling of group funds.

16. SATURDAY. Pressured. The atmosphere could remain strained today. Goats in a committed relationship might experience the gathering of storm clouds. Although there could be some positives relating to your financial status, the progress might seem to be too slow. The current lack of funds causes frustration and angst. Of all the signs in the zodiac it is Capricorn that knows that wealth has to be built on a solid foundation. So be patient, and your bank balance is sure to blossom eventually. A glamorous social event could disappoint by not living up to advertised hype. Those of you finding your own entertainment should have a good time, but keep tabs on spending.

17. SUNDAY. Variable. Even though you could be doing okay in the financial stakes, the Aquarius Moon impacting your second solar house could have you fretting over money. Whether you are sailing along or in a muddle with money, it is a good time to examine your current situation. You could find that there is still room to cut expenditure so you can save more. This isn't the day to enter into discussions with an ex over the division of property or child alimony. Words could soon become heated and hurtful. A yard sale could assist your quest for greater financial security. It is also a great way to clear away unwanted household and personal items.

18. MONDAY. Soothing. Stellar influences pick up now, and you should have a better day than yesterday. Work-related travel will add a dash of variety. Even though you might travel only short distances, these trips can put a measure of excitement into daily activities. Your imagination and flair can be used to impress. Capricorns with a writing project to complete should make swift progress. Settling down to study can be easier now. The ambitious Goat may consider enrolling in a refresher course or a training program that will aid your career advancement. A gathering of special friends should be stimulating and motivating.

19. TUESDAY. Busy. Prepare for plenty of running around today. If you have a heavy workload and planned for a quiet day to catch up on outstanding tasks, it may be necessary to eliminate superfluous activities. Endeavor to limit phone calls and postpone answering e-mails. That way you should free up a few extra hours to concentrate on meeting deadlines and completing duties. When it comes to decision making, be disciplined but also go with your gut instincts. Then the right choices can be made. Later in the day avoid discussing controversial topics. It would be very easy to say something that is misconstrued, misunderstood, or insensitive.

20. WEDNESDAY. Meaningful. This is a time to enjoy your home and family and to become involved in the interests and activities of loved ones. Needing to belong is important for members of your sign. You like knowing that people believe they can depend on you and that your opinion is valued. If solving family issues is a little tricky, open up discussions for every member of the household to participate in. You could be pleasantly surprised by the depth and understanding of potential solutions presented. Speaking or performing in public should progress smoothly. Celebrity Capricorns are sure to be signing photos for your fans.

21. THURSDAY. Peaceful. Keep arrangements on the simple side if possible today. There will be enough demands made by other people. Don't add self-imposed stress and pressure. The emphasis is on home and domestic concerns. Making changes to the home abode to increase comfort and to improve living conditions will claim your attention. You should find it effortless to come up with a number of attractive solutions to resolve sticky problems and to complete outstanding chores. Regardless of your age or current energy level, a quiet evening at home might be preferred instead of venturing out for a night on the town.

22. FRIDAY. Constructive. Lunar influences are mainly positive, although mid-morning could bring problems with clients or a business partner. If possible, steer clear of getting in the way of others. If you are not in front of the public or responsible for resolving problems, keep a low profile. Problems should be discussed while they are minor and easy to handle. If you have an issue to resolve later in the day, seeking advice from a family member would be wise. Mutual decision making leads to harmony. General household repairs and maintenance might cost you a bit of money, but peace of mind comes when everything is in good order.

23. SATURDAY. Heartening. If your professional life is not supplying enough emotional satisfaction and gratification, then perhaps it is time to reconsider available options. Taking a break to
think things through can be a positive first step. Then, when you are
relaxed and rested, a reassessment could take place. The Sun, the
bright star of our solar system, is now crossing into the sign of Leo
the Lion, the sign the Sun rules. Leo represents your eighth house
of sex, money shared with other people, and power. Although most
of you may be well aware of your financial status, this can be a good
time to take stock of personal as well as joint cash holdings, other
assets, and all liabilities.

24. SUNDAY. Trying. A tricky day is ahead. Planned social outings might be more about doing your duty than having fun. Some
of you may be pushed into making an important decision regarding a current love affair. It would be wise to wait until next week
when planetary influences will be upbeat. Children are likely to be
disruptive unless parents can find a fun outlet for the excess energy
of youngsters. Most Capricorns are cautious when it comes to gambling. But today you may be prone to making large wagers in the
hope of coming out a winner. If so, defer these types of activities.
There is more chance of losing money than winning it now.

25. MONDAY. Guarded. Mixed trends prevail today. Relationships and love affairs could be more rewarding later in the day.
A blind date should work out well for singles as long as the introduction comes from a friend or family member who knows you
well. Watch what you say. There is a danger of speaking first but
thinking later when it is too late to stop the words from spurting
out. Avoid taking on too much in your daily schedule over the
next couple of days. Endeavor to eliminate habits that could be
detrimental to your health and well-being. Drink plenty of fluids
if you are working outside. Liberally apply sun screen to protect
your skin.

26. TUESDAY. Manageable. Focus on your working environment.
Implement necessary changes to discard what is no longer needed.
Add what you do need so you can get where you want to go. Although this process is hard, you can do it. Capricorn ambition is the
driver. So if you are not moving in the right direction, depression
can set in. It is worth the time and energy to regain emotional satisfaction. If you have already made essential alterations, you can reap
the rewards of your courage and effort. Your efficiency is enhanced,
aiding progress on the job or in the domestic environment. An ap-

plication could be accepted. For some of you this might be an offer of employment.

27. WEDNESDAY. Thrilling. Exciting times appear on the celestial horizon as the vibrant Sun engages happily with unique Uranus. Believing that you can do something or make a difference is the first step to achieving your aim. Once you know that anything within reason is possible, you can then take the next step. Routine schedules and mundane chores are unlikely to hold the interest of even the most staid Capricorn now. So introduce a large dose of variety and change into your day to avert boredom and monotony. Ideas and plans could have a strong inventive flavor and flair, opening new doors and presenting interesting opportunities.

28. THURSDAY. Fortunate. A bevy of planetary patterns exists today. Good fortune could come your way. For some Goats a social or romantic chance may arrive suddenly. Venus, planet of love and money, enters your eighth zone of Leo adding a dramatic flair to emotional issues and shared finances. While Venus travels through Leo from now until August 21, your feelings will be more intense. Capricorn singles seeking love will be more interested in a deep and binding affair rather than a superficial and short-lived flirtation. This is also a good time to dig deep in order to reassess financial security. That way you will be on track to establish a strong monetary foundation for your future.

29. FRIDAY. Satisfying. Mercury, planet of communication and commerce, has just joined the Sun and Venus in your Leo solar sector of sex, death, and regeneration. A strategy to improve financial resources can be planned, developed, and implemented now. You don't need to cut out all luxury and comfort items. However, this is a good period to think about what you could do if you had more money available. Enroll in a course that gives advice on playing the stock market. Attend a class that discloses various options for investing funds in a pension scheme. These activities would be illuminating. Capricorn folk who would rather skip the hard work and hire a professional to do the work for you have good chances of finding someone suitable.

30. SATURDAY. Refreshing. Interesting lunar patterns form today. The highlight is a Leo New Moon activating your eighth solar sector of shared assets, taxes, inheritances, and regeneration. New beginnings can be expected. A windfall could help pay unexpected expenses that might crop up. For some Goats the birth of a child or grandchild could make this a very special period. It should be easier now to find practical solutions to difficulties with finances or basic security needs. Consider opening a separate account if you are saving for a special purpose. Capricorn parents can steer youngsters in the right direction by arranging their own savings scheme now.

31. SUNDAY. Fair. Pay attention to your dreams, Capricorn. Answers could come by recalling key visions. It might be time to think about changing things in your life even if this means making a few tough decisions. Your power of reasoning could be off target, especially when domestic concerns or family matters are under consideration. So listen to the ideas of loved ones before moving ahead any further. A social outing with the family should bring pleasure. There may be a few harsh words spoken to younger folk if they are not punctual. A romantic development could provide a sample of good things to come. Wind up the day with an early night.

AUGUST

1. MONDAY. Affectionate. Love and romance are to the fore as Capricorns greet the new month. With Venus steaming up your solar house of sex and meeting exciting Uranus, you can expect plenty of thrills and adventure in the emotional department. Take advantage of this passionate period to cement your relationship in the best possible manner. If you have been spending too much time on the job and your honey is suffering from neglect, rectify this situation. Organize some couple time in which you can share quality outings together. Those of you who are savvy about money management could consider purchasing an item that will increase in value and add to your future security.

2. TUESDAY. Encouraging. Developing your mind or gaining new skills doesn't always mean enrolling in a university. But if you do have higher academic studies in mind, this is a good period to find out what courses and options are currently available. With the Moon now in Virgo, any form of editing or publishing work should progress smoothly. Capricorn pet owners might consider saving money by bringing out the brushes and combs and trying your hand at grooming your pampered pooch. Messenger Mercury now begins retreating through Virgo, your solar house of travel and education, and will be retrograde until August 26. Delays or mix-ups with study grants, legal proceedings, or travel arrangements are likely to occur more frequently during this period.

3. WEDNESDAY. Social. With the Sun in your Leo eighth house, having fun and entertaining others should now be near the top of your list of priorities. If it has been some time since you held a dinner party or invited friends over for a casual barbeque, the coming weekend could be a good chance to show off your cooking skills. Motivation to share your dreams grows stronger, allowing people to see a side of you that might not be revealed very often. If music is your passion, listen to the local radio station to relax you while you work and commute. Capricorns who regularly enter competitions could be on the winning end of some sought-after concert tickets.

4. THURSDAY. Sparkling. Your mind and wit should be especially sharp right now. With thinking Mercury happily linked to dynamic Mars, this is a good time to begin a new course of study, to debate a particular issue, or to argue an issue in court. Promoting some of your initiatives and getting support from people should also be extremely easy. Practical solutions or new options with travel plans or a long-distance relationship could be found. Mental facility and attention to detail are at a peak, assisting those of you who have writing and study tasks to complete. If you are chained to your computer all day, make sure an occasional break is taken to reduce the chance of a sore back or eyestrain.

5. FRIDAY. Bright. Self-confidence rises today due to the constructive influences sent by the universe. The Sun and your ruler Saturn are harmonizing together. To prepare for leisure time this weekend, a spot of spring-cleaning may be in order. Organizing and rearranging furniture, your closet, or other belongings could be both energizing and therapeutic. Moderation should be the motto to follow even for the frugal Goat while saucy Venus challenges excessive Jupiter today. An important financial undertaking requires painstaking research, the sharing of information, and attention to detail before you should consider moving ahead any further. Love and romance are starred for Capricorn folk now.

6. SATURDAY. Guarded. Keep an eye on your energy level and make sure activities are not too strenuous. With the Moon moving through your solar eleventh zone of Scorpio, the emphasis falls on friends, acquaintances, and relatives. Call on friends, family, or faith if you need support or guidance. A group gathering attended now could have long-term benefits. Take care if someone other than a family member asks to borrow money. This could become an issue within a friendship. Money could come your way if you are not afraid to commit to extra responsibilities. Friends should be pleasant company, and this is a good night to hold an impromptu party.

Solo Goats could meet someone special through an associate or a pal.

7. SUNDAY. Abundant. It is a good day for love and money, and right now you probably would like plenty of both in your life. Penny-pinching is unlikely to have a place in your consciousness, but beware an overly generous attitude unless the bank balance is extremely flush. Capricorn shoppers are likely to head for quality over quantity when making purchases. An expensive piece of artwork could be an excellent investment for your long-term future. Recharging run-down batteries can be as simple as spending time in a natural setting or relaxing with loved ones. A swim in the pool or a trip to the beach could also be the perfect form of recreation later on when the Moon enters the sign of Sagittarius, your twelfth house.

8. MONDAY. Edgy. It is a day when the disciplined Capricorn might need to call on those formidable Saturn reserves to remain focused. A strong undertone of confusion prevails, and misunderstanding and mix-ups are likely to be prevalent. Think twice about divulging personal secrets to coworkers or associates. Some of them might use such disclosures in a negative manner. Issues from the past should be left there. What has happened is now history and cannot be changed. Errors made on the job could come back to haunt you, so better own up to any mistakes as soon as you make them. The solace offered within a place of worship can help to quell doubts and fears.

9. TUESDAY. Volatile. A cool and collected approach is the preferred demeanor of most Capricorn people. Most of you probably don't like it when emotions become heated, because ultimately it is remaining in control that is important to you. With current volatile influences prevailing, it will require extra effort to stay calm and composed. Resentment could rise to the surface regarding a family tradition or issue. Right now you may realize that it will be difficult to break away and do what you want rather than following the call of duty. Stepping out and having fun with your partner tonight would be far better than staying at home and becoming embroiled in an explosive argument.

10. WEDNESDAY. Productive. The Moon returns to your own sign of Capricorn, adding to an impatient but go-getting approach. Slow things down if everything appears to be moving too fast. Rushing through tasks and obligations is not always the smartest course of action. However, this is your time to shine. A good mood and an optimistic outlook can give you an extra boost of vitality to attack the many duties accumulating on your to-do list. Don't be afraid to practice spiritual and physical disciplines such as tai chi or yoga. These could be useful to Goats who are under extreme pressure and can be the key to maintaining overall good health and happiness.

11. THURSDAY. Fine. Capricorn strength remains high, although a more somber attitude could be on display. Even when others give in to pressure, you will more than likely remain firm and resilient. This isn't the time to look back. Instead, it is a period when you should be moving forward toward cherished goals and dreams. Start today to adopt methods that are motivating and self-empowering. Doing so will widen your horizons and provide a sense of accomplishment. Those of you who feel the need for an increased display of love and affection should let your partner or spouse know. He or she will surely respond with a show of support. Then you, in turn, can be demonstrative.

12. FRIDAY. Fidgety. A restless atmosphere prevails today. This could be destabilizing if energies are not applied productively. If you are involved in a team meeting or group situation, grasp the chance to demonstrate original ideas and an ability to think outside of the box. Keep in mind that elements of the unexpected are likely to arise suddenly, providing a reminder that things won't always go according to plan. This should be fine if you take a more easygoing approach than is usual for you, especially when schedules or plans are thrown into disarray. A financial arrangement might require more discussion before you decide to go ahead with a proposed loan or joint venture.

13. SATURDAY. Tricky. On this bumpy day you also have the added pressure of an Aquarius Full Moon taking place in your house of personal finances, self-worth, and values. Maintaining a balance with your cash flow may be stressful, stretching your ingenuity and resourcefulness to the limit and beyond. It would be wiser not to take fiscal action now. Waiting for a few more days could find a clearer view emerging. If you are in the middle of negotiating a major acquisition, careful analysis and consistent effort are required if your aim is to secure an investment for the future. Partnership issues appear to be under a cloud, with the possibility of a power play arising.

14. SUNDAY. Sensitive. Be thoughtful and kind in discussions with loved ones. Sensitive emotions linger on under continuing Full Moon influences. Not everyone is as cool, calm, and logical as a

Capricorn. If you haven't anything nice to say about someone, then
don't say anything at all. With a Pisces Moon arriving later, those of
you who play a musical instrument and write or read poetry should
find pleasure in your favorite pastime. Relax and have fun. If there
is a pool close by, a relaxing swim would be in order. A pedicure or
a foot massage might work wonders for Goats feeling a little foot-
sore and weary. Visiting the weekend markets can be a source of
entertainment if you just look and don't buy.

15. MONDAY. Variable. Communication flows freely and agreements are easily reached, during the morning hours. Later on in
the day, discussions are unlikely to flow as easily. You should bear
in mind that people around you could have an agenda of their own,
which will not mesh with your interests. It may be difficult to express in words exactly what you mean or intend. But body language
and subtle nuances should get your message across without risking
an argument. Reopening an unsettled matter with someone in authority could bring up overlooked factors. If you are persistent and
respectful, an accord can be reached.

16. TUESDAY. Happy. A positive glow arrives now, putting a rosy
perspective on current situations and concerns. Planning to leave
the office or store a little earlier to complete outstanding errands
and chores would be a great idea. It would help reduce some of the
pressure that might be building up. Don't' waste time on long phone
calls if a quick e-mail or text message would suffice. Financial paperwork could take up your time. This may relate to an investment
in your future, so be meticulous if you are applying for a special
loan or home mortgage. Evening hours are good for entertaining
guests or for visiting nearby relatives. Comfort and joy come from
mixing with people you love.

17. WEDNESDAY. Trying. The frugal Capricorn might balk at
spending money on beautifying your home unless the changes add
value to your net worth. The level of home comforts should also be
taken into consideration. If there are areas that require upgrading,
examine what is needed and begin implementing a few alterations.
With the Moon moving through your Aries fourth solar house,
spending quality time with parents and children increases in importance and should take precedence over work duties. If there are
problems brewing on the domestic front, nip them in the bud before misunderstandings and grievances spiral out of control.

18. THURSDAY. Positive. A renewed sense of optimism and enthusiasm arrives today. Energetic Mars is harmonizing happily with

generous Jupiter. So this is a favorable period to be more assertive so that you can make progress in any area that is important
to you. Capricorn energy, drive, and motivation are enhanced and
can be channeled into a business or intimate partnership, a major
public relations event, or a targeted advertising program. Those of
you considering a vacation abroad could look at a package that includes a variety of adventurous activities. You want to ensure that
your journey is different from the usual run-of-the-mill sightseeing
trips.

19. FRIDAY. Pleasant. Even if family relations start to get tense,
issues can be smoothed over quickly this morning. A pleasant atmosphere prevails now. Take advantage of the harmony. Seek favors, ask questions, and share your ideas and views. If you live by
yourself, you might want to catch up on overdue chores involved in
basic housekeeping. Savor the peace and tranquillity that having
your own abode can bring. Social plans are likely to need firming up
once the day gets under way. Love and romance would benefit by
more attention being applied in this area. Solo Capricorns can expect a buzz on the dance floor this evening. A promising encounter
could make your night one to remember.

20. SATURDAY. Good. Lunar trends are fine as the weekend begins. With the Moon in Taurus, your fifth house, the party may have
already begun. Although you might not have any qualms about
putting arrangements in place, maintaining those plans will be extremely difficult today. You or others are likely to want changes
made. So take a more flexible approach, and you can still have
plenty of fun. If there has been anything lacking in your life, you
could find that a book or a study course holds the answer to some
of your questions. Children bring joy for Capricorn parents now.
Think up ways to nip boredom in the bud when you take youngsters on an outing this afternoon.

21. SUNDAY. Misleading. Relationships that begin now might appear to be superficial and insincere. However, there may be something that you are not seeing just yet. Put some energy into the
relationship, and you could reap the rewards a few months down
the track. It might be time to find out more about a tax or insurance matter, especially if your partner is self-employed and you
are not privy to all his or her business dealings. Deceptive trends
abound today. Be wary of investing in something that looks too
good to be true. If you are tricked, your money could disappear
very quickly. Check your purchases when shopping, as you might

be shortchanged. Remember to request receipts and store them in a safe place.

22. MONDAY. Deceptive. Although you are renowned for a realistic approach, even cautious Capricorn folk need to take care today. Deception continues to abound. It could be very easy for a slick salesperson or con artist to talk you out of your hard-earned cash. Venus, the lover, has taken up residence in Virgo, your house of education and experience. Venus here gives you a chance to learn more about the mysteries of life and what continues to propel you forward. Enjoyment will come from pursuing creative pastimes or by visiting art galleries and other institutions of culture and learning. Surprise expenses are foreseen. Protect valuable personal items.

23. TUESDAY. Progressive. At dawn the vibrant Sun enters Virgo, your ninth house of long-distance travel and belief structures. You may now be ready to consider a variety of options regarding education, training courses, or journeying afar to broaden your experiences of life. The self-employed Capricorn could gain more success if dialogue is opened up with traders abroad. A new job out of town could offer a quicker chance of your moving up the career ladder. A spot of retail therapy should bring pleasure to the capricious Goat. If you are accompanied by a special friend, delight will be doubled. A long-standing or chronic ailment could be progressing toward recovery now.

24. WEDNESDAY. Restrictive. Contrary planetary influences mark this day. There isn't much you can do other than making the best of whatever does come your way. Whether for a personal or business matter, professional consultations could be helpful for Capricorns who need an unbiased outlook. Weigh all advice and options. You might be inspired to go about a financial or romantic concern in a new and different manner. However, think seriously before moving too far ahead with your plans. It might be that you are just bored with the same old patterns and routines. Taking a radical approach if the plan hasn't been well thought out might not be the wisest move.

25. THURSDAY. Uncertain. Although the planetary influences remain tricky, there is definitely a light at the end of the tunnel. You might not have a clear view of it right now, but it is there and things are improving. Taking a less jaundiced approach and adding a large dose of optimism can make life more pleasant for you and those in close proximity. This is only a passing phase. If your love life is looking a lot brighter, you can thank the stars, which are shining brightly on your romantic sector. A number of potential partners could be beating a pathway to your door. Capricorns in a committed union will be sharing loving and passionate times with your mate.

26. FRIDAY. Favorable. This is a good period to ask for a loan and to fill out important paperwork for a scholarship or special grant. Messenger Mercury is preparing to move forward in Leo once again, making the whole process much easier than envisioned. With the Moon in Leo, matters regarding joint finances, investments, or a retirement fund can be successfully pursued. A special labor of love should progress smoothly. An overseas project could hold appeal for some of you. Capricorn singles can expect to receive increased attention from romantic partners. He or she may be planning a surprise treat to be shared by just the two of you.

27. SATURDAY. Manageable. The power of attraction remains enhanced. However, feelings of agitation are likely to develop today, and you might not understand why. Remain active and on the go rather than trying to analyze something that you cannot control. Clean out your closets, Donate what you no longer wear or need to a favorite charity. Consider holding a yard sale with neighbors to make a few extra dollars. Surprise news could arrive, possibly setting off an emotional chord and a sudden need to make an about-face. An unexpected change at home or in the family could be upsetting. Try to take such alterations and adjustments in stride.

28. SUNDAY. Energetic. An extra boost of energy should enhance your physical vim and vitality now. Take advantage of it. Give your body a good workout or engage in tasks that require strenuous labor. Research various methods of growing your investment portfolio. Or work out a strategy to reduce debt. These activities would be a productive use of leisure time. The New Moon culminating in Virgo later this evening places emphasis on your ninth house of legal matters, philosophy, education, travel, and foreign affairs. With enthusiasm and energy applied, any new ventures relating to these areas should reach a successful outcome. Now is a favorable time to plan an itinerary for a journey abroad.

29. MONDAY. Heartening. Positive planetary influences reign today. If local business dealings are not bringing expected returns, then looking farther afield for new markets might be the solution. Initiating self-improvement methods should bode well. If you need further qualifications or training to enhance your value to a current or prospective employer, then this is the time to take action. Capricorn published novelists as well as hopeful writers can improve your output now. Get busy finishing a manuscript so you can soon send it to an agent or editor. Launching a literary project should be successful. Attending a reunion this evening can rouse pleasant memories.

30. TUESDAY. Exhilarating. A fortunate atmosphere surrounds Capricorns now. Just about anything is possible. Luck abounds for love and money. There should be plenty of income available to spend on children, a lover, or a luxury item. Art and beautiful objects could catch your eye. If you have money to spare, an acquisition made now could increase in value over time. You may be reaping the benefits of past efforts, which will also add nicely to your bank balance. Action in the love arena is promised by the positive link between sexy Venus and jolly Jupiter. Let your hair down and prepare for an evening of fun and frivolity.

31. WEDNESDAY. Strategic. Positive trends continue, although it may be essential to watch what you say and how you say it. There may be someone or something that gets in your way. However, thinking creatively can be the solution to finding answers. Negotiations or business meetings should reach desired outcomes. Be prepared to make a few adjustments first. You might be promised or offered something regarding employment that raises your profile and status. Give this proposition a lot of thought before you make a firm decision. Either way, emotional satisfaction comes by knowing that you have reached this lofty level and that you have received recognition for it.

SEPTEMBER

1. THURSDAY. Empowering. Travel, education, and adventure remain at the forefront of attention now with the Sun continuing to travel through your ninth house of Virgo. This is an auspicious time to pursue educational aims, open your mind to new possibilities, travel, and broaden your horizons. If you have opinions for improving procedures at work, it might be time to speak up and state your views. Capricorn folks involved in technical fields should find that this is a good time to advance your career and business interests. Socializing with associates or clients after work this evening will be pleasant. A number of productive ideas might begin to form and should be developed.

2. FRIDAY. Fortunate. Luck and good fortune surround Capricorn people now. Give serious consideration to your goals and dreams for the future. This may include gaining advanced educational qualifications. Enrolling in a place of higher learning to aid your career aims can provide long-term benefits for your future. The desire to travel and expand your views is also strong right now. This could be the impetus that sends some of you to the travel agent to arrange an exciting itinerary. Warm displays of affection are in store. Capricorn in a couple might want to make plans for the two of you to get together for an evening of loving. Spending time with friends could be a stimulating experience for those of you currently without a partner.

3. SATURDAY. Enlightening. Take advantage of good cosmic vibes. Lovely planet Venus is transiting Virgo, your solar ninth house of aspirations and cultural experiences. Many Capricorns will enjoy an involvement with the arts, planning a long journey, or researching educational options. Take the time for learning and exploring the finer things in life. Finances appear to be looking up, and you should receive a number of opportunities for advancement. Those of you in a permanent commitment could be tying the knot with that special someone. Singles looking for love may find that an older lover appeals right now. A blossoming love affair has the potential to go the distance.

4. SUNDAY. Enriching. Take it easy today, Capricorn. Lunar trends are not very helpful, so energy and enthusiasm may be depleted. Whenever the Moon slides through Sagittarius, your twelfth house of secrets and solitude, it signals a time to slow down and to spend time alone. Rest, relax, and take care of your body. Avoid overindulging or pushing yourself beyond reasonable limits. If you are recuperating from an operation or major illness, give yourself plenty of time to heal. A boating or fishing trip, swimming at the pool, or watching the breaking waves on a beach could be a wonderful and therapeutic method of unwinding and letting the world pass you by.

5. MONDAY. Beneficial. The workaholic Goat might experience bouts of frustration if a health problem slows progress down. Looking after your overall well-being is important, so don't neglect important signals advising that something might not be right. An offer on the table again may intrigue you. It might involve shared resources and gains through other people. Don't let previous mistakes of any ilk weigh you down or hold you back from taking advantage of a new proposition or opportunity. Passion could be slowly building in a situation where you didn't expect to find it. If you are currently solo and looking for a potential lover, participating in volunteer work for a good cause may lead to a romantic interlude.

6. TUESDAY. Accomplished. Power and assertiveness come to the fore for much of the day as the Moon enters your sign and impacts your first house of personality and self. This marks a two-day high in your lunar cycle, providing extra strength and charisma. This influence is enhanced by the conjunction of the Moon with intense Pluto in your sign. So beware coming on too strong to people who don't know you well. Your ambition rises, which is a plus for the hardworking Goat intent on steadily climbing the ladder of success. Accomplishing a goal or finally possessing something that has been a dream for a long time could be realized now. This evening attend to private tasks that make you feel good.

7. WEDNESDAY. Motivating. Capricorn people know that quality beats quantity every time. Although the image you portray is made up of more than clothes and accessories, dressing to impress can take you places and help you open doors. The introduction of small and subtle alterations that to others might seem inconsequential could be adding up to a major change of image and perspective for many Goats. If your wardrobe needs updating, this is a positive period for a spot of retail therapy. Most of you will know immediately what suits your style and enhances your appearance. Don't forget to complete the picture with a new hairstyle and smart jewelry.

8. THURSDAY. Complicated. A complex day dawns as a dose of practical application as well as deceptive influences are sent by the cosmos. Partnership ventures could appear uncertain. Maintain lighthearted conversation with people whose money or assets you share. If possible, steer away from financial discussions altogether. Guard your wallet and possessions all day, especially if you are out among the crowds. Capricorn shoppers should check receipts and change given. Be careful when handing over credit cards for purchases or obtaining cash at an automated teller machine. A tendency to splurge is strong now. It would be advisable to calculate how much you can spend beforehand. Organizing work procedures will increase efficiency.

9. FRIDAY. Challenging. Financial matters demand careful attention again. Apply your usual practical and conservative standards. Tackle important issues rather than wasting time in wishful thinking. If someone lets you down or is becoming more and more unreliable, discuss the problem in depth rather than allowing the situation to get worse. Your sign of Capricorn is known for a thrifty attitude toward money, which can sometimes border on stinginess. It would behoove you to change your attitude toward fiscal management, spending, saving, and earning in order to ensure that resources are used wisely. However, be careful that a poverty consciousness doesn't develop. A night out with colleagues could be relaxing.

10. SATURDAY. Varied. Money continues to rule the airwaves all day. Mercury has reentered Virgo, your house of travel. So those of you planning a journey soon can make headway on the preparation and plans. The Internet might be a good source of deals and possible destinations, and you might find just the vacation package to suit your requirements. Remain practical without succumbing to a gloomy outlook. Stimulating conversation and intellectual observations can lead to progress. Avoid shopping or socializing at expensive venues if your finances arc limited. Both of these activities could drain the bank balance. Participating in a favored hobby aids relaxation.

11. SUNDAY. Sparkling. Getting up close and personal with a special person this morning can start the day on a bright note. Capricorn creative talents might be waiting to be unleashed. Today's influences bring the perfect time to use your inspiration to produce. If people are shown the products of your imagination, an outlet to sell your goods could soon be found. Whatever activities you engage in outside of the home, be sure to take the proper safety precautions. Those of you who are traveling after dark should be extra vigilant. Heated discussions could erupt late in the day. Avoid going over and over the same problems. Be conciliatory to maintain harmony on the home front.

12. MONDAY. Bumpy. Challenging and emotional energies are in store today along with the power and passion to express yourself. With a Pisces Full Moon culminating in your communication house, verbal confrontations are bound to occur. However, some assistance comes from the cosmos. Whatever argument is presented, you should have the correct answer. Even if you don't want to make waves and speak up, you might feel that you have to do so whatever the outcome. Students taking exams, studying, or researching an assignment should do exceptionally well. Public speakers are unlikely to experience any problems holding the interest of an audience. The Goat on a debating team or part of a sales force is also in the driver's seat.

13. TUESDAY. Bright. Expressiveness is your forte today. Your ability to speak up and say what is on your mind is strong. Key intellectual insights abound. This is a period when you are more likely to give an articulate opinion and guidance to others. Past conditioning from childhood could be something that comes to the fore, and you might think about experiences from then until now. Pat yourself on the back if you have grown in that time span. If you haven't, then start finding ways to attract positive events into your life. The urge to put down roots could be keenly felt. This may be the motivation for younger Capricorn people to begin looking for your first home.

14. WEDNESDAY. Gratifying. It is a day when even the most stable Goat could find that your heart rules your head. Love and romance should bring delight. Vivid imagination can be a wonderful gift to use now, especially for those of you who are required to be creative and original. If reality does get you down a little, you can always escape into the world of dreams and fantasies for a short period of time. Something around the home or yard might need an overhaul, so be alert and look around. There may be a number of things that need to be repaired, recovered, restored, recycled, or just given away to people who have few material goods. Being charitable is its own reward.

15. THURSDAY. Satisfying. With the Moon slipping through the sign of Aries, matters relating to the home and family remain high on your agenda. Attend to whatever domestic tasks are required early in the day. Later on, the desire to have fun and party could take over. An idea or opportunity could roll around in your mind. But put the thought on hold until you have worked out all details to ensure that plans are viable. Love affairs should remain upbeat and happy. Capricorn singles could be blessed with an encounter that looks more than promising. If vacation plans need to be arranged, consider taking that cruise you have been dreaming about.

16. FRIDAY. Eventful. Pressures and stresses could come from unexpected or hidden sources this morning. Put things in their place, and issues should be resolved. Extra care and attention applied now can be time-saving in the long term. For the remainder of the day a positive mood should reign while the Moon moves through the sensual sign of Taurus. And transformational Pluto starts to move forward again in your sign of Capricorn. Plan to enjoy a night of happiness, love, and laughter. Goats in a committed union should arrange to be alone with your partner. Singles heading out for a night on the town should ensure that spending remains within a reasonable limit.

17. SATURDAY. Tricky. Today's celestial influences are sure to throw a few obstacles in your path. Capricorn on the job either as an employee or self-employed could find that career and professional matters are not in harmony with domestic or family needs. Be realistic about current challenges and responsibilities. If you act with logic and maturity, finding the right emotional balance that satisfies you and your loved ones shouldn't be too tough. Hidden expenses might begin to eat into your budget. So perhaps it would be a good exercise to look at where your cash is being spent. Take small steps in a new love affair. It is very likely that impulsive action now will be regretted at leisure later on.

18. SUNDAY. Vexing. Tense planetary influences prevail today. Power struggles could arise on the job, so take any frustrations out in a productive manner. A creative project could suffer due to a lack of support or funding. The expected sponsorship for a sporting event might be delayed. This is a good period to organize your closet, pantry, or home office. Send unwanted goods to a favored charity or homeless center. Capricorns who succumbed to overindulging in rich foods or alcohol should consider a day of detox. At least stick to fresh fruits, vegetables, and lots of refreshing water. A family member, possibly an elderly relative, could come to stay.

19. MONDAY. Uneasy. It is a day to be aware of your physical resources, health ailments, and minor symptoms of stress. The Moon is moving through Gemini, your house of health. So this is a positive period to consult a nutritionist, dentist, or medical practitioner to ensure that you remain in top gear. If anyone can stick to a fitness plan or diet, it is a Capricorn. However, your renowned workaholic tendencies can create extra stress and strain on your body. Remember to take an occasional rest. If you haven't had a decent break from work for some time, consider changing this. Arrange for vacation leave as soon as possible. Conflicts with clients or associates continue to make things a little awkward, creating more stress all around.

20. TUESDAY. Manageable. Scheduling problems on the job could bring angst for some Goats. If a no-nonsense approach is employed, it shouldn't be long before all concerns are ironed out. Dynamic Mars is now residing in your Leo eighth house of mystery and shared resources. This sector is also concerned with liabilities and fiscal management. You could make the decision now to reduce your current level of debt in order to maximize or at least maintain financial stability and security. Be wary of taking on staff unless absolutely necessary, especially if you own the business. Be vigilant when it comes to chasing down clients who owe you money.

21. WEDNESDAY. Problematic. Tricky stars make it more difficult to move forward. Intuition could rise, but be on guard. Trusting
your instincts might not be the best course to take. Organizing a
sale of some type could help if you are struggling financially or if
you need to increase company profits. Don't let personal concerns
consume all of your time today. It may be very important to connect
with a partner or loved one. Giving someone your full attention will
let them know that you care and that their problems do matter. An
application for a loan or home mortgage could be accepted. Make
sure that paperwork, especially the fine print, has been thoroughly
read and understood before you sign on the dotted line.

22. THURSDAY. Uneven. An up-and-down day appears likely. Be
available for others, the people who matter to you, and they should
also be there for you when the need arises. An existing union can
be strengthened if energy is exerted. See that your significant other
is made to feel that he or she is a top priority for you. Some Capricorns might be unwilling to face up to the cost of an entertainment
project until it is too late to pull out or to make other arrangements.
If you are disappointed, put it down to experience and make sure
that the mistake is not repeated. Being seen in public this evening
could be a strong motivation to dress up and put your best foot
forward.

23. FRIDAY. Mixed. Changeable influences are in play now. Following your dreams can be more easily obtainable and put you on
the road to success as long as your goals are realistic and firmly
in sight. Something in your daily surroundings might need to be
repaired or replaced. Organizing and getting rid of junk around the
household can free up space and freshen the environment. Today
the Sun enters your tenth house of Libra. So you can expect the
tempo of life to pick up as career and professional matters come
to the fore. Entrepreneurial Capricorns who supply goods and
services to clients should do yourself a favor by doing a thorough
background check on potential new accounts. Weed out the clients
who have already run up debt.

24. SATURDAY. Uplifting. A surprising business proposition or
career opportunity could be presented to you out of the blue. Be
flexible in your thinking. Consider the pros and cons before coming to a decision. It might be time to implement a reasonable but
not too restrictive household budget, one that your significant other
or roommates are happy and willing to comply with. Expanding a
special goal might be more challenging than anticipated. Just keep
trying, and success should follow. Some type of tug-of-war could

erupt over a joint asset, inheritance, or business partnership. Wait until the coming workweek to tackle this issue. On this leisure day you need a bit of peace and quiet.

25. SUNDAY. Diverse. Many Capricorn people are likely to display the capricious side of your personality today. Restlessness could encourage radical behavior, possibly surprising people who thought they knew you well. Make sure that your schedule is packed with a variety of leisure activities to keep you busy and to lessen the chance of boredom taking over. Quick-thinking Mercury now joins the Sun, Venus, and Saturn in Libra, your house of status and vocational interests. This influence will further motivate the career-minded Goat to improve your standing in the world. Your ability to speak up, contribute ideas, and share experiences is at a peak, raising your profile among peers and authority figures.

26. MONDAY. Good. A number of issues might need to be confronted, but with patience most concerns shouldn't take long to straighten out. Moving forward in your chosen field of interest is easier for the ambitious Capricorn. Those of you who require further training can attend seminars and conferences to increase your knowledge and also to get hands-on experience. You may win a grant or scholarship to pursue higher education. Goats who are interested in becoming an exchange student should receive promising news. Youngsters preparing for a driver's license are likely to do well. A legal proceeding might be delayed, but this could work in your favor.

27. TUESDAY. Unpredictable. Be prepared for the unexpected today. As the pace of life increases, many of you are bound to feel edgy, agitated, or hemmed in. Problems will arise if you constantly change your mind. So try to defer major decision making that could be hard to reverse sometime in the future. Utilize your dry wit and sense of humor to obtain a different perspective. The Libra New Moon accentuates your career and reputation, attracting support from colleagues and authority figures. Projects that are started now should flow smoothly. Capricorn who is seeking a new employment position or attending a job interview has a better than average chance of success.

28. WEDNESDAY. Trying. Today's scenario is highlighted by employment situations that may be very stressful. If your nerves are on edge or you are suffering overwhelm from too much work, try deep breathing to restore a calm and detached approach. Extra responsibilities or deadlines could be placing too much demand on your time. You must learn and practice the art of delegation. If there isn't a need for you to carry such a heavy burden, start to share the load. Cooperation is more productive than confrontation. A diplomatic approach can aid Goats working in a team or group setting. Take your mind off your worries by realizing that there is only so much you are capable of. An early night might be in order.

29. THURSDAY. Excellent. Many of you typical of the Capricorn Sun sign have no qualms about putting the needs of family before your own. If this is the case it might be time to reward yourself with a few special treats. Congratulations to those of you planning to walk down the aisle, as this is a positive period to cement a committed union. Accepting a marriage proposal, holding an engagement party, or selecting the ring bodes well now. An older, more mature or wealthier lover could hold more appeal to single Goats seeking a partner. If your bank account can afford it, this is a positive period to purchase a piece of artwork or jewelry that holds the potential to increase in value over time.

30. FRIDAY. Opportune. Vital and alive may be an apt description of Capricorn demeanor now. However, keeping abreast of schedules will require a concerted effort today. Many things are unlikely to run according to plan. Learn to be more flexible, which should help to keep your blood pressure and stress down to an acceptable level. The driving ambition that you currently possess can find you making adjustments to goals. You want to ensure that aspirations and long-range goals do merge with your current situation. Another opportunity arises for someone to pop the question. Setting up a home with a lover may occupy a lot of your time and attention.

OCTOBER

1. SATURDAY. Promising. The focus is on your career and standing in the community while the Sun travels through the sign of Libra from now until October 23. There are mainly favorable influences prevailing as the new month gets under way. However, Capricorns on the job and those of you self-employed could have a couple of uncomfortable dealings with an authority figure or supervisor. Inflated egos may be the problem, making it a wiser proposition to keep a low profile unless you are in charge. With the Sagittarius Moon in your twelfth house, it is the day to stand back and observe rather than going into battle. Unless plans for tonight are exciting or cannot be changed, a quiet evening at home might be useful.

2. SUNDAY. Reflective. It is another day when self-nurturing and pampering are in order. A more contemplative mood could find many Capricorns planning rather than actually taking action. When it comes to the business and professional sphere, a spot of thinking could go a long way. This is the time when you can mull over career offers or business propositions before you come to any concrete decisions. Quiet entertainment might be in order again, as the urge to socialize may be very low. A casual meal with friends, a trip to the park with the family, or a drive to the weekend markets could be all the activity you can manage.

3. MONDAY. Tricky. Moving forward with personal decisions and interests may be what many of you are eager to do now. If you haven't decided what pathway to take, considering your options now could bring a number of answers. A solution to a few niggling problems could also come to mind. However, proceed slowly. Haste makes waste. Being careful with money and resources is the trademark of your sign of Capricorn. But today's influences could encourage you to be overly generous, even to the point of squandering money on children, gambling, or a new lover. Confusion and deception abound, sending a warning for you to verify information regarding a new job, a salary boost, or a promised bonus.

4. TUESDAY. Trying. Another tricky day dawns. Learning and then using the art of compromise will be essential, given the planetary aspects now in force. Enhanced egos could create issues and upsets on the job over the next week, especially if you or another feel unfairly targeted or criticized. There are some things in your personality that you might need to face and own up to. Be honest with your appraisal. Then be prepared to embrace changes in both your personal and business life. Taking a flexible approach rather than digging your heels in can make the process of transformation easier to handle. An early night is recommended, particularly if you are a little down in the dumps.

5. WEDNESDAY. Fine. Goals can be achieved as long as your focus is sharp. The chance of ridding yourself of negative patterns of behavior is strong through the morning hours. So consider looking for professional assistance or help if you are unable to go it alone. Later in the day money matters come to the forefront, and how much you earn and spend might be a priority. Working with groups can be beneficial. Issues that were confusing just recently could begin to be clarified. Buying and selling carried out now should bring a healthy profit. For some Capricorns the opportunity to start something new will be exciting. Prepare for a busy time at home this evening.

6. THURSDAY. Satisfactory. Capricorn practical judgment is sound under present star patterns. The Moon is still moving through Aquarius, your house of personal finances and possessions. So this is the day you might decide to upgrade or acquire a special item of value. Inspired ideas for improving your income could come to mind. However, don't neglect details; otherwise, the project could fizzle out. With a logical and methodical approach to everything undertaken now, you can reduce troublesome costs related to certain machinery and technology that you use for your work. A shoulder to cry on may be needed by an associate or colleague. They will pick you as the likely candidate because your opinions and guidance are highly valued.

7. FRIDAY. Pleasant. A dream quality spreads over today's activities. Your capacity to listen and understand remains enhanced, although you might be a little cautious when it comes to voicing things as you see them. Wasting time on superficial matters will irritate you. But those of you attending work meetings or business negotiations may find that this is exactly what happens. Guard against spending too much money on luxury goods or frivolous items. Your urge to splurge, uncharacteristic of Capricorn, may be heightened. Ambitious Goats should find that now is a very good time to mix business with pleasure. Couples can share loving rapport. Singles are prone to falling in love with love.

8. SATURDAY. Happy. The Moon dances into your Pisces solar house of communication today, enabling you to express yourself fluidly. Capricorn inspiration and imagination are on the rise, assisting those of you talented to get busy and create the masterpiece that could set you off onto another pathway. Parents can use the next couple of days to have a heart-to-heart with a youngster who has not been listening or responding to your good parenting skills. A romantic outing could recharge any Goat who has settled into a rut. Apply effort and add a little zing into a permanent relationship. Singles might experience a head-turning experience that sends you into fantasyland.

9. SUNDAY. Reassuring. Friends and associates may be a wonderful source of comfort and support from now until November 2 while Venus moves through Scorpio, your eleventh solar house. Romance could blossom with a friend or someone you already know on a casual basis. Your social life is about to lift, with many invitations arriving to fill up the social calendar. Fitting in with the wants and desires of others should be easier. Associating with people who share common interests with you can bring pleasure and delight. This is the time to expand your circle of friends. Be alert for signals from various newcomers who are expressing interest in meeting on a regular basis.

10. MONDAY. Comfortable. The suggestion of spending more time at home with family could be taken on board now. The urge to remain close to the domestic abode is stronger. For some Capricorns the thought of having to go out to work might be frustrating. Venus, the planet of love and money, continues to play a prominent part in your solar horoscope. Venus conveys a warning to those of you who frequent upscale department stores. You might not notice how much money is being spent or wasted on incidentals. Singles, be wary of any romantic approaches; mutual interest is unlikely to remain for long. A night at home curled up in your favorite chair might appeal to many Goats.

11. TUESDAY. Tense. Today's Full Moon in Aries activates your solar fourth house of home and family, increasing the anxiety and emotion on the domestic front. Endeavor to resolve issues and tie up loose ends quickly in order to avert tension. A property settlement could occur for potential home owners. A long-term roommate might move out, bringing the end of a cycle as well as some sadness. Finding the right balance between employment duties and family responsibilities could be tricky. An authority figure or a boss might demand more effort from you or expect you to work overtime, creating friction with loved ones. Hurry home after work, and surround yourself with your nearest and dearest.

12. WEDNESDAY. Creative. Your intuition is heightened and inspiration flows swiftly under today's link between intellectual Mercury and dreamy Neptune. Fertile imagination assists Capricorn folks in many facets of your daily life. Those of you who write, compose, or play music should be in your element. Filmmakers and photographers won't have to look far for subjects. Some of you will create a little magic in a favored field of interest. An ability to listen with compassion and empathy could find that you are sought out by others. However, it may be problematic to set your own clear and firm boundaries. Don't fall into the trap of fantasizing about unrealistic ideas and wishes. Instead, draw on your innate common sense.

13. THURSDAY. Inspirational. Capricorn creative powers reach a peak now due to the phethora of planetary influences holding sway in your solar horoscope. Inspirational ideas backed up by good judgment can make this a very productive period for the talented painter, musician, designer, and dancer. A bunch of fresh flowers on your desk might arouse the inner artist and also make for happiness. Those of you in a romantic relationship can enjoy the little things that make love go around. If time permits, arrange a lunchtime date with your honey. Singles should have some luck in love. Partnered Goats can expect more passion and zest. Look forward to more contact with friends now that Mercury is in your Scorpio eleventh house.

14. FRIDAY. Productive. Capricorn organizational skills are enhanced. Concentration and energy can be poured into work and business activities, with the likelihood of successful outcomes. Precision tasks or duties that require a high degree of focus and skill can be handled smoothly today. Managing your money may be a priority for those of you who like to keep an exact record of income and expenditure. Go over bills, check credit card statements, and ensure that all monthly accounts are paid on time. If an organization or a club that you belong to is now taking up too much time or is no longer providing stimulation and satisfaction, then it might be time to call it quits. Just think of the money you will save on membership fees.

15. SATURDAY. Gratifying. A lighthearted and laid-back morning should be enjoyed. Your creative juices are still flowing, and inspiration can be used to refurbish your home office, brighten up a living room, or create a magical space in the garden. A sports event or concert featuring one of your youngsters should be a highlight for Capricorn parents. Romance heats up. Freely giving more of your time to a significant other can reduce the possibility of friction developing. Later in the day your thoughts might wander to matters regarding a current diet or exercise program. If losing weight is a goal and to date you have been unsuccessful, consider hiring a personal trainer for a few weeks to direct a fitness regime.

16. SUNDAY. Bright. The Gemini Moon could find many Goats in a rush to finish things. Energy and enthusiasm climb. However, this is a time to tackle one task at a time. That way your productivity will be paced and you won't have to redo anything. Over the next few days, your ability to grasp and understand even the most complex of issues and equations will be at a peak. Your comprehension of various topics will rise. Students taking exams should excel. Public speaking, selling, and debating are activities in which Capricorn folk are unlikely to experience any problems. Those of you involved in scientific and research projects will make solid progress.

17. MONDAY. Challenging. Expect intense emotions to bubble to the surface as adverse planetary trends prevail. Reacting strongly to something that normally wouldn't be a bother can be a problem today. Remain cool and focused if you hope to make headway. It is also essential to pace duties and obligations in order to ensure that you have enough vim and vitality to complete tasks to your usual high standard. Avoid junk and sweet foods. Taking the healthier option should provide the energy boost you need to tackle an overwhelming amount of work. Consider any potential negative impact of your actions or behavior before you do something that you might later regret.

18. TUESDAY. Fair. Take a sensitive and conciliatory approach toward others this morning. It certainly is not in your best interests to upset intimate or business partners or alienate important customers. So tread softly. The feelings of a significant other could be easily wounded unless a little extra tender loving care is directed his or her way. By mid-morning trends are looking up. Those of you involved in a fund-raising event should be pleasantly surprised by the success of collective efforts to date. Have your say this afternoon, but be prepared for someone else to also take center stage espousing their ideas, thoughts, or demands. Romance is starred for tonight.

19. WEDNESDAY. Exacting. Adverse planetary vibes are in effect today. The Moon is continuing to move through your opposite sign of Cancer. So compromise and cooperation will be essential if enlisting help and support from other people is a priority. This isn't a good time to force your opinions and views on others. Instead, keep discussions practical and to the point without becoming overbearing. Someone close might be eager to provide the currently unattached Capricorn with a helping hand now. Don't turn down a blind date. The worst that can happen is a few hours spent with someone who doesn't meet your expectations. The best could be the start of a satisfying romantic attachment.

20. THURSDAY. Good. Today's Leo Moon is sure to bring a spot of drama and commotion. The deeper mysteries as well as the cycle of life could be a source of fascination now. More involvement with money belonging to others also appears likely. Major financial incentives could get the green light. For some Capricorns there may be additional money available to invest into company expansion or issuance of stocks. Outstanding debtors might be slow in paying money to those of you self-employed. There could be a holdup in an expected legacy or insurance claim. Lovers can share greater intimacy. The single Goat should be extra choosy about potential romantic partners.

21. FRIDAY. Accomplished. Trust your intuition today. Covering a debt might be worrying for some of you, especially if you don't have the money to pay an account in full. Take a proactive approach. Contact creditors directly and arrange to make regular payments, which should ease the strain. Capricorns who are employed in the field of debt collection should make strong progress in this endeavor, especially after lunch. Special projects are likely to be tackled with enthusiasm, although your energy could be a little low. Empathy and compassion will be used constructively by Goats in the counseling fields. Now you may prefer socializing with people who are more experienced, older, or wiser than you.

22. SATURDAY. Uneasy. Stable and security-conscious aptly describes today the majority of individuals born under your sign. However, there are times when the yearning for travel, adventure, and change becomes so overwhelming that the tried-and-true takes a backseat. This often occurs when the Moon is moving through Virgo, your ninth house of long-distance journeys, learning, and wisdom. Just make sure that the urge for variety doesn't also extend to your love life now. This isn't the time for rash or unpredictable behavior in this area. Friends and money are not a good mix. Lending money is not in your best interests unless you do not care whether or not the debt is repaid.

23. SUNDAY. Sociable. Your social calendar will fill up rather quickly now as the Sun moves into Scorpio, your house of friends, associates, and goals. Remaining open to new experiences can be soothing to the soul. A meal at a restaurant offering cuisine different from the usual fare can be an interesting way of sampling the customs and culture of another land. If you are conducting a long-distance love affair, plans to meet could come together now. Capricorns on vacation might find romance with someone in a far-off country. You are being encouraged to demonstrate your skills to the world and mingle with people who share common interests with you.

24. MONDAY. Fidgety. Increased agitation could lead to restlessness today. Introduce variety into your routine. Find activities that hold your interest in order to reduce the possible onset of boredom. Exams, lectures, and legal concerns should bring successful outcomes this morning when cosmic trends are supportive. As you move into the day, professional and business issues take over. By mid-afternoon the increased pressure could create tension and stress. Mixing business with pleasure can bring rewards, but effort and adjustments to original plans or ideas might be necessary beforehand. An outing with member of an organization might not live up to your expectations, but some benefits can be gained if you attend.

25. TUESDAY. Demanding. Your standing and prestige in the community could be in focus today. Many Goats seek a high profile and become respected members of your social and professional network. Meaningful work is always a positive experience for you. But it is essential to cater at times to loved ones. They also require your company and attention in full measure. Working longer hours or overtime could add pressure for the family-oriented Capricorn. Follow a time management plan and learn to delegate some of the lesser responsibilities so that quality of life can be enjoyed. Being connected with the right people can help you achieve some of your social objectives.

26. WEDNESDAY. Stable. Most of you should revel in today's celestial climate. Energetic Mars is in a positive link with stable Saturn, your ruler. So positive and directed action can be taken. Any obstacles encountered yesterday can be forgotten as your ability to resolve most problems returns full force. Conducting business affairs, negotiating tricky financial transactions, and furthering your career prospects are areas where advancement can be made. Be prepared to take the lead. Colleagues and superiors are likely to rely heavily on your expertise and experience. Be wary of divulging confidences. If you do reveal a secret, make sure it is to someone who can keep it.

27. THURSDAY. Smooth. It is another day when Capricorn folk should be feeling that all is right within your own world. A few minor problems could arise, but nothing that you cannot take care of with speed and efficiency. Moving up in your field of expertise may be the main priority, so taking on more responsibility is unlikely to faze most of you. Small gains may be on offer. Meaningful perks could arrive because of your efforts on the job. Many Goats are probably becoming more confident about sharing ideas. This confidence should be reflected in your ability to speak up with plenty of self-assurance and finesse. Seek stimulating company tonight.

28. FRIDAY. Powerful. By mid-morning the Moon enters Sagittarius in you twelfth house and represents your lunar low period. Nevertheless, today you can assert authority and leadership in a positive manner. It is essential that you do not let the power go to your head or let an inflated ego spoil your chances of gaining more respect and status. Arguing with others can be a time waster. So rather than insisting that they follow your lead, conserve your energy and demonstrate your capabilities by example. Also express your thoughts and plans with a large dash of humility. Then you should find that people will join your cause fairly quickly. A special celebration should be a joy to attend.

29. SATURDAY. Mixed. With the Sagittarius Moon impacting your twelfth house, your energy might be slightly lower. But your ambition and the will to succeed remain high. Confidence and caution should be well balanced, providing just the right amount of incentive to follow your cherished dreams and desires. Sudden technical problems could find many of you rushing out to acquire new equipment. However, seek advice before spending too much money. Otherwise, your bank account could suffer instead of remaining moderately healthy. Friends and group members will offer a good variety of social activities. Steer clear from raucous gatherings. A peaceful environment will appeal.

30. SUNDAY. Relaxing. Rest, relax, and recharge run-down batteries this morning. A good beginning to the day would also include breakfast in bed. Tackle personal tasks or small duties that don't require much thinking on your part. The urge to assist people in a charitable manner may arise. Providing support to the needy can be an emotionally fulfilling experience and help Goats of all ages build your karmic bank account. Once midday arrives, many of you will be ready to emerge from your cocoon and join the social whirl. Vim and vitality also rise later in the day, a gift of the Moon entering your own stable sign of Capricorn.

31. MONDAY. Chancy. The artistic and gifted Capricorn should experience lots of imaginative and inspired ideas as well as a few fantasies today. Your charm and magnetism remain enhanced. This is a good day to showcase your innate capabilities and strengths. However, it isn't such a great period for love or money matters. Those of you in committed relationships can receive loving and affectionate benefits. However, a vulnerable and naive demeanor could prove disastrous for those of you in a new love affair. Hold on tight to your money. Don't let anyone talk you into any get-rich-schemes. Take off the rose-colored glasses and avoid placing a child or lover on a pedestal. Have a happy Halloween!

NOVEMBER

1. TUESDAY. Pressured. There are strong indications of memory lapses as this new month gets under way. The fact that the year seems to have disappeared could also have something to do with any increased pressure you might be feeling in some areas of your life. However, as the Moon is in your sign of Capricorn, there is plenty of incentive to progress based on new ideas and plans and to move steadily ahead. Your popularity remains high, with a bevy of social invites continuing to arrive in verbal or electronic form. There is a need to understand people's motives. An associate or friend may give you misleading information, which might be intentional rather than innocent.

2. WEDNESDAY. Significant. Major planetary trends gather today. Savvy Mercury and saucy Venus both slide into Sagittarius, your twelfth house of secrets and solitude. These planets here give you a chance to review the past, examine the present, and make plans for the future. Many of you are bound to keep most of your thoughts to yourself rather than sharing them. There is a possibility that you could become involved in a secret love affair. Feelings may develop for someone who is currently unavailable. Ignore rumors circulating through your friendship network. More than likely this gossip is just the product of someone's fertile imagination.

3. THURSDAY. Lively. Your social calendar continues to fill up. Be careful not to overcommit; otherwise, burnout could occur. Sometimes, various comforts are just what you need to restore your joy in life. This isn't the time to place limits on yourself. Instead, be ready to have some fun and excitement. New emotional experiences, especially of the loving kind, can be a confidence booster as old inhibitions and insecurities are left behind. Enjoy the thrills that come with a new love affair, but be prepared for the romance and exhilaration to fade quickly. Curbing the urge to splurge could require a strong dose of willpower even for the thrifty Goat.

4. FRIDAY. Reassuring. Mixed vibes descend today. Although not everything will go the way you hope, dreams and thoughts are active. So this can be a good period for decision making, calculating, and planning. Cherished goals should be pursued vigorously, especially if you feel that these aims are worthwhile. Have faith and put plans into motion. Friends are important now, and there can be plenty of social interaction. Look to people in a high position of authority for any guidance and support that you are currently seeking. This coming weekend can be a great time to organize a special retreat to a place that makes you feel relaxed and refreshed.

5. SATURDAY. Uncertain. Adjustments to plans might be needed to avoid friction today. This isn't the time to go along with a plan just because someone else wants you to. Be your own person. Ultimately, you are responsible for your decisions and choices. Sorting out the truth of an issue could be difficult as you may be caught in the middle of a situation. Don't be disappointed if someone you thought was reliable lets you down or makes a promise that cannot be kept. Capricorns who are involved in a clandestine relationship might need to face the facts that perhaps you are wasting your time and that the romance is unlikely to go the distance.

6. SUNDAY. Affectionate. Love is in the air, and this is a day to spend time with a significant other. Quiet pleasures such as staying in bed a little longer this morning could provide emotional comfort. Those of you contemplating a vacation should consider a quiet and cozy retreat with a lover rather than an action-packed trip jammed full of sightseeing and tourist traps. You might need to look to the past to review a lesson that remains relevant now. If you are still learning from the experience, the next time around you will know the right way to respond. Reading or researching a topic of interest will be worthwhile for the Capricorn who is determined to expand your knowledge.

7. MONDAY. Deceptive. Domestic affairs create angst as your list of chores begins to pile up. It might be time to divide up the household duties among all family members so that you are not overburdened with all of the tasks. The career-minded Goat may become frustrated with a partner if you feel that he or she is not as ambitious or as motivated as you are. The actions of others could be loaded with deception, and your interests are likely to be ignored. So take care. Make sure that there is enough money on the credit card or in the bank if you go shopping today. Otherwise, an embarrassing situation could occur and you may come home empty-handed.

8. TUESDAY. Difficult. Adverse planetary trends prevail throughout the day. Don't continue to play along with emotional games if you no longer want the same drama continually repeated. Persistence is needed to make lasting changes because old patterns and habits may resurface. However, the determined Goat has the ability and the power to make lasting transformations now. Making minor changes can involve varying the order in which you do routine daily tasks. That may avert boredom. A few personal items or touches can brighten up your work or home office. Defer seeking a pay raise if that is your intention now. Wait another nine days to do so.

9. WEDNESDAY. Fair. The day ahead looks rosier than yesterday. Trying to change a family member may be fraught with difficulties and unlikely to work. Change can only be initiated by those who desire it enough to take personal action. Just be there to provide support. Seeking pleasure may be your aim once the working day is over. Thrifty Goats shouldn't have a problem with overindulging and splashing money around. However, some of you less disciplined might need to marshal a strong measure of self-control while the Moon wanders through Taurus, your house of pleasure, leisure, and treasure. Use moderation; enjoy a comfortable evening, and your head and wallet will thank you in the morning.

10. THURSDAY. Sensitive. Highly charged emotions and sensitivities could creep to the surface today. The Taurus Full Moon accentuates your house of play, leisure, children, romance, and creative talents. This lunation bodes well for projects or issues relating to these areas. Fruition or closure is foreseen. Extra inspiration can enhance artistic ventures. Capricorns negotiating a sports grant or sponsorship could be pleased with the results. Goats in a romantic relationship should experience increased zing. However, power struggles might occur if tension already exists in your union. Discussions regarding the cost of a hobby, entertainment, or children's needs should be deferred or handled carefully for the next few days.

11. FRIDAY. Motivating. Mars is on the move, sojourning into Virgo, your house of travel, education, sports, and philosophical beliefs. Expect plenty of action to take place in these arenas from now until the end of the year. If climbing up the ladder of success is your motivation and ultimate goal, now is an excellent period to review educational options, training courses, or an apprenticeship that can help you to eventually realize your goals. Capricorns organizing a class reunion should make positive headway, with the promise of a successful event. If at all possible, defer legal action. The outcome is far from certain when dynamo Mars is visiting analytical Virgo.

12. SATURDAY. Uneven. Begin your day in a healthy way. Take a brisk walk, if the weather is reasonable, followed by a nutritional breakfast. Stretching for thirty minutes can be advantageous. Those of you who have a home gym should endeavor to use it every day instead of allowing it to lie idle and unused. Avoid rushing around. Watch where you are going whether you are a pedestrian or a motorist. Issues with in-laws could arise, so defer visiting now. Keep a low profile if you are attending social gatherings with extended family. A marriage or religious ceremony could hold special significance, but prepare for a few obstacles or alterations to plans.

13. SUNDAY. Disconcerting. It is another day when things might be a little bumpy. Your energy level may be a little low, especially if you went to bed late last night. Take action now if battling the bulge isn't working. Renew your gym membership, take up a sport, or change your diet so that you can be fitter and slimmer as the festive season approaches. A hunger to gain more knowledge can be satisfied in various ways. Attend a conference or seminar relating to current interests or join the local library and read up on selected subjects. Be careful of joining fringe groups or blindly following a guru. Such a move could leave you dissatisfied and angry.

14. MONDAY. Cooperative. Changes around the home or on the job may be disconcerting. However, if you take a flexible and easygoing approach and you embrace the changes, this small bump shouldn't become a hurdle difficult to climb over. Cooperation makes things flow in a positive direction, whether this is with domestic chores or with employment tasks. Capricorns attending a community meeting, working on an advertising promotion, or dealing with the general public should find that your ability to compromise works strongly in your favor and keeps everyone happy. Around mid-afternoon it may be necessary to use a larger dose of tact and diplomacy with a business partner or client.

15. TUESDAY. Mixed. Lunar trends are quiet because the Moon is connecting with only one planet today. Keep the lines of communication open with a loved one. Even if you don't agree with their views or opinions, be honest and calm while still standing your own ground. That can result in a better outcome for all concerned and will reduce the chances of an argument occurring. Parents, be alert for signals from a child. A youngster might be keeping a secret that would be better divulged. Friends or associates could expose you to a new topic of interest that will have you heading for the bookstore to learn more.

16. WEDNESDAY. Restrained. Several astrological patterns form in the cosmos today. Keep your expectations fairly low. Not everyone can maintain the same high standard that you expect of yourself and loved ones. If you are in a loving union, keeping secrets from your partner is not something that you normally do. So now would be a good time to confess anything that has been kept hidden. Mood swings are possible as the day progresses and the Moon shifts into your Leo eighth house. If an intense atmosphere develops, endeavor to maintain a lighthearted approach. Steer clear of discussion involving money or resources shared with other people. Be moderate in all things now and over the next few days.

17. THURSDAY. Satisfactory. A happier day emerges for most Capricorns. Overindulging, being extra secretive, and promising more than you can deliver are all areas that need watching. If you cannot meet a deadline, inform whoever is waiting. Otherwise, your reputation, something that you strive to maintain at a high level, could suffer. Your ambition is strong. If you choose the right moment to ask the boss for a pay raise, you could receive an affirmative response. Moving forward one step at a time is sensible and should please the stable Goat. You know that you can handle more responsibility, so put in the extra effort for all to see.

18. FRIDAY. Empowering. Belief in yourself is rising and will continue to do so over the coming years. Even if the day has a few rough patches, there isn't any reason to be displeased. Most important, transformative Pluto is moving through your sign and impacting your first house of personality. You will come to realize that change is unavoidable and that you need to be yourself. The travel bug may bite. Those of you taking a vacation over the festive period should begin planning an itinerary that suits you and your traveling companions. A grant to study at home or abroad could please the dedicated Goat. Those of you competing in a debate team should be happy with your effort.

19. SATURDAY. Stable. You can make whatever you will of the day ahead. The trends are a little discordant. But if effort is applied, minor adverse trends can be overlooked. The call for travel and adventure lures you. A weekend trip or even an overnight stay in the country might be just what is needed to rest and relax your weary body and soul. Contacting in-laws and other relatives at a distance would be better done via e-mail or phone now rather than a visit in person. The timing might not be right for you to drop in unexpectedly. A goal could be finally realized. Attending a local political caucus or a community business conference should be worth the time for the knowledge that you will gain.

20. SUNDAY. Low-key. Your physical resources may be a bit depleted and the thought of conducting daily activities could be distasteful. Going out to socialize might be entirely off the agenda. However, make the effort, and an outing can be enjoyed. Choose quiet and relaxing entertainment. Keeping an open mind may be difficult. Understanding the beliefs of someone close might be hard, especially if he or she has grown up in an environment different from yours. Childhood conditioning can be overcome. Give people the benefit of the doubt and listen to their opinions. You might find that they really aren't that different after all.

21. MONDAY. Slow. A lethargic mood lingers on, which can be very unhelpful for those of you with a heavy workload. Pace yourself and distribute tasks among coworkers if possible. Ask yourself what makes you happy now, Capricorn. If your answer is career or business advancement, talking to people higher up the ladder can be enlightening. They might provide a few pointers on how to climb to the top more quickly. Young Goats attending a job interview or audition should be very clear about your expectations. Be honest when describing your expertise and experience. Prepare the guest room, as you might be receiving visitors from afar.

22. TUESDAY. Calm. Although you are heading into the busiest time of the year, your preference might be to sit back and observe rather than participate. Your vitality and initiative may be low, which could create frustration for the hardworking and energetic Goat. Be patient. Today the Sun enters Sagittarius, your twelfth house, signaling a period for you to stop, rest, and rejuvenate body, mind, and spirit. However, Sagittarius is an outgoing sign. So having fun will be of interest. But keeping a lower profile is also something that you will covet more. If you need a vacation, make reservations now and begin preparing to take off to a wonderful exotic destination.

23. WEDNESDAY. Productive. A boost of power, ambition, and energy sent by the friendly meeting between Mars and Pluto can raise your vim and vitality. Contracts and agreements should work out favorably, although making sense of complex paperwork and legal jargon might require more effort and attention to details. Your resume might benefit from a few extra qualifications. Online courses via the Internet could provide various options for upgrading your skills. Capricorn students shouldn't suffer too much stress or pressure while taking exams. Those of you taking driving lessons are likely to demonstrate a good understanding of the rules and regulations required to pass the test and get a license.

24. THURSDAY. Sizzling. Becoming more in tune with your instincts could be an apt description of what is happening in your life right now. Trust your gut reactions. Also record your dreams and visions. Important messages may be bubbling up from your subconscious. Lovely Venus is happily engaging with mystical Neptune now. So ask for favors from people close to you and from the universe. Your wishes may be granted. Inspiration could come through another. Capricorns with talent can put creative skills to work. Handmade gifts could be a hit with family members and a money-saver for the conservative Goat. People will delight in the products of your imagination. Love is in the air, so spread it around.

25. FRIDAY. Charitable. A romantic atmosphere lingers on. A Sagittarius New Moon shines the spotlight into your house of secrets and solitude. Keeping to yourself can bring a sense of peace and well-being. A secret love affair could develop now. However, be prepared for the consequences if one of you is already attached. Someone is bound to find out about this clandestine relationship in the next month or two. Kindness, consideration, and compassion you have shown to people sometime in the past may be repaid. A continued involvement helping the needy can be a wonderfully fulfilling experience. If you have time to spare, consider volunteering a few hours of your time to a community organization or charity.

26. SATURDAY. Serene. Prayer and meditation can be a beneficial means of stress relief. A class in yoga could also keep your emotions balanced as well as bring peace and contentment into your life. Clearing your head of thoughts that are no longer relevant or that serve a useful purpose can be the beginning of obtaining a fresh perspective that will lead to a new start. Take care while shopping. Impulse buying could cause havoc with your budget. If you cannot return goods for refund or credit, you will be stuck with purchases that you may not want and really cannot afford. When it comes to matters of the heart, beware jumping to conclusions or rushing into a commitment. Practice due diligence.

27. SUNDAY. Loving. Romantic trends continue to heat up the atmosphere. This can be a wonderful day for couples in a committed union. Use quality time together to strengthen loving bonds. Enjoy the pleasures of being in a twosome. However, Capricorn singles do need to be wary of jumping into a love affair without having some idea of what you could be letting yourself in for. Be prepared for the consequences. If you go into a romantic encounter with your eyes wide open and no expectations, a thrilling experience is foreseen. Pleasurable pursuits are bound to be more expensive than envisioned. Take extra cash along to ensure that you have enough money to pay for the cab fare home.

28. MONDAY. Renewing. A new cycle has begun now that Venus has settled into your own sign of Capricorn. A more magnetic and charming demeanor should be on display. You can project yourself with confidence and self-assurance. Just about everything will seem to be possible from now until the end of the year. You are ready to embrace new responsibilities, adventure, and excitement People will grant favors. Someone close could become your personal fountain of wisdom and knowledge. Those of you seeking a sense of accomplishment are bound to find it now. You can revel in the romantic trends prevailing. For some Goats, however, a love affair might be sweet but short-lived.

29. TUESDAY. Spirited. A generous approach toward others may be rewarded in numerous ways that make you feel happy and contented. Take care of the myriad of small tasks or details that have been neglected recently. Repairing, mending, or recycling objects around the home can free up more space and is great feng shui. Several alterations or transformations have probably taken place over the last couple of years, and these may have changed your life forever. Although at times it might not feel good, regeneration can be healthy and will put you on the desired path. Begin purchasing odds and ends needed for the upcoming festive season.

30. WEDNESDAY. Helpful. A short trip into the countryside or to a new shopping mall could quell restless feelings today. Beware gifts that are supposedly free, especially through telephone or Internet offers. Most of these specials are not free and can be quite costly in hidden fees. Flattery and exaggerated compliments could come your way, but most Capricorns are too savvy to fall for that type of trickery and deception. Money can attract money. For some of you this could be a day when you receive a moderate boost of cash that will help cover a few festive expenses. You can mix business with pleasure now as long as you are not overly generous giving special deals or promotions.

DECEMBER

1. THURSDAY. Intense. Passion and desire rise as the new month begins. Lover Venus merges with powerful Pluto, increasing the depth of feeling and emotion within a personal partnership. Capricorn singles should experience progress on the love front, with a blossoming romance flourishing quicker than expected. Doing things your way should be easier. People may be more willing to provide assistance and support. If you have a special wish, practicing creative visualization could help turn what you imagine into reality. Seeking a salary increase, promotion, or sports sponsorship could bring the desired outcome. Just ask the right person the right questions.

2. FRIDAY. Varied. Meetings, gatherings, and get-togethers may be more frequent than usual. A dose of the dramatic could color your day. Everyone is likely to be more aggressive now as the Sun and Mars link up in a challenging formation. If this dynamic energy is used constructively, progress can be swift and you can get what you want. Responsibilities that you fulfill will earn you a pat on the back from colleagues. Your reputation will benefit. Physical exercise, housecleaning, and repair work are excellent ways to release excess energy. Social pursuits are unlikely to proceed smoothly and could cost more than expected.

3. SATURDAY. Supportive. There is a chance that some Capricorns will be busier than usual today, although this might not be what you want on a leisure day. However, being on the move can help keep your motivation and enthusiasm elevated. Your energy could be lower, so avoid labor-intensive tasks and jobs that require endurance. You may run out of steam before completing the work. You could meet a person who offers a few words of wisdom, so listen and learn something of value. If you are concerned about a family issue, sharing the load with a sibling could help to relieve any stress you may be experiencing. Even if the problem isn't solved, at least a dear one knows of your worries.

4. SUNDAY. Trying. With a bevy of celestial patterns forming, you can expect various obstacles, challenges, and achievements to occur on this erratic day. Everyone is likely to have an opinion, so be prepared for a few disagreements or debates when people disagree with your point of view. Devoting some of your time to volunteer for charitable deeds will be emotionally fulfilling. Many Capricorn folk gain satisfaction from sacrificing your own interests in order to benefit others. The failure of another blind date could bring frustration, but don't worry. Romantic bliss is unlikely to elude you forever, and might be just around the corner.

5. MONDAY. Happy. This can be a fun day as sexual Mars happily engages with loving Venus. It is a good period for Capricorn shoppers in search of that special sexy outfit or that perfect festive gift for your lover. Romance can be magical. A sincere and heartfelt gesture to a significant other can heal any issues in a love affair and will strengthen the ties that bind. Those of you unattached could find an irresistible romantic partner with whom you soon become one half of a couple. If you have a manuscript ready for publication, this is a positive period to take action and send the fruits of your labor to an agent or editor.

6. TUESDAY. Buoyant. A friendly and outgoing mood prevails today. Socializing with relatives or friends could be a wonderful way to use this happy energy. It is difficult to cut back on spending at this time of year, but you can reduce the chance of going overboard by implementing a few economic measures. Steer clear of the shops, leave the credit cards at home, and invite people over for a casual meal if you are in a hospitable mood. Goats who live alone or who commute at night and want to feel safer should consider signing up for a self-defense course. You can learn a few moves to protect yourself. Martial arts also help you reach a high level of fitness.

7. WEDNESDAY. Watchful. Members of your sign of Capricorn are known to be frugal and cautious. Both of these innate characteristics need to be in play today. Even those of you who can stretch the budget further than most other people may find the cash flow tightening up a little now. Be firm about good money management. Be wary of heavily discounted goods, check the quality of your purchases, keep receipts, and count your change. Mistakes can happen, and are very likely to happen now. When it comes to a special person in your life, an adjustment in your thinking may be needed to avoid placing someone on a pedestal. Wishful thinking is bound to set you up for future disappointment.

8. THURSDAY. Good. Quick thinking can save the day, and you have the facility to make things happen. Your ability to tackle complicated or demanding tasks can raise your profile. However, show modesty. There is a chance that you will display a big ego or a domineering attitude. If you do, appreciation for your efforts will soon dissipate. Be advised to take an open and less critical attitude. Then your popularity is sure to rise. Contracts and agreements can start to be negotiated now. But thoroughly read any documentation that relates to financial matters while Mercury is still in retreat. Children might be more disruptive than usual, so you will need to find suitable distractions to keep youngsters amused.

9. FRIDAY. Difficult. A trying day looms. Handle problems and issues with your usual aplomb and calm demeanor. Then the pressure should be successfully managed, if not reduced. For some Capricorns, the job may be extra demanding as the workweek ends. Errors made by other people are not your fault, so don't take the blame or feel guilty. Health and diet come under scrutiny now. You want to make a few changes as the festive season approaches. It will be easier to gain weight at that time of year. If this will be a problem, cut down on your food and alcohol consumption to avoid putting on the pounds. Clearing the pantry and fridge of junk food can be a good start to implementing healthful eating patterns.

10. SATURDAY. Stressful. Another day dawns when you could feel the strain of too much work and not enough time to complete designated tasks. The Full Moon culminates in Gemini, your house of health and service. This lunation will heighten your emotions as well as the emotions of the people around you. Tread gently. A large dose of tact and diplomacy might be required if anyone begins to show signs of strain from an overflowing workload. Alternative health treatments such as hypnosis or acupuncture could prove effective if orthodox methods are not helping to cure minor ailments. Consider writing your New Year resolutions a little early, with emphasis on overall well-being.

11. SUNDAY. Fair. There is not much relief in sight from the cosmos again today. Lunar trends are mixed and require adjustments to your thinking, strategies, and plans. When it comes to loved ones, the right words can make a difference. So remember to think about what you are going to say before you speak. If effort is applied, your relationship can be revitalized and a successful transformation should take place. Be realistic when organizing holiday social activities. If expenses are climbing, now is the time to implement cost-cutting measures. A change of mind or the departure of another could provide a professional opportunity that would be worthwhile for you to follow up.

12. MONDAY. Nurturing. With the light of the Cancer Moon shining into your relationship and marriage arena, your partner will appreciate the tender loving care that you bestow now. For many Goats, personal transformation and change have occurred over the last couple of years. This should have led to increased self-empowerment and growth, and will continue to make a positive difference in your life. Moving to another area or renovating your current home could have been the big event that gave a new start. Now the enhanced living conditions contribute to your overall well-being. If you haven't started your holiday shopping, you are missing out on all the fun. Head to your favorite department store and embrace the festive atmosphere.

13. TUESDAY. Useful. The time for retreat is nearing an end as planet Mercury prepares to move forward in the zodiac once again. If things haven't been going that well recently, you can breathe a sigh of relief. Some of the delays and bumps experienced lately should begin to disappear. If you know someone has been keeping a secret from you, the wait might be just about over. A confidence could be finally revealed. Capricorn folk who have been held back in your attempts to complete a special goal, especially one relating to an educational pursuit, could find things starting to fall smoothly into place now. Would-be travelers waiting for a passport or a visa should soon receive good news.

14. WEDNESDAY. Strategic. Delicate negotiations on a financial matter could demand attention. But it would be better to wait before making major plans. There may be a number of issues that still need to be resolved before the transaction can be successfully completed. If you are owed money by friends or relatives, it might be time to ask for repayment. Capricorn business owners should chase up debtors to ensure that you have enough money coming in to pay your creditors when accounts become due. This is a good time to clear out your desk and to get rid of old business files that are no longer required. If you expect visitors are coming during the holiday break, start now to remove clutter from the guest rooms.

15. THURSDAY. Promising. The day ahead looks promising, especially through the daylight hours. Productivity should rise, and plenty can be accomplished if consistent effort is applied. This is a period when it is easier to experience a close and loving bond with a personal partner and to enjoy harmony on the home front. Financial deliberations with a business partner should also run smoothly. If one of you is eager to buy the other out, coming to an agreement on the worth of joint property should be amicable. Once nightfall arrives, a few issues are likely to arise. So it would be wise to defer deep and meaningful discussions until a more opportune time.

16. FRIDAY. Helpful. Some tension marks the day. For many Goats, this could be a certainty. Consider splurging on a head and shoulders massage or start planning your next vacation. Check out the Internet for last-minute deals, and you could find a package that is just right for your travel needs. For many Capricorn people it is time to stop and consider where you are going and how you want to get there. Facing your fears might be the first step. Then you won't act in an uncharacteristic manner and run away from issues instead of confronting problems head-on. Use the power sent by planet Pluto as it transits your sign and your first house of personality. Act in a way that best serves your interests.

17. SATURDAY. Vibrant. Energy and enthusiasm arrive in abundance. Studying for a special exam, attending an interesting seminar, or organizing a ceremony are activities that can bring joy for many Goats. A special celebration held today should be a highlight. A public speaking engagement might be the beginning of a new and lucrative sideline. Any product or service you advertise in the papers or via electronic media should do well and generate good financial gains. This is a favorable day to finish promotional material, a thesis, or a book review. Capricorns beginning a full-time or part-time enterprise should find it easy to design a business logo and slogan.

18. SUNDAY. Guarded. A mixed bag of astrological influences descends today. The demands of employment duties are likely to clash with domestic concerns, adding a little stress. Those of you planning to attend a festive business function should plan to share your time with colleagues and family members so that no one feels neglected. A best friend or a significant other might be detached and evasive, making you wonder what you have done for this attitude to occur. More than likely it has nothing to do with you. Your loved one probably just needs a little space and freedom to sort out his or her issues. Keep a low profile if you attend a gathering of older family members.

19. MONDAY. Pleasant. A much better day seems promised. Most things should proceed smoothly, except some issues regarding money. It might be hard to get much work done when a dreamy quality permeates the air. But perhaps this is a positive and might encourage some of you to take a more leisurely approach to the day. As a hardworking and diligent Goat, you are entitled to a day off every now and then. It is good for the body, mind, and spirit. For the career-minded Capricorn, your business reputation will be your main priority. Ensure that all responsibilities under your control are moving ahead as expected. A holiday atmosphere will make life very pleasant for those of you on the job.

20. TUESDAY. Upbeat. The celestial heavens bring a welcome lift to the day. However, forget the saying that you can never have enough good cheer. It will not be the case today. A tendency to go overboard is evident, and you could easily overindulge on desserts, splash money around, or drink more alcohol than you should. Exercising self-control is something that most Capricorns are very good at. Apply moderation today, or you might regret your actions tomorrow. Love and romance are starred as long as moderation is also observed here. Steer clear of the casino, and be wary of speculative investments. You can still go out on the town and have fun without stinting yourself.

21. WEDNESDAY. Positive. Luscious Venus is now sliding through Aquarius, your house of personal possessions, and is harmonizing happily with excitable Uranus. This is a positive, and you can expect to receive lots of lovely goodies during the festive season. Something that you have always wanted could finally arrive, generating pleasure and exhilaration. A longtime link with a good friend could turn romantic. Capricorns without partners could also experience a number of thrilling encounters that might make your heart flutter wildly. Don't rush headlong into a relationship, though. Under current planetary trends you do need to move at your usual slow and steady pace. Long-term lovers are content to share affectionate accord.

22. THURSDAY. Happy Birthday! Well before dawn the Sun moves into your own sign of Capricorn, marking the beginning of a very powerful and empowering period. New projects and plans can move ahead smoothly and successfully. Life should become exciting and lively. A very optimistic outlook surrounds you. It gives a big and energetic assist to your overall well-being and health. Your ability to attract money increases. This can be the perfect time to approach a superior for a salary increase or a promotion. You might receive a better than expected end-of-year bonus. Those of you who work on commission or tips are also likely to experience a boost to income.

23. FRIDAY. Lucky. Good luck abounds now. Even though the Moon is moving through Sagittarius, your house of solitary action, your urge to socialize and have fun remains strong. Restlessness could also account for your need to mix and mingle. You want to pursue the many activities that are accumulating in your social calendar. Challenges arising on the job could be testing your patience and resolve. However, your ability to straighten things out despite the pressure is admirable. Teammates appreciate your tenacity and perseverance to see a job through to the end. Grasp all opportunities that have the potential to bring you closer to your cherished goals.

24. SATURDAY. Empowering. A wonderful day is foreseen. A New Moon in your own sign of Capricorn offers loads of chances to move ahead in whatever area holds your interest. People will flock around you. Your popularity rises and social invitations pour in. Those of you in the public eye will make a good impression on your audience. An honor or public accolade could come your way. A social event might present an interesting opportunity to network. Special personal plans are likely to move quickly ahead. Volunteering at a charity function, singing in a choir, or wrapping festive gifts with loved ones can provide plenty of emotional comfort and joy.

25. SUNDAY. Merry Christmas! The celestial heavens are smiling on Goats today. However you choose to spend this holiday, sharing hospitality with near ones and dear ones can bring a wonderful sense of personal peace and tranquillity. Make light of any obstacles and challenges that come along. These will quickly dissipate if a sense of humor and fun is displayed. Don't rush through the day. Slow down and savor the magical moments spent with guests and loved ones. Keep your camera close by to capture a lasting keepsake of family pride and happiness. As a bonus you can provide guests with a memento of one of the highlights of 2011.

26. MONDAY. Active. Capricorn energy remains enhanced as lively cosmic trends ensure that most of you will be kept busy. For those of you who don't mind the crowds and are seeking a few bargains, the post-festive sales could be calling. This is a good day to head to the department stores. Unwanted gifts can be replaced with more appropriate items. Faulty appliances or clothing that doesn't fit can be returned for credit. Money and how to make more of it will remain of interest. This can be a positive period to find methods of improving the bank account, reducing expenditure, and building personal assets. Take a break and rest this evening.

27. TUESDAY. Beneficial. Some Capricorns could be wishing that you hadn't been quite so generous with your holiday gift giving and socializing. Stop worrying. Right now you are unlikely to be splashing your money around. Remember, every now and then it can be enjoyable to open up your wallet and share the wealth with those who deserve it. Mixing business with pleasure can lead to positive contacts that may increase the bottom line next year. Don't be afraid to cultivate people who can help you advance. Vacationers should really spoil yourself a little. You have earned the fruits of your labor throughout the year. New Year resolutions should already be well thought out, and you might consider putting some into action now.

28. WEDNESDAY. Manageable. Capricorn people who are faced with going off to an unexciting job every day should take a closer look at your life, expectations, and experience. Routine work could seem boring even for the disciplined Goat, so add variety to spice things up a little. There may be easy ways to introduce more variety or excitement into your daily activities. Some of you may look for another job that offers better compensation. Finding good methods to improve effectiveness and efficiency will occupy your time. However, this aim is constructive. Saving time in the long run can be of benefit to you, your employers, and your employees. Financial gains are foreseen.

29. THURSDAY. Fruitful. You will feel the full force of positive astrological aspects today because the life-giving Sun is merging with powerhouse Pluto in your sign of Capricorn. Confidence and self-assurance rise dramatically now, along with heightened ambition and the will to succeed. Many of you could experience the sensation that your identity is in the process of transformation and is continuing to evolve. Be willing to experiment with new options that hold the promise of greater opportunity and self-growth. You are ready to climb higher toward the summit. This is a favorable day to contact friends, casual acquaintances, and colleagues to arrange a social gathering for New Year's Eve.

30. FRIDAY. Favorable. Capricorn charm and charisma continue to attract favors and support. Your popularity remains high. Still, there may be a few rough patches to make today challenging. Those of you seeking a home mortgage, a personal loan, or an extension on credit cards shouldn't have any problem now if the paperwork has been filled in correctly. Answers to questions could come through general discussions. So listen intently and you should learn something to your advantage. Don't push siblings or relatives too hard. Leaving others to their own devices and allowing them the freedom to make their own choices can aid their personal growth.

31. SATURDAY. Motivating. As 2011 comes to an end ready for the new year to begin, put self-doubts in the past and move confidently forward. Contact friends and extended family that you haven't spoken to recently. Catch up on gossip and the highlights of their year. Immerse yourself in celebrations. Forget about pressing worries for now. Just concentrate on all the good things occurring in your life. A casual get-together or even a formal party at home may suit some Goats this evening. Other Goats might prefer to mix and mingle and to be seen out in public. There is a hint of romance in the air. A surprise proposal could end this year on a very high note indeed.

CAPRICORN
NOVEMBER–DECEMBER 2010

November 2010

1. MONDAY. Favorable. Pleasant trends greet Capricorn folks as the new month begins. Try not to get too bogged down with the finer details in your search for the truth. You could find yourself chomping at the bit, wanting to rush ahead and take risks. On the other hand you may have an urge to analyze and dissect every situation and issue. Taking time to research and plan what you hope to achieve can lessen self-inflicted pressure and tension. Sometimes dreams are the way your unconscious can communicate and provide answers. So paying attention to them can be the means of receiving universal benefits. Couples should make plans for togetherness this evening, and singles may experience luck in love.

2. TUESDAY. Constructive. Sharing valuable information with like-minded folks could prove gratifying. Just be wary of preaching. Not everyone is ready or willing to listen to your pearls of wisdom, so choose to share with those who are genuinely seeking. Your memory should be sharp, which can be very useful if you are called upon to speak in public or asked to train other employees on the job. Don't be discouraged if you encounter a technical or electronic fault. If you cannot fix the problem yourself, call on someone who can; then watch how it is done, gaining information that can be useful later on. An interesting documentary may be a good choice of entertainment this evening.

3. WEDNESDAY. Cooperative. Diplomacy and tact are today's weapons of choice. If your expertise and common sense are called upon to settle a workplace argument, take a firm and fair approach. Keep in mind that more can be achieved if the team is in harmony than when there is discord and tension. Capricorn folks tend to be happy when their work or community efforts are noticed by others. Performing good deeds can raise your profile, earning you respect from other people as well as making you feel good about yourself. You might even receive well-deserved public acclaim, or an honor may be bestowed in recognition of your services.

4. THURSDAY. Manageable. The focus remains on career, business, and the work environment. Beautifying your surroundings to provide more comfort and aesthetic pleasure on the job could find you opening your wallet to purchase a few special items that will add color and style. A business matter might need more effort, increasing the time you must spend dealing with it. It is important to get it right now in order to reduce the chance of the matter becoming drawn out. If a good friend seems upset or distant, don't take it personally; their distress is unlikely to have anything to do with you. Try not to question and probe for the reason. This person will confide in you when and if ready.

5. FRIDAY. Fruitful. Capricorn home lovers and artistic types might have an urge to use their special skills on a personal project. Restoring old pieces of furniture to their former glory can be immensely satisfying for the savvy Capricorn eager to demonstrate creativity and also to save money. Laughing is a wonderful way to unwind from the working week and get in the mood for weekend excursions. Including plenty of humor in the day should make you and your colleagues feel good. Couples can make the most of increased passion, while the currently single can express affection through a romantic dalliance with a special person.

6. SATURDAY. Diverse. A bevy of planetary patterns is forming, with most of the prevailing energy involving mischievous Mercury. Prepare for confusion and unexpected events to shake you out of any self-imposed rut. Plans to meet with friends could be disrupted, or messages that are received or forwarded may be misunderstood. Pay your own way when socializing with a group. Refuse to loan money to someone you don't know all that well; the chance of the money being returned any time soon seems slim. The New Moon in Scorpio conveys opportunities to begin a new business project or an enterprising fund-raising venture with a group or organization. A pay raise or a promotion might be the source of increased income for you.

7. SUNDAY. Relaxing. Recharge your batteries for the workweek ahead. Spending quality leisure time curled up in bed with a good book or reading the Sunday newspaper might be your idea of heaven this morning. You have an increased need for solace, and you could utilize this time productively to write, read a fantasy novel, attend a religious service, or take care of personal duties. Going to the movies is another good form of escape, and today could find you at the theater enjoying an imaginary world with a friend or special companion. Neptune, the planet currently reigning supreme in Aquarius, your house of personal finances, moves forward now. Neptune going direct will help you to regain control of money management.

8. MONDAY. Revealing. There may be a time today when the urge to stop work or whatever you are doing and ponder the true meaning of life becomes overwhelming. The realization may dawn that not everyone has the same values and ethics as you, since everyone matures at a different pace. Choose low-key activities that require very little energy, and allow yourself time to contemplate, read, meditate, and generally just feed yourself with knowledge. Capricorns who like to wager should use restraint when placing a bet because optimism might be misplaced. Mercury now moves into Sagittarius, your twelfth house of secrets and solitude. Mercury here is likely to persuade you to keep thoughts, ideas, and opinions to yourself for a while.

9. TUESDAY. Liberating. Appearance and personal grooming take on more importance as the Moon whizzes into your own sign of Capricorn. Everything in your wardrobe may seem too old, too tight, or just not right. Perhaps it isn't entirely about the clothes, but also a need to create a new and trendy image that provides a big boost to your self-confidence. Fluctuating emotions could be an issue, especially if this adversely affects your working day. Intense feelings will pass, although for writers and other creative types this could be a day when some great work is produced. Enjoying a coffee break with friends could be good for the soul, especially if lighthearted banter creates plenty of good humor.

10. WEDNESDAY. Noteworthy. Whoever said that life wasn't meant to be easy obviously spoke from experience, and might have been a Capricorn! You're likely to confront challenges on the job scene, but this is where you can come into your own and produce your best effort. Take the reins and don't hesitate to showcase innate leadership qualities if required. If you are having a bad hair day, take yourself off to the local spa or salon for a relaxing full makeover. Pay extra attention to your skin and teeth. If you need to have any procedures done, make an appointment now before you find reasons to put off visiting the dentist or doctor or other specialist.

11. THURSDAY. Smooth. This is a good day to check your credit card balance and then head to the stores for a few essential items and treats just for you. Take along a shopping friend or a workmate if you'll need advice on what suits you best. A happy and friendly workplace is important, but there will always be an invisible line between the staff and the boss. If you are the one in charge, be friendly but beware talking over management issues with employees who are under your authority. Capricorns who recently moved to a new location and are a little lonely shouldn't remain that way for long. Strong, positive energy surrounds friendships, so expanding your circle of acquaintances should come with ease.

12. FRIDAY. Encouraging. If you have been dreaming about a new computer or the latest electronic gizmo, the opportunity to purchase up-to-date technology may come through work. Or you may spot a sale on the most recent gadget while out browsing the stores and decide that you must have one for home. If your working environment is in need of an overhaul, today might find Capricorn bosses being willing to pay for improvements. Just be sure to first check with the staff about what is lacking and what is needed for more efficiency on the job. This is a favorable period to finalize plans for a festive work party or other function designed to maintain good employee morale.

13. SATURDAY. Uncertain. Memory lapses could strike as the Moon prepares to cross over dreamy Neptune, creating a foggy atmosphere. Don't be alarmed if you find yourself forgetting the simplest of things or having to ask someone to repeat what was just said. It would be wise to record monetary expenditure, especially when using credit cards, so you are spared any unpleasant surprises later on. On the positive side, the current creative spell can produce bright, inspired ideas. However, it may be wise to wait a few days before actually attempting to turn these thoughts into concrete form. Charities may prove the biggest winners today, as your increased compassion and empathy will probably lead you to give more.

14. SUNDAY. Idyllic. Capricorn sensitivity is strong as this day begins, and your shoulder is apt to be the one that other people want to lean on or even shed a few tears on. Because your feelings are heightened, recording your own thoughts should be easier than usual. Signing up for or attending a short course that requires creative or imaginative input may be perfect if you are eager to evolve spiritually or artistically. Singing in a choir may be an emotional experience for some, while other Goats find crooning along with the radio or a karaoke machine a truly uplifting experience. Listening to relaxing music or attending a musical performance can also help calm frayed nerves.

15. MONDAY. Fortunate. Lucky Capricorns have a great day to begin the workweek, even if that involves going off to the daily grind. Positive planetary trends send auspicious vibes along with the ability to work hard. Concentration rises to a high level as energetic Mars happily entwines with serious Saturn. This is a favorable time to schedule duties that need extra care and attention. Tasks that are long enduring can also be undertaken with a high degree of confidence that the work will be successfully completed. Good fortune could come your way. Opportunities for travel that combines business with pleasure are likely to put a smile on your face. Social pleasures should be plentiful and memorable.

16. TUESDAY. Bright. Lucky vibes continue to come your way. Buy a lottery ticket, enter a competition, or ask the boss for a pay raise. Whatever you do, you should come out a winner one way or another. Including plenty of variety in your day-to-day activities will reduce boredom and keep restlessness from becoming overwhelming. Walking around the office or taking a stroll through the mall at lunchtime can help keep your motivation high. You may be inspired to write or to express yourself in some creative form as brilliant ideas flow freely. Capricorn parents who have been experiencing problems relating to children on their own level shouldn't have any trouble today.

17. WEDNESDAY. Accomplished. Your renowned practicality and good common sense should be to the fore as intellectual Mercury connects positively to your life ruler, serious Saturn. Secret deals and plans that are being pursued behind the scenes should proceed without a hitch. Your natural ability to organize and to do more than one task at a time increases your overall efficiency and effectiveness on the job. Pressing financial business could spur you into action if you have slacked off where money is concerned. Capricorns who are in charge of purchasing office or store supplies should put a limit on such spending. Before making any large purchase, obtain a few price quotes to ensure you are getting the best deal available.

18. THURSDAY. Perplexing. Experiencing a sense of not being part of the scenery or of whatever is taking place could be disconcerting. It might seem as if you are watching a movie and not taking an active part. If you feel that your workplace has become dull and boring, it may be time to look elsewhere in order to keep enthusiasm and motivation alive. Don't underestimate a financial challenge; the situation could be more complex than first thought. The pressure could be on to complete a demanding project, but you will need to proceed slowly and steadily. Rushing could lead to a number of errors occurring in your work. Family issues might need attention tonight, so try to return home from work earlier than usual.

19. FRIDAY. Positive. Originality and the ability to think outside the square are the gifts of today's planetary aspects. You need to take an open, flexible approach or you risk being busy all day without accomplishing anything of significant value. A dramatic new slant on a problem could be the breakthrough you need to resolve an ongoing issue, further boosting your star on the job. Accept an invitation to a special reunion or other gathering; it is apt to be a memorable experience that has far-reaching positive consequences. A child could make Capricorn parents glow with pride and happiness. Tonight do something entirely different from your usual run-of-the-mill pursuits.

20. SATURDAY. Interesting. You may feel more talkative than usual as Mercury and Mars get up close and personal. Your choice of words is likely to be succinct and assertive, although you could have a cutting edge when conversing with certain people. Speaking without thinking first may also occur more frequently; guard against putting your foot in your mouth. Although as a Capricorn you are not usually prone to gossiping, be careful that secrets confided in you by other people don't inadvertently slip out. Physical resources may be lower than usual. So if a busy social evening is planned, an afternoon nap might be in order. Choose fun pursuits for entertainment tonight.

21. SUNDAY. Sensitive. Proceed with care. Your emotions are heightened, and planetary trends are not very helpful. A sharp mind and tongue continue to aid concentration and efficiency. The Taurus Full Moon could contribute to a number of power struggles and conflict with friends and loved ones. Be on your best behavior if socializing. Make sure a consensus is obtained when choosing entertainment so that clashes of opinion don't spoil your day. Children could be more troublesome than usual, and a baby might be hard to settle down. Pregnant Capricorns nearing the delivery date should have a bag packed and ready for a quick trip to the hospital.

22. MONDAY. Nurturing. Today's positive atmosphere should get you off to a flying start. Lunar influences encourage expression in whatever mode of communication you prefer. Sharing opinions and viewpoints will provide satisfaction. An eager, receptive audience will be on hand to applaud your ideas and beliefs. Heed signals from your body over the next four weeks if tiredness and lethargy become more frequent. The Sun now moves into optimistic Sagittarius, marking the beginning of the upcoming festive celebrations. However, Sagittarius is your twelfth house of solitude and secrets. The twelfth house being accentuated may trigger an inclination to withdraw from the social scene.

23. TUESDAY. Enriching. Mixed energies are in play. However, with the Moon in communicative Gemini, you should be able to talk your way out of any troublesome situation. Avoid the lure of trying to compete with other people; offer assistance instead. You may want to do something on the spur of the moment, which is unusual for the staid Capricorn. If there isn't any risk involved, being spontaneous for a change should be an enriching experience. Unless the bright lights of the city beckon, find a constructive way to release stress and relax close to home this evening. Romance may call to singles on the job scene. Those of you already committed could share a pleasant evening on a double date with a coworker and their partner.

24. WEDNESDAY. Tricky. The day ahead contains a few bumps and potholes that you will need to navigate carefully. Your cool, calm demeanor is apt to be put to the test, especially if you work directly with the general public. Expect more product returns than usual as well as more customer complaints. If you are unable to keep your temper under control, it might be wise to ask a colleague to stand in for you. Money matters could grow more complicated unless action is taken as soon as possible. Not everybody will like what you are doing, perhaps considering your efforts misguided. Be willing to take a closer look to see if there is any merit in their views.

25. THURSDAY. Guarded. You should be brimming with confidence, which is basically a good thing. Although being sure of yourself can be a positive approach to take, there is an undercurrent of being too sure which could be your undoing. Information overload increases the likelihood of your concentration being focused on the big picture, with the result that you miss or ignore important details. Mind what you say to other people, and refrain from entering into gossip or spreading rumors. Otherwise by the end of the day you may become the subject of an exaggerated story and be very sorry that you were foolish enough to spread unfounded gossip.

26. FRIDAY. Inspired. If you have been looking for more purpose in life, this is the time to turn the page. You probably know what is needed, and now it is just a matter of acknowledgment. Capricorns currently in a serious union may need to offer more support to their mate or partner. Business relationships are likely to flow more evenly through the morning than later in the day. This timing also pertains to those considering applying for a mortgage, credit increase, or business loan. Make sure your in-basket is empty before signing off work; you will appreciate coming in to a clean slate on Monday morning. The fires of love are stoked, so enjoy a loving weekend.

27. SATURDAY. Diverse. Contrasting and contradictory influences prevail. Intellectual Mercury is unhappy with chaotic Uranus but in love with dreamy Neptune. Indulgences of fantasy await the creative and imaginative Capricorn. If you can sit still long enough, this is a wonderful time to write, paint, or learn to play a musical instrument. Whatever activity you undertake, make sure to include a variety of pursuits and to move around to offset your restless energies. Romantic vibes are strong. This is a great time to make an important announcement or to celebrate a special event or anniversary. For singles, love could be close; you may be in the right place at the right time.

28. SUNDAY. Purposeful. Don't sit around and do nothing. If you are expecting visitors during the festive season ahead, now is the time to begin decluttering the house, guest room, or garage. Selling what is no longer needed could be lucrative for those who have a number of items to dispose of, or a local thrift store might be very glad to receive good-quality donations. Visiting out-of-town relatives may be worthwhile because they may be feeling extra generous. Capricorn shoppers poking around local antique stores might come across a special item that will fit in well with an ongoing collection. Viewing a humorous or satirical movie this evening could provide wonderful light relief.

29. MONDAY. Vibrant. Overconfidence and a lack of moderation are problems that may arise under today's planetary conditions. If you can manage to stay in your usual Capricorn frugal mode without succumbing to temptation, this can be a very productive day. Postpone major decision making because you could also be too quick to reach conclusions without thinking about all of the likely consequences. Try to do something new to satisfy your adventurous spirit, which could be yearning for variety and excitement. Keep track of your social plans. Your social calendar could begin to over- flow while good-time girl Venus moves through your friendship zone.

30. TUESDAY. Supportive. Attention turns to status, recognition, and career pursuits as the Moon moves through Libra at the top of your solar chart. If you need to ask coworkers or a superior for a favor, a day off, or a promotion, making your request early in the day should produce better results than waiting till later. These conditions also apply for business owners who need to contact an important customer, service provider, or goods supplier. Mercury continues on a merry round, now moving into your own sign of Capricorn. Confidence to speak up and say what you mean comes with a flourish. On a cautionary note, choose words carefully be- cause it will be easier to speak first and think later.

December 2010

1. WEDNESDAY. Gratifying. Capricorns are natural-born lead- ers, but today you may find yourself needing to work with a part- ner. This is not a day when you are likely to shine, so working in a team environment and supporting other people is a favorable way to utilize the energy you have as an innately hard worker. Someone in authority is apt to be watching, increasing the chance of your efforts reaping benefits in the future. Quick and clever Mercury is making an easy aspect with charming and attractive Venus. So folks are likely to respond positively to your ideas, initiative, and positive demeanor. An evening spent with special friends should provide all the mental stimulation you can absorb.

2. THURSDAY. Insightful. Inattention on the job could reduce work efficiency substantially. Don't allow inspired and imaginative thoughts to be wasted. Insights could lead to methods of gener- ating more income. A special friend may consume much of your thinking. If you are unable to meet up with friends, consider orga- nizing a social function where you can get together and exchange the latest news and gossip. New contacts who have the potential to become friends can be made as a result of combining business and pleasure. Your intuition is high, assisting the clever Capricorn to see through superficial appearances and to get right to the heart of any matter.

3. FRIDAY. Unsettling. Restlessness threatens to derail a few good intentions. As you prepare to wind down work duties and head into the weekend, your thoughts are likely to center on socializing with friends or a lover. However, with fiery Mars making a challenging aspect to explosive Uranus, caution is necessary. Take extra care when traveling, watch where you walk, and steer clear of fiery or flaming situations. Your fuse as well as that of people in close proximity to you may be shorter than normal, which can all too easily create a volatile atmosphere. Social commitments can provide welcome relief this evening. A girls-only night out should ease pressure for female Goats.

4. SATURDAY. Purposeful. Relaxing with good friends can be a refreshing change. However, with the Moon continuing to weave a path through Scorpio, social chitchat without any depth might not provide required stimulation. To find answers to vital questions, dig deep to find out why, how, who, and when. Visiting a new restaurant with family members or friends could be enough of a change from your normal routine to satisfy your need for variety. Chatting, buying, or selling online can be beneficial; you could end up with a new friend, more money in your pocket, or a number of bargain purchases. A quiet night at home could be enjoyable if you are not inclined to socialize.

5. SUNDAY. Renewing. Today a New Moon in Sagittarius is being ushered in, highlighting your twelfth house of solitary activity. The energy that comes in now is one of new beginnings. However, don't rush right off to start new projects; finish uncompleted tasks first so that you have a clean slate to begin with. You may even feel the need to withdraw from interacting with others so you have time to organize plans and strategies. Expanding your knowledge is more important now, and you might choose to widen your horizons by studying religion, traveling, or enrolling in a new academic course. This is a perfect day to write down hopes and wishes that you would like to see come to fruition.

6. MONDAY. Uneasy. Your desire to again spend time alone could present minor challenges due to current work and social commitments. It might take a little extra effort to get yourself moving this morning, to plan an agenda, and then stick to your schedule. Dreams and visions that have filled your nights may be your subconscious helping to unveil secrets that have been hidden. With a little bit of work and research, the meanings of these visions should become clearer. Innovative planet Uranus is now going forward in Pisces, your house of communication. Uranus in direct motion helps to remove many of the confused thoughts you have experienced over the past few months.

7. TUESDAY. Liberating. This new day dawns with fresh challenges and opportunities. Consider setting new goals that you will be able to achieve through hard work and personal effort. For Capricorns considering work-related studies, this is a prime time to research areas that will provide the best long-term advantages. Energetic Mars now moves into your sign, impacting your first house of physical resources and personality. Mars here provides an extra burst of encouragement to channel your energy and efforts into new interests and pursuits. Even though your Sun sign is usually stable and reserved, the chances of impulsiveness and of beginning too many tasks all at once increases considerably with Mars in your sign.

8. WEDNESDAY. Rewarding. With the positive link between saucy Venus and intense Pluto, the cosmic heavens are sending a plethora of romantic trends that are sure to increase pleasure, desire, and passion. Plan a dinner for two at a favorite restaurant, and take advantage of loving attention from your special honey. Luck also comes in monetary matters; profits for work done now should be plentiful. Capricorns who are working in the area of retail sales can make good headway, especially if currently on a commission basis or eligible to earn a substantial bonus. If there are dreams waiting to be realized, this is the time to give an extra push since good fortune is on your side.

9. THURSDAY. Satisfying. To gain fresh ideas and different perspectives, take action to expand your circle of friends and acquaintances. Working with groups of people and being part of a team can also provide emotional satisfaction. A rigid or fixed approach may limit possibilities, but answers should come by thinking outside the box. A costly electrical appliance may be high on your shopping list, or maybe you just want to ignore the budget and buy some wacky gadget or gizmo that is more fun than practical. Regardless of what ends up in your shopping cart, you would be wise to postpone making any major purchase at least until after lunch.

10. FRIDAY. Guarded. Pleasure and finance are apt to consume your thoughts. Although it is not in your Capricorn nature to fritter money away, be careful when browsing stores selling small and trivial items, especially festive incidentals. Such purchases can add up to spending a larger sum than envisioned. Although you might still be intent on buying costly electronic equipment, extra care will be needed. Messenger Mercury now goes into retrograde motion, highlighting your own sign of Capricorn for the next three weeks and possibly crimping your style somewhat. Don't trust rumors or become involved in spreading gossip. Make sure computer files are backed up on a regular basis.

11. SATURDAY. Favorable. Check the fine print before signing anything important. It would be even smarter to delay putting pen to paper if there isn't a get-out clause. If anyone knows the rules about working hard for money it is a Capricorn, so count your change, keep receipts, and look for quality when shopping for gifts or special family treats. A party or other social event should provide a welcome release from the strains of this busy week. For both single and married Capricorns, passion is likely to increase. Just be sure that the other person fully understands your feelings, and that you understand theirs. The thought of a candlelight dinner and a romantic rendezvous can keep you buzzing all day.

12. SUNDAY. Smooth. Fresh new ideas should begin to percolate, giving you the necessary inspiration to rethink goals. This may mean tackling a number of your plans from a different angle. Family members could preoccupy your thoughts, particularly a sister or close female relative. Catching up with family members and reconnecting on an emotional level can be beneficial if you have been spending long hours on the job. Attending a religious service may be comforting and a good way to interact with other people. If you don't know your neighbors, perhaps it is time to reach out and get to know them a little better.

13. MONDAY. Compassionate. As a caring Capricorn you may find yourself lending a sympathetic ear to someone close to you. This could be a bit awkward and uncomfortable because you don't want to become emotionally involved, but probably all that is required is practical advice and guidance. The challenge is to balance what your head tells you to do with what your heart feels is right. Photos may play an important part in your day. This could include everything from taking new pictures to reminiscing over past memories. Being able to put pen to paper can be a creative way to release pent-up emotions and share what is on your mind.

14. TUESDAY. Agitating. If you are feeling more frustrated than usual, you can thank the Moon, which is now racing through fiery and impulsive Aries. Losing your temper could be all too easy unless you take precautions. A positive way of channeling this yang energy is by participating in physical exercise or some form of cardiovascular workout. Housework, yard work, or going through files are also good outlets. However, don't become overly obsessive with cleaning or let self-inflicted pressure to complete everything in one day lead to a stress-related headache. A night spent unwinding with that special person in your life should aid relaxation.

15. WEDNESDAY. Bumpy. Today's planetary influences, although small in number, expose possible problems around your home base, making those you live with more edgy. As a Capricorn your home is your castle, and you have extra energy to exert around your living quarters. However, if you have been waiting for other people to finish home repairs or just clean out the garage, your patience is likely to run out, leading to an inclination to roll up your sleeves and do the work yourself. Check that arrangements are in order and clutter has been minimized in anticipation of invited or unexpected visitors for the upcoming festivities. Be sure to stock up on plenty of snack food.

16. THURSDAY. Cautious. Venus and the Sun are both linked unhappily to Jupiter, planet of excess. Although these connections shouldn't be negative, you need to apply moderation in all areas. Inner harmony, courage, and confidence rise considerably, although there is also a risk that the pendulum could swing a little too far. This will result in arrogance, pomposity, and not heeding other people, especially when it comes to taking risks. The desire for romance sparks for the unattached Capricorn, but caution should be applied. There may be a tendency to venture into a romantic rendezvous without thinking of possible consequences.

17. FRIDAY. Social. As the festive season fast approaches, having fun is apt to be on your mind even for the most serious Capricorn. Today will find artistic types able to take creativity and expertise to a new level, which can certainly help in producing original items for sale to the public. Children can be a grounding influence, although many parents might find that they are doing the grounding of youngsters, especially of unruly teenagers. Whatever you are involved in, your senses are likely to be more highly tuned than usual. When it comes to enjoying fine food, it will need to taste, smell, and look good, which will increase the likelihood of overindulging.

18. SATURDAY. Diverse. A plethora of celestial activities lights up the skies. Prepare for an interesting and exciting day, but don't expect everything to run smoothly. Postpone purchasing gifts today. Even the astute Capricorn could pay more than a fair price for the quality of goods available, even those on sale. Your significant other may be feeling a little neglected, particularly if you have been working long hours and not spending much time at home. Make amends by bringing home a feel-good gift of flowers, chocolates, or anything that will tickle the pleasure senses; your thoughtfulness is sure to be a hit, putting you firmly back in the good graces of your loved one.

19. SUNDAY. Meaningful. Communication is a key theme, although Capricorn folks may prefer to work alone on the computer, writing, answering e-mails, or chatting online rather that engaging in face-to-face interaction. If you have been tardy with health habits, you could find yourself feeling rather tired and exhausted. Take time out to rest rather than continuing to rush around. Use the quiet stillness that you create for yourself to unwind and restore a relaxed state. Your increased sensitivity to the feelings of other people may encourage a visit to someone who is confined in their home or is hospitalized. Go out of your way to spread some festive cheer.

20. MONDAY. Disquieting. A restless attitude could prove difficult to contain as the new working week begins. To utilize this energy in a positive manner, make some changes so that life becomes more comfortable. As a Capricorn you are known for finishing what you start and for your ability to work long hours. However, this trait could prove to be your undoing if you stubbornly press on through illness or when you are just not feeling very well. You are in tune with your body, with an urge to heal yourself, so perhaps it is time to research alternative treatment methods if you are not receiving desired results from current medical practices.

21. TUESDAY. Happy Birthday! Another bright and busy day graces the horizon as the planets combine to make their presence felt. You are likely to feel extremely positive, which is wonderful. However, be sure to watch what is going on all around you. A Full Moon in Gemini brings a warning to be careful with words and actions because other people may be more sensitive than you. This is also a day when your head might be in the clouds, leading you to neglect details, blurt out secrets, or promise more than can be delivered. Later on this evening the Sun sails into your own sign, a time to take your place center stage and shine.

22. WEDNESDAY. Uneven. Partnerships and teamwork are in the frame. As the holiday season fast approaches, trying to separate work from home and personal life will become more challenging, especially if overtime is required to keep on top of festive orders. If you have any deep emotions secreted away, these could make an unwelcome appearance. Unwanted or painful thoughts and memories that have been holding you back should now be tossed away. Release negative energies and you may be amazed at how good you feel. Office gossip is apt to flow freely, but what you hear could be misleading; check the information before accepting it as truth.

23. THURSDAY. Sparkling. Surprises in the form of money or a gift could come your way, uplifting your spirits and providing much happiness. Enjoyment comes from giving as well as receiving, and you still need to watch that the dollars don't disappear too quickly from your wallet. If you haven't finished gift shopping, the reward for facing the mall crowds will be plenty of good-quality bargains, reducing the amount of money you'll spend on your celebrating. For the artistic Capricorn, your imaginative side can be displayed in a multitude of ways, including making handmade gifts that will be appreciated by those lucky enough to be on the receiving end.

24. FRIDAY. Pressured. The lunar goddess isn't showing any favors even though it is Christmas Eve. If you have uncharacteristically left shopping to the last minute, you can expect to run into a myriad of obstacles that leave you tired and grumpy by day's end. Your credit card should be used sparingly in order to avoid facing a large bill in the new year. Thoroughly read through the terms and conditions if signing up to pay on time; it can be very easy to get in over your head financially without realizing it. Romance is in the air as thoughts turn to good times, love, and intimacy. Attending a caroling service as a family could strengthen ties.

25. SATURDAY. Merry Christmas! A flair for the dramatic can be a big help with preparations for a family get-together. Although it will require plenty of hard labor to produce a day full of excitement and fun, you should relish being busy and working to please loved ones and friends. Stimulating conversation is likely to flow freely. Those attending a church or community service may be uplifted by the prevailing spirit and love. If you know of someone who is spending the holiday alone, add pleasure to their day by offering to share your hospitality and good cheer. Whatever you do, have fun relaxing with loved ones.

26. SUNDAY. Fair. Hopefully the hectic pace that has been keeping you on the go will now slow down. The Sun is merging with Pluto, which could add vitality or drain energy; it just depends on your own personal physical resources. Try to incorporate restful pastimes as well as periods of activity, enjoying the best of both. Aim to be busy and energetic enough at the end of the day to feel good. A get-together could play an important part in today's activities. You'll have an enjoyable time socializing with friends and meeting new people in your neighborhood or community. Younger Capricorns out to have a good time should avoid any area that may be a threat to personal safety.

27. MONDAY. Erratic. An adaptable approach is needed to get through the day unscathed. Your strong desire to control every situation is likely to increase tension in your life, so avoid this as much as possible. Unexpected circumstances are bound to occur due to the current celestial climate, possibly upsetting a set routine. A tendency to worry needlessly is a Capricorn trait, and this could discourage you from going after cherished goals. Keep in mind that your sign is known for tenacity and resolve, which you should use to overcome stubborn obstacles. As the end of the year approaches, you may find yourself wanting to clear away clutter and dispel chaos.

28. TUESDAY. Resourceful. If you are back on the job, career and professional matters are likely to be a main priority. Employment problems may be creating such an overload of work being assigned to you that you have little time to spare for social or family pursuits. Meeting powerful or influential people could inspire career-focused Capricorns to look far and wide in seeking a new work-related direction or to realize current ambitions. If you are in search of a new job, your ability to please prospective employers increases and you could be on the way to taking another step up the ladder of success. Hold out for what you know you are worth.

29. WEDNESDAY. Mixed. Patience is a virtue, so the saying goes. However, it might be in short supply for you today, as well as a dearth of energy. Working alone and minimizing contacts with the outside world could work well. Try not to worry if sudden feelings of inadequacy or a lack of self-confidence arises; this is a typical reaction to current planetary trends. Employed Capricorns could feel frustrated by a lack of power and authority on the job. Or you may feel that you have reached the glass ceiling and are being held back. Exercise can be a way to release frustration; literally or figuratively climb a hill to blow away cobwebs and clear your mind. Gear up for an exhilarating challenge to come.

30. THURSDAY. Challenging. As a Capricorn you are known for your self-sufficiency, but today the focus is more on teamwork. Decisions may be a little harder to make due to having to consider loved ones; you are now seeing how your long-term goals and ambitions impact other people. Your leadership ability could be tested as an employer turns over a couple of major responsibilities to you. Just be wary of being manipulated into taking on tasks that you don't have the means or license to do. An end-of-year social event that you host or have organized should be just what you need to demonstrate your creative and coordination skills.

31. FRIDAY. Happy. With trickster Mercury now going in forward motion, contacting distant friends and family members should be easier. Socializing with friends will top your list of priorities. Your positive feelings and outlook will act like a magnet to attract like-minded folks, resulting in an energy-charged day. New goals can be established. If you are really serious about realizing certain ambitions, write out a list of New Year resolutions so you have a record of your aims. Whether you are attending a glamorous event this evening or a low-key get-together, enjoy the close of 2010 surrounded by close friends and those who love you the most.

NOTES

NOTES

Train at home in your spare time to

Be a Medical Billing Specialist

*U.S. Dept. of Labor projects significant growth for specialists doing billing for doctors' offices.

Take the first step to earning up to $40,000 a year and more!

Now you can train in the comfort of your own home to work at home or in a doctor's office, hospital or clinic making great money...up to $40,000 a year and more as your experience and skills increase! It's no secret, healthcare providers need Medical Billing Specialists. In fact, the U.S. Department of Labor projects a significant increase in demand for specialists doing billing for doctors' offices!

Nationally accredited training... be ready to work in as little as four months!

Our experts train you step by step to perform the job of a qualified Medical Billing Specialist. Everything is explained in easy-to-understand language with plenty of examples. You learn exactly what to do and how to do it! You can graduate in as little as four months and be ready to take your first step into this exciting, high-income career.

No Previous Medical Experience Required. Compare the Money You Can Make!

We make it easy to learn how to prepare medical claims for Medicare, Medicaid and private patients. And since every medical procedure must be properly billed, there's plenty of work available. You'll make great money working with doctors as a part of the medical team doing a job that really helps people.

WORK AT HOME!

Because of the demand, more and more billing specialists work from home!

You Get Toll-Free Support!

You are never alone with USCI training. Just email us or call our toll-free hotline if you ever need help from our expert instructors.

❝ I would like to thank you from the bottom of my heart for the WONDERFUL course of Medical Billing... I want to encourage others who are thinking about taking the course. Go ahead! IT'S THE BEST DECISION YOU'LL EVER MAKE! ❞ Sincerely, Scarlet M.

Get FREE Facts! Call 1-800-388-8765 Dept. SPHB2A70

SENT FREE!

U.S. Career Institute, Dept. SPHB2A70
2001 Lowe Street, Fort Collins, CO 80525
www.uscareerinstitute.com

Or mail this coupon today!

Yes! Rush me my free information package with complete details about training at home to be a Medical Billing Specialist. I understand there is absolutely no cost and no obligation.

Name:_____ Age:_____

Address:_____ Apt:_____

City: _____ State: _____ Zip: _____

E-mail: _____

CL210

FREE
PARTY LINE

Make new friends, have fun, share idea's never be bored this party never stops! And best of all it's FREE!

**Never Any Charges
Call Now!**

712-338-7722

WHAT DOES YOUR FUTURE HOLD?

DISCOVER IT IN *ASTROANALYSIS*—

**COMPLETELY REVISED THROUGH THE YEAR 2015,
THESE GUIDES INCLUDE COLOR-CODED CHARTS FOR
TOTAL ASTROLOGICAL EVALUATION,
PLANET TABLES AND CUSP CHARTS,
AND STREAMLINED INFORMATION.**

ARIES	0-425-17558-8
TAURUS	0-425-17559-6
GEMINI	0-425-17560-X
CANCER	0-425-17561-8
LEO	0-425-17562-6
VIRGO	0-425-17563-4
LIBRA	0-425-17564-2
SCORPIO	0-425-17565-0
SAGITTARIUS	0-425-17566-9
CAPRICORN	0-425-17567-7
AQUARIUS	0-425-17568-5
PISCES	0-425-17569-3

Available wherever books are sold or at penguin.com

B093

Incredible Psychic Solutions!

5 Minutes FREE!

Speak to one of our highly trained
professional psychics for
answers to YOUR questions!
LOVE, ROMANCE, MONEY,
HEALTH, HAPPINESS!
Your answers are only a call away!

1-888-799-2428